RELATED POTOMAC TITLES

*A Talk in the Park: Nine Decades of Baseball Tales
from the Broadcast Booth*
—Curt Smith

Pull Up a Chair: The Vin Scully Story
—Curt Smith

KEEPERS OF
THE GAME

KEEPERS OF THE GAME

When the BASEBALL BEAT
was the BEST JOB
on the PAPER

DENNIS D'AGOSTINO
FOREWORD BY DAVE ANDERSON

Potomac Books
Washington, D.C.

Library of Congress Cataloging-in-Publication Data
D'Agostino, Dennis.
   Keepers of the game : when the baseball beat was the best job on the paper / Dennis D'Agostino ; foreword by Dave Anderson.
       p. cm.
   ISBN 978-1-59797-691-6 (hardcover : alk. paper)
   ISBN 978-1-59797-870-5 (electronic)
1. Sportswriters—United States—Biography. 2. Sports journalism—United States. 3. Newspapers—Sections, columns, etc.—Baseball. I. Title.
GV742.4.D34 2013
070.4'497960973—dc23
                                                                                  2012043924

Printed in the United States of America on acid-free paper that meets the American National Standards Institute Z39-48 Standard.

Potomac Books
22841 Quicksilver Drive
Dulles, Virginia 20166

First Edition

10 9 8 7 6 5 4 3 2 1

As always, for my family:

For Helene, and Jeanne and Freddie, and Emilie and Charlotte. And most of all for Mom and Dad, with very belated apologies for reading these guys when I should have been doing my homework.
—D. D.

I don't want to be a millionaire.
I just want to live like one.
—Dick Young, channeling Joe E. Lewis

Billy, always have your dime.
—Milton Richman

I never lived a normal life.
But I lived the life I wanted to live.
—Bob Hertzel

CONTENTS

IN MEMORIAM

Maury Allen

Rod Beaton

Furman Bisher

George Cantor

Mike Celizic

Matt Dobek

Red Foley

Trent Frayne

Bill Gallo

John Halligan

Bobbie Isaacs

Bruce Keidan

Phil Jasner

Neil MacCarl

Bob Mandt

Phil Musick

Jesse Outlar

Arthur Richman

Bill Shannon

Mark Wagner

Vic Ziegel

FOREWORD

Baseball's past, present, and future converged for me on a sunny spring day in Mobile, Alabama, in 1954. I was the *Brooklyn Eagle*'s beat writer covering the Brooklyn Dodgers as they wound their way north by train with the Milwaukee Braves from spring training in Florida. Before an exhibition game in the old Mobile ballpark, I happened to be standing near Jackie Robinson as the Braves took batting practice.

"See that kid in there," Robinson said, nodding toward a slender rookie outfielder who was slashing line drives. "You're going to be watching him a long time."

The slender rookie's name was Henry Aaron, and twenty years later at a night game in Atlanta, I watched him hit his 715th home run, breaking Babe Ruth's record. Known as Hank by then, he would hit 755 homers and set major-league career records for runs batted in, total bases, and extra-base hits. But whenever I think of him, I always remember what Jackie Robinson said to me that day in Mobile.

Little moments like that were the best parts of being a beat writer. You followed the team you covered, for better or for worse, and you went to the World Series, just as all the other big-league beat writers did. But sometimes you were the only one listening when somebody said something memorable.

Like the time in the Dodgers dugout at Ebbets Field when Roy Campanella turned to me. "To play this game," the three-time National League MVP said, "you got to have a lot of the little boy in you."

I was the *Eagle*'s beat writer for less than two full seasons, but I was the last beat writer to cover the Brooklyn Dodgers for the *Brooklyn Eagle*, the last of only about half a dozen *Eagle* beat writers since the late 1890s.

When the *Eagle* folded just before the 1955 season, I moved to the *New York Journal-American*, where I was a backup beat writer on the Dodgers before they departed for Los Angeles after the 1957 season, and later a backup on the Yankees and Mets. I went to *The New York Times* in 1966, again covering the Yankees and the Mets occasionally, and I've been a *Times* sports columnist since 1971, writing dozens of baseball columns each year and writing from virtually every World Series until my semiretirement in 2007. But I still cherish my time as a beat writer with the Dodgers.

In those early '50s, young sportswriters didn't come out of journalism schools at Columbia, Missouri, or Northwestern. The word "intern" didn't exist. All I knew about journalism was what I read in newspapers growing up in the Bay Ridge section of Brooklyn— sports columns by Red Smith, Jimmy Cannon, Frank Graham, W. C. Heinz, Arthur Daley, and Tommy Holmes, and baseball writing by Dick Young, Herb Goren, Bill Roeder, Harold Rosenthal, John Drebinger, and Dan Daniel.

Two months out of Holy Cross (where I was the sports editor of the college paper when Bob Cousy was an All-American), I was lucky enough to be hired in 1951 by Lou Niss, the *Eagle*'s sports editor, as a $40-a-week clerk in the sports department. I went for coffee, answered the phone, filed photos, and wrote two or three paragraphs on high school football and basketball games and sandlot baseball games.

But in 1952 Lou let me cover some Yankees and Giants home games. I was doing that again early in the 1953 season when Harold C. Burr, the *Eagle*'s beat writer with the Dodgers, fell and broke his hip in Cincinnati. He would be hospitalized for weeks and then walk with a cane.

"When the Dodgers come home," Lou told me, "you're covering them."

Everything about being a beat writer was different then. The word "computer" didn't exist. The words "cell phone" or "tweet" or "blog" or "Web" didn't exist. ESPN was about twenty-five years away, sports talk radio about thirty-five years away. The word "media" didn't exist. The newspapers were your only connection to a team. The words "interview area" didn't exist.

If you were a beat writer, you were simply one of the "writers," a member of a rare and hallowed herd who worked in a rare and hallowed era. Before a game, you sat in the dugout or in the clubhouse, sometimes alone with a player or the manager, and had a conversation. Not always about the team or about baseball, sometimes just about the world around you.

Before a game at Ebbets Field, I often sat on an equipment trunk near the corner lockers of Pee Wee Reese, Jackie Robinson, Gil Hodges, and Duke Snider. The day after Preacher Roe confessed in *Sports Illustrated* that the "outlawed spitball was my money pitch," I was sitting on that trunk across from Hodges, the big first baseman who had a reputation for sleight of foot when taking an infielder's throw on a fast baserunner. I had never mentioned this to Hodges, but he had a dry sense of humor and with Preacher Roe's headlines, I couldn't resist.

"Gil and I are going to do a magazine piece after he retires," I said quietly as all four sets of Dodger eyes turned toward me. "We're going to call it, 'I Never Touched First Base.'" Gil chuckled. So did Pee Wee, Jackie, and Duke.

Yes, being a beat writer was different then. You wrote on a portable typewriter with real paper. In small, sweaty, or cold press boxes, Western Union telegraphers, sometimes clicking dots and dashes, sent your stories. You traveled with the team by overnight train on a "Western trip" where St. Louis was the frontier. Not only did the club pay your sleeping-compartment fare and your hotel room, but the traveling secretary handed you an envelope with daily meal money in cash. Of the New York papers, only the *Times* and later the *Daily News* paid their own way.

On the train, you ate in the team's dining car where the steaks were great, but the custom was for the writers to wait until most of the players had eaten. You rode the team bus to the ballparks. Believe me, all those perks never influenced what you wrote. The term "conflict of interest" didn't exist, either.

Deadlines were different, too. With the Dodgers, you had four morning-paper writers for the *Times, Herald Tribune, Daily News,* and *Daily Mirror* and five afternoon-paper writers for the *Journal-American*, *World-Telegram & Sun*, *Post*, *Brooklyn Eagle*, and *Long Island Press*. Except for the club's play-by-play announcers, the radio or TV reporters not only never traveled with the team but seldom came to Ebbets Field.

The afternoon-paper writers like me could wait until after a night game ended to compose their stories after going to the clubhouse to talk to the manager and the players. The morning-paper writers wrote straight game accounts, except for Dick Young of the *Daily News*, a great reporter who was always hustling for a meaningful early-edition story (and a back-page headline) that was on the street about when a night game began.

Dick Young was my journalism school professor. In the Ebbets Field press box during a night game, somebody would always send out for an early-edition copy of the *Daily News* to see what Young had written.

As the youngest beat writer with the Dodgers, I didn't know much, but I knew enough to keep my mouth shut most of the time. In the press box I always listened to what the other writers were saying about the manager or the players. After a game I'd mostly listen to what the other afternoon-paper writers were talking about as we went down to the Dodgers clubhouse, or to what they would ask the Dodgers manager—Chuck Dressen or Walter Alston—or sometimes the opposing manager, especially if it was Leo Durocher. The next day, I always checked the other papers to see what the other beat writers had written about.

As the *Eagle*'s young beat writer, I learned the newspaper business and the baseball business in self-defense. I wasn't merely young; I was younger by decades than most of the other beat writers. I remember them more for what they were like than what they wrote.

On losing at gin rummy, silver-haired Roscoe McGowen—the "gentleman from the *Times*"—would throw his cards to the ceiling. Gus Steiger of the *Mirror* advised me, "Never check your typewriter." Mike Gaven of the *Journal-American* taught me that Miller High Life was "the only beer that goes with an outside cut of prime rib." Harold Rosenthal of the *Herald Tribune* warned me that "the road makes bums of all of us." Whenever it was on the menu, Bill Roeder of the *World-Telegram* would order Baked Alaska for dessert.

For beat writers, the newspaper business was different, too. Some writers worked virtually every day, from pitchers-and-catchers through the regular season to the last game of the World Series, which was always played on early October afternoons, often with the sun slanting into left field at Yankee Stadium or slashing between the lower and upper third-base stands at Ebbets Field where, quite understandably, right-hander Billy Loes once lost a grounder in the sun.

And after a Series game at Yankee Stadium, you wrote and then hurried downtown to the Series headquarters at a midtown hotel to have a drink or two, enjoy the prime-rib buffet, and rehash the game.

In that era long before agents and free agents, you mostly were off in the off-season unless your team made a managerial change or a trade. If you were a beat writer on a New York paper, you acted in the skits at the annual New York Baseball Writers' Dinner at the Waldorf-Astoria, a theatrical rite of baseball's off-season that eventually perished along with the words "beat writer" when the New York newspapers had more baseball writers than they knew what to do with in 1958, after the Dodgers and Giants departed, until the Mets appeared in 1962.

Which reminds me of covering the Dodgers' last game at Ebbets Field as a backup beat writer for the *Journal-American*. Long after Danny McDevitt, a little left-hander, had blanked the Pirates, 2–0, on September 24, 1957, Bill Roeder and I were the last two writers in the press room. After finally filing our stories, we took the small elevator down to the field level and walked around to the night watchman's exit to Ebbets Field's marble rotunda and the outside world.

As we approached the door, I motioned for Bill to go ahead of me, then I followed him. I hadn't planned it, hadn't thought about it, but suddenly I realized that I was the last writer to leave Ebbets Field after the Dodgers' last game there.

Not the last person, as other people were still cleaning the stands. But I was the last *writer*. What more could a former beat writer ask?

—Dave Anderson

New York Times *columnist Dave Anderson won the 1981 Pulitzer Prize for sports commentary. From 2000 through 2007, he held the coveted card number 1 as the longest-tenured active member of the Baseball Writers' Association of America (BBWAA).*

PREFACE

It still rests in my wallet today, its corners frayed and its orange stock fading. Issued decades ago, it serves no current use. It provides no admission to any ballpark, no passage to any clubhouse or press box. Yet I am as proud of it as I am of any physical possession.

It is my 1982 Baseball Writers' Association of America card.

At the tender age of twenty-four, albeit for just one year, I was a member of the greatest sportswriting fraternity in the world.

There was a time when the most prestigious, most sought-after, most-read, and most competitive job on a major newspaper belonged to the baseball beat writer. It was a job that carried unparalleled longevity and influence within the sportswriting profession—when the Baseball Writers' Association of America (BBWAA) was probably the most powerful and respected voice within the game's structure. The baseball writers whose careers began in the 1950s, '60s, and early '70s epitomize a time when the beat writer was the unquestioned primary source for any and all baseball news, opinion, and analysis.

That world doesn't exist anymore.

Through a variety of events and circumstances—television, expansion, technology, all-sports radio, lifestyle changes, and ultimately the Internet revolution—those days are long gone. The baseball beat writer endures, but the job is no longer the best at the paper, the one position that could go unchanged and unchallenged for decades.

Today, the newspaper beat writer is only one of a dizzying array of information options available. Connect your laptop, Blackberry, iPhone, or tablet to any one of dozens of national sports news websites, each of which promises "twenty-four-hour coverage" of your favorite team. Sign up for e-mail alerts and tweets. Tune in to non-stop sports television or talk radio. Log onto one of hundreds of websites and blogs, some run by media giants and others by teenagers, some well-written and scholarly, others saying little more than "Look at me!" Become an instant media celebrity by starting your own website, blog, or Facebook page . . . all from the comfort of your living room or your local Starbucks.

Today, anyone with a computer and an opinion can proclaim themselves a baseball writer. But the men whose careers were rooted in teletype machines and ten-team leagues were the game's last true custodians and guardians, yielding a singular influence that would be unthinkable today.

*   *   *

Organized in 1908, the BBWAA quickly became the single most powerful organization of its kind. Its members were not only the game's gatekeepers but played the lead role in determining how baseball—its teams, stars, and inner workings—was perceived around the nation and the world.

Even though its membership spans the entire country (and now Canada, Japan, and Latin America), the BBWAA has always been an exclusive and selective organization. You can't just send a dues check to a post office box and join the club. Your name, credentials, and personal qualifications are submitted by your employer (your newspaper, wire service, or, in recent years, website) for approval. The association's earliest bylaws warned against "careless acceptance of doubtful eligible members," and the rule holds today.

From the start, baseball was quick to realize the influence held by the writers. A BBWAA card granted the bearer access to every major league ballpark, press box, and locker room. The association controlled press facilities throughout the majors, handled the duties of official scoring (a practice that ended in the 1990s), and was in charge of credentialing the game's major attractions such as the World Series. If you were a radio or television guy, well, tough luck. Many baseball press boxes (including Shea Stadium and the remodeled post-1976 Yankee Stadium) had separate sections strictly for broadcast media and non-BBWAA members.

In 1931, the BBWAA began the annual selection of baseball's official Most Valuable Player awards, and it now votes on (and owns the rights to) virtually every major postseason award. In the mid-1930s, the BBWAA assumed responsibility for selecting the recipients of the game's highest honor, the entry into the newly formed Baseball Hall of Fame in Cooperstown, New York. The association's veteran members (with at least ten consecutive years of membership) have made the selections ever since, often inspiring lightning-rod controversy and criticism.

A source of pride within the BBWAA—then and now—is each writer's individual membership number, which is maintained during a member's full-time employment. The numbers are based on individual longevity; in other words, the older you get, the lower your number. For nearly a decade, Pulitzer Prize-winner Dave Anderson of *The New York Times*, who joined the BBWAA in 1952, held card number 1. When Anderson retired from full-time duty in 2007, his number 1 status went to Seymour Siwoff of the Elias Sports Bureau, another 1952 alumnus.

At the core of the BBWAA's influence was the work of the beat writer, who covered his team, home and road, from the first day of spring training to the last day of the season. In the days when the beat writer was the primary source of information, he would practically live with the team. Today we'd call it being embedded; back then, it was a way of life.

The beat writer would ride the same special trains and chartered airplanes as the team. He would stay at the same four-star hotels, share the same buses and taxis, and quite often—clear into the 1960s, in some cases—have all expenses paid by the club he covered. This constant, near-24/7 access enabled vintage baseball journalists to establish deep and trusting personal relationships with those they covered—players, managers, and executives—in a fashion impossible to imagine today.

The beat writers—many of whom stayed on the job for decades—became synonymous with the teams they covered, their names familiar to fans of all ages. From the '50s through the '70s, a staple of each team's annual yearbook was the "Meet the Press" section in which bios and photos of the traveling writers were often as prominent as the players'. (Today, only the Dodgers still carry on that quaint tradition, the photos scaled down to tiny head shots.) In Cleveland, Indians baseball meant reading Gordon Cobbledick, Hal Lebovitz, and then Russell Schneider. In Cincinnati, following the Reds meant the venerable Lou Smith, then the youthful Bob Hertzel. In Pittsburgh, Les Biederman presided over decades of bad Pirate baseball, after which Charley Feeney became the Steel City's conduit to the heroics of Clemente and Stargell. In New York, Phil Pepe and Maury Allen *meant* baseball for generations of readers.

The baseball writer became a star in his own right, a local celebrity often romanticized in film and print. Both Spencer Tracy (in 1942's *Woman of the Year*) and Walter Matthau (in 1968's *The Odd Couple*) could list portrayals of baseball writers among their most memorable roles. In New York, the streetwise Jimmy Cannon counted both Joe DiMaggio and Ernest Hemingway among his closest friends. Jimmy Powers, Bill Corum, and Stan Lomax, all based in New York, were among the many who became early stars of sports on radio. Damon Runyon and Paul Gallico started their fabled literary careers as baseball writers. Vincent X. Flaherty (in Los Angeles), Furman Bisher (Atlanta), Sam Levy (Milwaukee), and Ernie Mehl and Joe McGuff (Kansas City) doubled as political movers and shakers whose influence, both on the sports page and in the boardrooms, helped bring major league baseball to their cities.

The writers themselves saluted their own with lavish events such as the New York chapter's annual black-tie dinner, which began in 1924 and immediately became the sport's premier off-season event. The beat-writer-as-local-celebrity still lives today in provincial cities like St. Louis and Cincinnati, where Rick Hummel and Hal McCoy are regularly pursued by autograph hunters. But in time, the beat writer's longevity and influence has fallen victim to a changing world, and the fanciful depictions of the past have degenerated to farcical depths with no basis in reality. When asked about Ray Romano's longtime portrayal of *Newsday* columnist Ray Barone on the TV show *Everybody Loves Raymond*, the paper's *real* columnist, Steve Jacobson, replied, "We'd never hire anybody that dumb."

My own first exposure to this world came in five marvelous years spent on the New York sports desk of The Associated Press, fresh out of Fordham University, class of '78. I learned more about writing, more about journalism, more about *life* in four weeks at the

AP than I did in four years at college. The Jesuits could teach theory and philosophy and explain the inverted pyramid, but there was absolutely no way they could prepare you for Dick Joyce, Hal Bock, Fast Eddie Schuyler, Murray Rose, or the host of Runyonesque characters who awaited a wide-eyed twenty-year-old the first time he walked through the revolving door at 50 Rockefeller Plaza.

*   *   *

Keepers of the Game owes its format and tone to the late Jerome Holtzman's seminal work *No Cheering in the Press Box*, first published in 1973 and revised in 1995. Holtzman's oral history spotlighted the first-person stories of two dozen famed sportswriters from the first half of the twentieth century. The book has since become required reading for every serious baseball or sports journalism historian, and any similarity between the overall look of this work and *No Cheering in the Press Box* is purely intentional. (Indeed, each of the men interviewed for this book had a copy of Holtzman's classic, many presented and autographed by the author himself.) In a very real sense, I hope that *Keepers* will be looked upon as an "update" of Holtzman's pioneering work, with the emphasis now on the longtime baseball beat writer.

I interviewed twenty-four vintage baseball writers, either in person or via telephone, during an eleven-month period from February to December 2010. To borrow a line from Holtzman, "The author is entirely responsible for the choice, emphasis and juxtaposition of material." The interviews have, in some cases, been lightly edited for clarity.

My criteria for selecting the book's subjects are basically twofold: historic "reach" and influence, and each man's longevity solely as a baseball beat writer (and *not* as a national or general columnist, as several later became). For a few, their historic reach goes back more than sixty years. Stan Isaacs became a BBWAA member in 1951, the same year Joe Giuliotti drew his first newspaper paycheck. Phil Pepe's initial major league assignments were at Ebbets Field and the Polo Grounds, while Gordon Verrell covered games at Wrigley Field . . . the one in Los Angeles.

Included here, I am proud to say, are nine winners of the Baseball Hall of Fame's J. G. Taylor Spink Award, the baseball writing profession's highest honor. (A complete list of the award's recipients since its inception in 1962 is included at the back of this book.) In addition, I interviewed each living Spink Award nominee from 2002 from 2011 as well. Unfortunately, health issues prevented Charley Feeney, the 1996 Spink winner, from conducting an extensive interview. But you're here in spirit, Pally.

Granted, several Spink winners (such as Peter Gammons and Tracy Ringolsby) are still active and may be a bit younger than the majority of writers included. But I'm of the opinion that a Spink Award (or nomination) is certification enough for a lifetime of distinguished baseball reporting. Writers like Gammons and Murray Chass achieved nationwide notoriety, and deservedly so, but just as important are the voices that reverberated on a local level, the Wayne Minshews and Jim Hennemans.

I've attempted to create as complete a representation of writers from around the country as possible. Space and time constraints forced me to omit (but certainly not overlook) several additional writers who should have been included. To them—especially several old friends from my New York days—I extend my sincerest apologies.

*   *   *

I wrote this book for many reasons, some of which I didn't realize until after I had started the process.

- The baseball beat writing profession, as defined by these men, has been transformed by the warp-speed communications and journalism revolution. As long as there is baseball, there will be baseball writing. But what form that writing takes, no one can know for sure.
- Save for the annual Spink Award recognition, the writers depicted in these pages—and their contemporaries—are quietly being lost to history. Most are retired, and only a few still work on a regular basis. The press room walls of my local ballpark, Angel Stadium of Anaheim, are filled with portraits of past Spink winners, yet few who visit the room can identify them or know their significance. A similar display of legendary writers at New York's new Citi Field brings the same lack

of attention. When Maury Allen—one of the iconic figures in New York baseball journalism and the very first writer interviewed for this book—died in October 2010, his passing did not even rate a mention on ESPN or MLB Network.

- Whether they knew it or not, these men have been—at various stages of my life—inspirations, mentors, coworkers, and friends. Connecting with them (and in some cases, reconnecting) was an absolute joy.
- I've grown weary of the wave upon wave of talking-head "experts," "historians," and "award-winning authors" spawned from cable TV documentaries, homemade damn-I'm-brilliant websites, and "research" conducted via Google. "The secret of life," Leonard Koppett was fond of saying, "is simply showing up." Frankly, I don't see too many of these folks in press boxes, dugouts, and locker rooms. Let Ken Burns stick with his poets, actors, and politicians; I'd rather listen to these guys. After all, they were *there*.

But please don't misunderstand. This book isn't meant to be a two-hundred-plus-page bitch session about the evils of the Internet or twenty-four-hour sports talk. Instead, it's meant to be a celebration and remembrance of both a time and a profession that are most likely gone forever.

*   *   *

You'll see some terms and names frequently mentioned throughout the book, and a brief explanation is in order.

Many writers will refer to working for "AM" and "PM" papers. In the days when most major league cities had multiple daily newspapers, most were AMs, hitting the streets with an early edition the night before and later editions first thing the next morning. Several, however, were PMs, afternoon papers that came out in multiple editions for the lunchtime and rush hour crowds (and, quite frequently, included scores and details of games played that very day). Today, virtually no PM papers exist.

The influence of several writers extended far beyond their home markets, and their names echo throughout these pages. Frequently referenced will be New York legends Dick Young, Jack Lang, Leonard Koppett, Joe Durso, Red Smith, and Jimmy Cannon. In Chicago, Holtzman, who died in 2008, remains the gold standard for baseball reporting. Based in New York, the bylines of Joe Reichler and Milton Richman were known throughout the country via their decades-long work with the national wire services The Associated Press and United Press International, respectively.

In the late 1940s, Young, of the *New York Daily News*, broke new ground when he became the first AM writer to consistently cover postgame locker room reaction, enabling him to unearth new stories, quotes, and angles each day. To keep up with Young, the most dogged and outspoken of reporters, you had to "cover the room." Previously, only the PM writers (who, naturally, had later deadlines) could be found amid the post-game scramble. Lang's bulldoggish tenacity and dedication to the BBWAA, Koppett's analysis and eye for the offbeat, Durso's and Smith's elegance, and Cannon's New York–bred blue-collar style all resonate today, long after their passings. Holtzman, with his trademark bushy eyebrows and fat cigar, defined Chicago baseball writing for decades (humming as he typed), originated the definitive "save rule" that is still in use for relief pitchers today, and later became Major League Baseball's official historian. Reichler and Richman used their widespread contacts and the wire service credo of "A Deadline Every Minute" to break stories of national interest and impact.

Later, expansion and franchise movement enabled dozens of writers who previously covered minor league ball to burst onto the major league scene, most notably Bob Hunter, George Lederer, and Frank Finch in Los Angeles; Bob Stevens in San Francisco; Phil Collier in San Diego; Bob Wolf in Milwaukee; and Lou Hatter and Bob Maisel in Baltimore.

I and thousands of others first encountered many of these men through their bylines in *The Sporting News* during its final years as the self-proclaimed "Bible of Baseball," reporting every week from their faraway outposts. In the pre-Internet days, we felt we knew them, even if we'd never met them.

Several of the Eastern-based writers profiled here were part of the New Journalism revolution of the 1950s and '60s. Dubbed "Chipmunks," they were often criticized by the older generation for being irreverent, witty, and immune to the trappings of athletic celebrity. This new wave of baseball writer looked for stories, issues, and angles far beyond the box score, an effort that crystallized with Jim Bouton's groundbreaking 1970 book *Ball Four*, which was conceived and edited by an original Chipmunk, the *New York Post*'s Leonard Shecter.

The brash, young Chipmunks of the '60s are now the industry's elder statesmen, sometimes leveling the same kind of criticism at today's new Internet-based breed of writer/commentator that they themselves endured half a century ago.

These, then, are the first-person histories of a group of journalists whose influence, power, and dedication to the game of baseball made them the last of their kind, that final generation of writers who were the unquestioned keepers of the national pastime. The emphasis is strictly on the personal and anecdotal. If you're looking for a day-by-day, play-by-play breakdown of the Phillies' 1964 collapse or the Mets' 1969 championship, you've come to the wrong place.

This is a celebration of baseball *writers*, life on the beat, and the special camaraderie that was once found in press boxes across the land. For decades, the words of these men shaped the history of the game. Now, they tell their own stories.

*   *   *

I interviewed twenty-four writers for this book. Twenty-three are included here.

For nearly half a century, Bill Conlin was the conscience of Philadelphia baseball. He was many things, none of them dull: acerbic, opinionated, brash, bombastic, controversial, and fearless.

A master of cadence and pacing, Conlin's reputation was forged over twenty-two stormy years as Phillies beat writer for the *Philadelphia Daily News*, beginning when he succeeded Stan Hochman in 1966 and stretching through early 1987. His confrontational, in-your-face style was evident both on and off the printed page, especially through his complex relationship with Hall of Fame pitcher Steve Carlton. Conlin's long career climaxed when he was named winner of the 2011 Spink Award, an honor many felt was long overdue.

Conlin's impact and greatness as a baseball writer cannot be denied or ignored. But nor can the horrific allegations of child molestation that were brought against him in late 2011. Hours before the allegations became public, he retired from his columnist position after forty-six years at the *Daily News*.

I interviewed Conlin a year earlier, and our two-hour conversation was easily the funniest, most colorful, and most emotional that I had with any of the writers. In typical Conlin fashion, he told of covering the 1965 Watts Riots during a Phillies road trip, surfing with Hobie Alter and Phil Edwards off the Southern California coast, and his battles with the likes of Carlton, Richie Allen, and Gene Mauch. As he did so often in print, Conlin turned a phrase that perfectly described the profession he embodied. "It was," he told me, "like being a jazz musician with a typewriter."

His was a riveting story. But ultimately, in light of the allegations that ended his newspaper career and sent shockwaves throughout the baseball and sportswriting worlds, I do not feel it is appropriate to include it here. The decision is entirely mine.

*   *   *

Perhaps the most gratifying thing about doing a book, I've found, is the help and support afforded along the way by a very special group of people.

My biggest and most heartfelt thanks, of course, go to the men—each one the epitome of the vintage baseball beat writer—who so willingly gave me an intimate look at their personal and professional lives.

This book couldn't have been done without the support and encouragement of Jack O'Connell, the longtime secretary-treasurer of the BBWAA and among the first to whom I broached the idea. The very first was Stan Isaacs, over lunch in the Citizens Bank Park press room in April 2008. After listening to my hurried description, he replied, "I'd buy that book even if I'm not in it!"

Thanks in large doses go to Jeff Idelson of the National Baseball Hall of Fame and Museum, Marty Appel, Janet (Mrs. Maury) Allen, Ron Cook, Billy DeLury, Randy Galloway, Joe Gilmartin,

Karen Guregian, George King, Larry Merchant, Rick Monday, Kay (Mrs. Bobby) Murcer, Tim McCarver, Jim O'Connell, Vin Scully, Mike Shalin, Dewayne Staats, Charley Steiner, Suzyn Waldman, Chris Wheeler, and several of my old PR brethren, including Matt Bourne of MLB Network, Bob DiBiasio of the Cleveland Indians, Maria Jacinto of the San Francisco Giants, Rob Butcher of the Cincinnati Reds, and Greg Johnson and Sally O'Leary of the Pittsburgh Pirates. Closer to home, thanks as always to Mark Langill, Joe Jareck, Jon Chapper, and Colin Gunderson of the Dodgers, and to Tim Mead, Eric Kay, Ryan Cavinder, and Adam Chodzko of the Angels—along with distinguished alumni Josh Rawitch (Dodgers) and Nancy Mazmanian (Angels)—who provide me with safe haven and work space all summer long. To Jay Horwitz of the Mets, along with Tiki, Leo, Stanley, and Lilly . . . well, we fooled 'em again.

A special thank you to Dave Anderson, the very last man out of the Ebbets Field press gate, for contributing the book's foreword.

Thanks to my intrepid agent, John Monteleone, for once again pulling the rabbit out of the hat, and to Elizabeth Demers and the staff at Potomac Books for their kindness, patience, faith, and indulgence. And thanks—again!—to all my friends at the NBA, the New York Knicks, MLB on Fox, Turner, and ESPN for keeping me busy (and gainfully employed!) between book assignments.

And, most of all, to Helene. If anyone ever gets around to doing a hockey version of this book, I call dibs on chapter one.

—Dennis D'Agostino
Huntington Beach, California
June 2012

1

STAN ISAACS

With a wry, offbeat style that typified not only his own career but the philosophy of an entire sports section, Stan Isaacs was the anchor of Newsday's *baseball coverage for nearly four decades.*

Joining the Long Island daily in 1954 (after the folding of the long-forgotten Daily Compass, *where he worked under the legendary editor Stanley Woodward), Isaacs covered all three New York teams in 1956–1957. After the Dodgers and Giants headed west, he took over the Yankees beat in 1958. He covered both the Yankee and Mets beats until 1965, when he became a columnist. With its signature title "Out of Left Field," Isaacs's column not only covered sports but, eventually, the local and national sports media beat. He retired from* Newsday *in 1992.*

As an original Chipmunk, Isaacs was responsible for three signature moments in modern baseball writing, two comical and one deadly serious: his role in the heisting of the Brooklyn Dodgers' 1955 world championship pennant, his infamous "breast or bottle" question directed at the Yankees' Ralph Terry in 1962, and his 1964 two-part feature on Alvin Dark, in which the Giants manager was quoted as criticizing the team's Latin and African American players.

A BBWAA member since 1951, Isaacs is a regular contributor to TheColumnists.com and also serves on the twenty-man committee that elects the Hall of Fame's annual Ford Frick Award winner (the broadcast equivalent of the Spink Award). Since 1960, first in Newsday *and now on the Internet, he has published his annual Isaacs*

Ratings of Esoteric Distinction, which include his anxiously awaited rankings of the world's great chocolate ice creams.

The Ebbets Field press box was way up on top of the upper deck, and to get there you walked down a gated runway into the box. The first game I ever worked in Ebbets Field, I walked down the runway, and there was a seat right as you walked in. I sat down, and two minutes later Jack Lang comes over to me and says, "Kid, get to the end!" That was Jack Lang being Jack Lang.

Once I started on the high school paper, I wrote sports and realized that it was really all I cared about. I advanced to the Brooklyn College *Vanguard* and then became a sports stringer for the *Herald Tribune* and the *Times*. That gave me an entrée into the New York newspaper business.

The *Daily Compass* was a newspaper from the 1950s that was really significant for its time. It didn't have any advertising, the feeling being that advertising corrupted newspapers, which was completely wrong. The more advertisers you have, the less advertisers can tell you what to do.

When the *Compass* started, I got a job under Stanley Woodward, the great sports editor. Woodward had been fired years before by the *Tribune*, and the *Compass* brought him back. The famous story about Woodward was that the *Tribune* was trying to cut staff. The editor-in-chief sends a note to Woodward, telling him to designate the two most expendable people on the staff. Woodward wrote back, "Stanley Woodward and Red Smith."

Woodward was a gruff guy who loved college football. I was awed by him, naturally. He was the editor, and I dealt more with the subeditors, the guys on the desk. He instilled a journalistic integrity that carried over not only to sports but to the whole paper. It was a muckraking kind of paper, and we all had high ideals.

When the *Compass* folded in 1952, I freelanced, which is a glorious word for "struggling," writing little pieces for magazines and hanging around the New York sports scene, going to the basketball writers lunches, that kind of thing. I also had a job on some crappy magazine that put out mild girlie editions. This was before *Playboy*. I wrote captions for it and left after one summer. Joe Goldstein, who at that time was still a writer before he became a great press agent, told

Bob Zellner, the sports editor of *Newsday*, that I was a bright young guy. In October of 1954, I started at *Newsday* writing high school sports. Four years later, in 1958, I started traveling with the Yankees.

I always felt I wasn't part of the mainstream of the New York baseball press. You had guys like Dick Young of the *Daily News* and Lou Effrat of the *Times*, they owned the place. I was a marginal guy, first at the *Compass* and now at *Newsday*.

I had this vision of being the equivalent of a cityside reporter— the guys who covered politics and crime and things like that. You do a good job, cover the story, and you don't become pals with those you cover. One day, when I was starting out, Joe DiMaggio was involved in a weird play. I asked him about it, and he gave me a non-answer. I walked away, and Joe Trimble of the *Daily News* came over to me and said, "Stan, you don't go over and ask Joe about the play. You wait until he lets us know he wants to talk to us." I was stunned. That's not the way a cityside or political reporter would do it.

I came at it from a different angle. We were serious journalists who weren't in awe of who we were covering. We were trying to write and cover things well, but with an irreverent air combining good reportorial instincts with a sort of an irreverent feeling and an honest skepticism. We were not part of a club; we weren't awed by covering the exalted Yankees. And they were a very tough team to cover, because they weren't used to people coming around and asking tough questions.

Jack Mann was the guy who set the tone for *Newsday* back then. He was a mild, sweet guy. Not a strong-minded sports editor, but that was fine with me because I was pretty strong. It was basically me and Mann who determined what *Newsday* was like: irreverent, hard-hitting, funny. We were cityside-type guys who felt strongly about doing good work. Today's expression, I guess, would be "outside the box."

As a newspaper, we always seemed to be on the outside. We were never part of the establishment. In fact, I was the one who said, "I won't be an official scorer." *Newsday* was the first paper to not allow official scoring. I said it was counter to what we were doing as newspapermen. One, we weren't part of the establishment. Two, it can hurt your stories. You make a scoring call in a game, and then you have to go down to the locker room and justify it. It wasn't worth

4 KEEPERS OF THE GAME

it. Other papers later followed. Then it bothered me years later when *Newsday* guys started scoring again.

*   *   *

Certainly I was a Chipmunk. The whole Chipmunk thing has been so distorted. The three people who gravitated toward each other were me, Leonard Shecter of the *Post*, and Larry Merchant from Philadelphia. Larry was a great guy for knowing what was going on around the country. He was reading me when none of the New York City editors were reading *Newsday*. He was sharp, and he recognized that sharpness in the way I wrote, the offbeat approach. We were kinsmen in a way. So the three of us would get together after games, and we thought of ourselves, lightheartedly, as the Rat Pack, a take-off of Frank Sinatra, Dean Martin, and their pals. That was the three of us.

A year or two later, Jim Bouton won a game he pitched at Yankee Stadium. Bouton was a guy who liked the press, and we gravitated to him because he was funny and he liked to talk to us. There's a lot of revelry around his locker; I was there, Shecter, Phil Pepe, we were kidding and laughing with him.

From across the clubhouse, Jimmy Cannon looked at us all laughing and said, "Look at them! Look at them!" And Pepe's teeth protruded a little. Cannon said, "Look at them, they're a bunch of chipmunks!" So we said, "That's a good name." Forget the Rat Pack, we're the Chipmunks. Then you had other young guys come along, a lot of them from *Newsday*, like Steve Jacobson and George Vecsey.

The Chipmunks were part of a generational thing. Young people come along and shake things up from the old guard, and then eventually the young people become the old guard when a new group comes along. So now *we* don't like some of the things that have been done over the years, like the personal stuff and the sex stuff.

When Roger Maris came to the Yankees, he was kind of a grouch. It was sort of refreshing that you had a guy who wasn't awed by being a Yankee. We looked upon him—a guy who, if you were in the army with him, he'd complain. And you liked him complaining because you'd agree with him, but you might not complain like he did.

When Maris and Mickey Mantle started hitting home runs in 1961, the traditional guys liked Mantle and were rooting for him.

They weren't anti-Maris, but Mantle was the guy. We, meaning Shecter and I and guys like us, liked Maris. While it might not have been part of our stories, I know I wanted Maris to be the guy. He had a surliness that at times was inappropriate, which if you didn't know him might have turned you off. That's what hurt him with Cannon and Oscar Fraley from UPI the next spring.

The run toward sixty-one homers was symbolized with two incidents. There was a game in Chicago that was delayed by rain. We're killing time in the press box and got word that Maris was down in the runway outside the Yankee clubhouse, talking to fans. So we run down, and it's a gated runway, and we're able to talk to him through the gate. Here's a guy who's supposedly running away from the press, and he comes out, and now we're interviewing him along the runway. He wasn't hiding.

The other incident was at Detroit toward the end of the season, and unfortunately it typifies Maris and why he got in trouble. He hits one into the upper deck; the ball bounces out of the stands and back onto the field. Al Kaline picks it up, throws it back in, and they give the ball to Maris. In the clubhouse afterward, Watson Spoelstra of the *Detroit News*, asks him, "Wasn't that a nice thing that Kaline did?" I'm saying to myself, "Roger, say yes!" But he said, "Anybody would have done it." That's typical Roger. He's being honest and doesn't mean to be mean. Well, Spoelstra writes it and frames the story around it. The next day, people are booing Roger.

Sometimes Roger would say no in a surly way that would work against him. That's why it started, that people hated him. If sixty thousand people were cheering and a thousand were booing, somehow Maris remembered the thousand who were booing. But Yankee fans were rooting for him. Once Mantle got hurt, Yankee fans were rooting for Maris. It's a myth to say they weren't.

Bill Veeck once said that only one team can win, but does that mean all the other teams can't have any fun? I looked at the early Mets and saw that they weren't going to win, but they had guys who were interesting whom you could write about. Casey Stengel set the fun tone, and so did Richie Ashburn. Ashburn clued us in on things about Stengel and Marv Throneberry that helped us realize that this was a team you could look at lightheartedly. It was ridiculous to think they were going to contend for the pennant. You like fun in this world, and this is a game, not high science. The logical thing was to cover them that way.

Throneberry had failed with the Yankees, and he was looked upon as a bum, a big, lazy Southerner who didn't amount to anything. People seemed to really dislike him. It struck me at some point that the opposite of hate is love. So I wrote a column that said, in effect, "Mets fans are bound to love Throneberry. He is going to be the guy they love." And that's what happened. It's one of the few things I can point to where I was right on. *Best Sports Stories* picked that one up.

A big part of the Throneberry thing was that Ashburn was egging it on. He'd come up to us and say, "Did you hear what Throneberry said yesterday?" Throneberry moaned a lot, but Ashburn turned the moaning into humor. Ashburn was also good for telling you things about Stengel that we didn't know.

I'll tell you the definitive 1962 Mets story. First day of spring training, Stengel takes the team onto the field, then at lunchtime they come into the locker room. I go over to Sherman "Roadblock" Jones, a pitcher who had come from Cincinnati. I say, "Hi, I'm Stan Isaacs of *Newsday*." He said, "Is that a newspaper?" I said, "Yes." He said, "I only believe 12 percent of what I read in newspapers."

I looked at him and said, "12 percent? Why 12 percent?" He gave me sort of a mystical air and said, "12 percent." I said to myself that no matter what I write, people are going to believe only 12 percent, so why should I get too worried about it?

*   *   *

When we stole the Dodgers' 1955 world championship pennant, there were four of us: me, Jack Mann, Steve Weller of the *Buffalo News*, and a friend of mine who had been born in Brooklyn but was now working for the *Los Angeles Times*, Chuck Sutton.

This is at the 1959 World Series in L.A., and this would be after Game Five. At the World Series press headquarters, we're eating and drinking. On the big curtain in this ballroom was the 1955 championship flag, pinned to the drapes. We're sitting there, and I said, "They took the team out of Brooklyn and now even the flag. They shouldn't have the flag." So we said, "Let's steal the flag."

I must say, liquor was not involved here. I'm not a drinker. But Weller was encouraging us, going, "Yeah, yeah!"

We're among the last few people sitting, and we're going to stack the tables on top of each other to get to the flag. We call the busboys, and Sutton says to them, "I'm Chuck Sutton of the *New York Herald Tribune*, and we must have the tables stacked up there, and we also need a pair of scissors."

I guess something about the *Herald Tribune* sounded good to them, because they helped us stack the tables. I got up, and I snipped the cord that tied the flag to the wall. We wrapped it up and ran out of the building, figuring that the cops would be following us the whole way.

We thought that when the Dodgers found out about this, they'd come to Mann and me. So we gave the flag to Sutton, who lived in L.A., and we'd get it later. Jack and I went back to the hotel, figuring that at any time, we'd be caught. We went to the airport the next morning to fly to Chicago, and Sutton came and gave us the flag. All the time, we're thinking that Walter O'Malley and his police are going to come. We go to Chicago for the rest of the Series and then home to New York, and I put the flag in my house in Roslyn Heights.

We figured we'd take the flag to Brooklyn, but in those days, Brooklyn was in a down time. There was no place to display the flag. So it stayed in my basement, wrapped in plastic, for years. I finally said, "This is ridiculous. We want this flag to be seen." So I gave it to the Hall of Fame in Cooperstown, but they didn't do anything with it, either. They kept it in their basement, and it just as well could have been in mine. Finally, they put together an exhibit honoring old ballparks and displayed the flag. Years later, Peter O'Malley persuaded them to give the flag to the Brooklyn Historical Society, where it is now.

Long after all this was over, I once asked Buzzie Bavasi, the Dodgers GM, "How come you didn't try to get the flag back?" He said, "Ah, it belonged where you had it. We just had another one made, and it cost us $92."

*   *   *

The bottle story. Ralph Terry wins Game Seven of the 1962 World Series in San Francisco. We're around Terry in the clubhouse. Terry was a shy guy, amiable. We liked him, and we had a lot of easy banter with him. In the middle of it, somebody tells Terry that his wife is on the phone. So he says, "Excuse me," and he went back. When he came back, he told us that the call was from his wife. We asked him what she was doing, and he said she was feeding the baby.

So I said, "Breast or bottle?" My wife had given birth not long before, so I knew about things like that. I said it as a flippant line. Some people laughed, but some were amazed that I would say this. Terry gave a shy grin, and by the way, we never got the answer. I thought of my question as a joke, just as part of the banter.

Some people saw it as the lighthearted thing that it was, but some saw it as typical intrusive Chipmunk reporting, and the state the business had come to. It's been distorted over the years. People have had it under different circumstances, like after the Mazeroski homer off Terry in the 1960 World Series. The History Channel made that mistake. To me, it was just having fun. To some who wanted to be negative about it, they saw it as intrusive.

In any case, I didn't write it. Not that I had any desire not to write it; it just didn't seem that important. I laugh now when it's mentioned. People say to me, "Oh, you're the breast or bottle guy. . . ."

The Alvin Dark thing came about because I was going out west to cover the U.S.-USSR track meet in L.A. in 1964. I stopped in San Francisco on the way. I'm thinking, I'll get a column while I'm there.

I liked Dark; so did Koppett. He was a Christian, a very ethical guy. Now I'm in San Francisco and I stop in the clubhouse before the game, and Dark is beside himself. The Giants have been losing games with stupid plays, and he was really venting about why they were doing so badly and making all these mistakes. I suggested that, well, isn't it the manager's fault? He said, "No, it's something else," and that's when he started saying that the Negro players aren't that smart and that's part of the problem.

I said that if the Negro players aren't that smart, look at the Boston Celtics. They're the best team in basketball, and the smartest team, and they're almost all black. Why would those black guys be smarter? And he said, "I don't know about that, I know that you just can't make the Negro and the Spanish players have the pride in their team that the white players have." By Spanish, which is what we said back then, he meant Spanish-speaking.

I'm not taking notes. I'm listening to him and certainly paying attention, and I paraphrase what he said in the column. I write it over two days, and the second day's column is mostly on Orlando Cepeda. He's really upset at Cepeda, and I wrote it as such. Because no one paid any attention to *Newsday*, it didn't get any publicity. The managing editor, Alan Hathway, tried to get the AP to pick up the column, but they wouldn't. But black players all around, they knew about it. It was an underground thing. Finally, it exploded about two weeks later when the Giants came to New York.

I had mixed feelings. On the one hand, I knew that I was accurate—I knew I wasn't making any of this up. I knew there were other managers who said these things who were not quoted. I thought I was bringing out into the open a feeling that existed in baseball about black and Hispanic players. But I was naïve; it didn't work that way. All that was seized upon was Dark saying that black and Hispanic players weren't that smart.

When Dark came to New York, he had a press conference. I felt bad about what was happening; you quote somebody and it blows up, and you can't protect him. This wasn't what I wanted to happen. I thought I was making a sociological point. Before Dark came to New York, I went down to see him in Philadelphia, and I explained the best I could that I wasn't trying to get him. But it was meaningless because he denied that he was a racist and that he hadn't said it. I, again protecting him, said, "I could see where he thinks that what he said was taken out of context." He threatened to sue later on, but I knew that other people had heard things like this, and he didn't sue. In later years, when we were on the field together, I looked at him, but he looked away, and I could understand that.

I felt bad for him. And the irony is that, as some people have told me, the Giants were foundering so much that Horace Stoneham was ready to fire him. But because of the flap at that time, he felt he couldn't fire him, and instead he did it at the end of the year.

*   *   *

I was known for doing offbeat stuff. Behind the right field fence at the old ballpark in Kansas City, there was a grassy incline. Charlie Finley, who was trying to outstunt Bill Veeck, put sheep out there so they could eat the grass. At the end of a long trip you get bored, and I decided I would sit with the sheep and cover the game from there.

Afterward, when I came into the clubhouse, Whitey Ford asked me, "Are you writing for the Stockyard News?" Mantle said, "How many blades of grass were out there?" You know, kidding, the kinds of questions we asked.

I think I could be a beat guy today, but I wouldn't like to do the job the way it's done now. Having to write so many stories, so many early edition stories, and writing for the Web. It's constantly feeding the maw, this gigantic maw. It doesn't seem very satisfying. On the other hand, you have to earn a living, and there are worse things than writing about baseball.

There's a lot more centering on insignificant stuff. I'm reading the Philadelphia papers, and there's two days in a row on "The Psyche of Cole Hamels." Hey, the guy's a pitcher, and he had a bad year. But they're squeezing the blood out of it. I don't see the New York papers, but I would assume that what I'd see there wouldn't thrill me. But if I'd had to do it, I'd do it.

One last story. One year we're in California, and it's a late game against the Angels. The game is running long. We're going to have a tough time making deadline, and we find out that we probably won't make the team bus out to the airport. Joe Trimble of the *Daily News* says, "Well, I know Peter Lorre. He's here and he has a car, and he'll take us." So after the game we go to the car, get in, and there's Peter Lorre behind the wheel. I kept thinking to myself, this is something out of *The Maltese Falcon*. Peter Lorre is driving us to the airport, and who knows what's going to happen? However, Sydney Greenstreet was nowhere to be found. Neither was the black bird.

2

ROSS NEWHAN

To find Ross Newhan, the elegant bard of Southern California base-ball, drive south on the 91 Freeway, take the cutoff at Corona, and stop along the side road at the Foothill Fruit Stand.

There, among bushels of fresh avocadoes and boxes of newly-picked tangerines, the 2000 Spink Award winner plies a new trade after a half-century of newspaper work, starting with the Long Beach Independent Press-Telegram *in 1958 and then the* Los Angeles Times *for thirty-six years starting in 1968.*

One of the original beat writers for the expansion Los Angeles Angels in 1961, Ross handled the Angels beat for the Press-Telegram *from 1961–1968 and again for the* Times *from 1980–1985. He also covered the* Times' *Dodger beat for the bulk of the 1970s. In 1986, he was promoted to national baseball columnist for the* Times, *serving in that capacity until his retirement in 2004. He's been a BBWAA member since 1961.*

In 1999, Newhan's career took on a new dimension when his son David reached the major leagues as an infielder with the San Diego Padres. It was a subject that Ross steadfastly refused to address in print . . . until David's successful return to the majors with Baltimore in 2004 after a shoulder injury had sidelined him for nearly three years.

Joining Jim Murray (1987) and Bob Hunter (1988) as Los Angeles–based Spink winners, Newhan is still an occasional contributor to the paper and also teams with son David for the blog "Newhan on Baseball." He'll also sell you some of the juiciest oranges this side of Anaheim.

11

My son David was once quoted as saying that he knew he'd never want to be a sportswriter because he came home too many times to find me screaming and cursing at my typewriter. That's very accurate. There's no doubt about it, I cussed out typewriters, computers, whatever.

I covered baseball for forty-plus years. I kind of divide it into four sections and consider myself extremely lucky to have had them.

The first section was with the Angels, when I was just breaking in and there were these terrific characters you could write about off the field as easily as on the field.

The second part was covering the Dodgers in the '70s when they had those great teams. I was fortunate to get the last years of Walter Alston and the early years of Tommy Lasorda.

Then came the period when I went back as the Angels beat writer from 1980 through 1985. They had an All-Star lineup then: Don Baylor, Rod Carew, Fred Lynn, Doug DeCinces. Talk about learning a lot of baseball from those guys, and then from Gene Mauch. God, how I loved Gene Mauch. He was probably the most fascinating manager I was ever around.

And then, finally, came the opportunity to become national baseball columnist. The labor issues would weigh on you and weren't a lot of fun to cover, but they were important stories. We bopped around the country covering labor stories, which enhanced my reputation nationally.

Those last fifteen or sixteen years as national columnist were absolutely incredible. Peter O'Malley sold the Dodgers to Fox, Fox sold to the McCourts, the Angels were sold to Disney, and Disney sold them to Arte Moreno. I mean, I never had to look for a column to write.

* * *

I absolutely fell into the only job I've ever had. I took a journalism course on a whim as a senior in high school. The instructor was this huge bear of a guy named John Gartner who kind of lit a spark in me. Hemingway's *The Old Man and the Sea* had just come out, and it was serialized in one of the magazines, and he read it to us, making points along the way. During that year, he told me that the

Long Beach paper, the *Press-Telegram*, was looking for somebody to phone in results of our high school's games, at $5 a week. He asked me if I wanted to do it, and I said sure. That started it.

From there, they asked me to work in the office and take games over the phone, and they also sent me out a little to write. I'd never had any real feel that I was a writer or anything like that. Not at all. But one assignment led to another; I'd do a sidebar for a college game at the Coliseum or a Rams game or something like that. They also let me work the slot at night, laying out pages, which was great fun.

At that point, the Long Beach paper had a terrific sports section. When the Angels were created, I was next in line for a major beat. I was working full-time hours but not on a full-time basis. I had started at Long Beach State with an interest in history and was thinking maybe I'd go in for teaching. But I was having so much fun at the paper and discovering that I had a little writing ability that my grades, let's say, deteriorated. It wasn't just the fun at the paper that hurt my grades—it was having one too many beers sometimes. The dean said to me, "You've got more on the ball than what you're showing. We'll let you have one more chance," and that just led to more of the same.

I was put on the Angels beat in 1961. Was I ready? Oh, no. Oh, my gosh, I didn't have a clue. But I would say three things helped me along.

One was that, with the Angels being an expansion team, I was dealing mostly with veteran players who were just happy to have a job. It was a different era from now in that there was a lot more trust between player and writer. "Can I have ten minutes of your time?" the young writer said. That wasn't a problem. The Angels were a group in the early years that had a lot of characters, so it was pretty easy to find stories.

Two, I broke in on the beat with Bud Furillo, John Hall, Braven Dyer, and Dan Hafner, so I learned a lot in a hurry. Bud was little zany, but he had a great passion for newspapers, as did John. I don't remember being intimidated. Those guys were so friendly, and we enjoyed going out for dinner at night. We were competitive, but it was a great experience to travel with those guys. Braven was the Dean; he'd been around for a long time. He sort of went his own way.

And the third thing was that Bill Rigney, the manager, was just great. He was very quotable after games. He was very social. He'd played and managed in New York, so when we went to New York, he'd take us to Toots Shor's and great restaurants. He made it real easy that way.

The players were so willing to share their stories. We had one crazy guy after another, so you could write what happened on the bus—and these were the days where we rode the bus with the players. You didn't even have to write the ballgame. The guys . . . Bo Belinsky and Ryne Duren and Art Fowler and Leon Wagner and Lee Thomas.

Fred Haney was the Angels' general manager, and he'd gotten the scouting reports from Buzzie Bavasi of the Dodgers. Meanwhile, Rigney had gotten the scouting reports from the Giants from Chub Feeney, his old boss who had fired him just months before. So they were able to draft several players who became famous. Jim Fregosi became an All-Star shortstop, Buck Rodgers became a terrific catcher, and Dean Chance turned into a Cy Young Award winner.

The first day that Bo Belinsky reported, we had a poolside press conference in Palm Springs. He'd come out of the Baltimore organization and had a reputation as possibly one of the Orioles' big pitchers. He and Steve Dalkowski and all those flamethrowers, although Bo wasn't really a flamethrower. He was more of an off-speed guy. Then he starts off that year five-and-oh with a no-hitter, and he's dating all these stars, Ann-Margret and Rita Hayworth and Mamie Van Doren. God, we wrote all of that stuff. There was one breaking-curfew story after another, one fine after another. You couldn't avoid it.

Here's this streetwise guy, handsome, with a swagger. Dean Chance latched onto him, and Dean's this hayseed from Ohio. They became running buddies. Another guy who latched onto him was Walter Winchell, the gossip columnist. Winchell was friendly with us, he was okay. That lasted for about a year, until Bo's career started to go south.

Remember the old dugout seats at Dodger Stadium? Well, frequently during day games, I would go and watch Bo pitch from those seats, sitting with Mamie. You could write a story from that perspective. What could be better for a young writer?

During spring training, Palm Springs was a haven for celebrities. I once walked into the dugout at that little ballpark one morning, and who's sitting on the bench but Dwight Eisenhower. Bud Furillo was real close to Frank Sinatra at the time, and we went over to his house one night for a party. That was fun. Frank was dating Jill St. John at the time.

If you look at the Angels' thirty-six years under Gene Autry, there were long periods that were just comical. In the '70s, they changed managers every year, it seemed. The years Alex Johnson played—1970 and 1971—were terrible, literally terrible. One time, Dick Miller of the [*Los Angeles*] *Herald Examiner* and I flew into Cleveland on the day of a game. We're getting our bags out of the cab in front of the hotel when we hear this guy screaming F-bombs all over the place, and people are looking up and all. It's *Alex* leaning out of his window, screaming at *us*. That's the kind of thing that happened. Dick was the guy that Alex took the coffee grounds and dumped them into his typewriter.

Alex could be such a great player when he wanted to be. One of the fastest right-handed hitters I've seen getting to first. But the off-the-field stuff got to the point where one of the headlines the *Times* ran during that time was, "Where Angels fear to Tread."

Here's my favorite story from the Alex Johnson years: Lefty Phillips is the manager, and never should have been. A wonderful, beautiful guy who just should have been a scout. Lefty had asthma, and when he got excited he'd stutter.

So we're in Arizona in spring training, and Lefty takes the writers out to dinner. He's driving us back to the hotel, and as he turns the corner, he almost hits this guy crossing the street. We realize as we drive off that it's Alex! And Lefty says, "I-I-I-I-I-I should have k-k-k-k-killed the SOB!"

*   *   *

I probably had a nervous breakdown every time I was on deadline. The Long Beach paper was both morning and afternoon, so we'd write the morning story at the ballpark. At that time, they had a Western Union operator right there, and you'd give the story to the operator and hope he'd transmit the same story that you wrote. Then I'd drive to the paper. I wouldn't have to do a whole new story, but I'd have to put a new top to it, maybe six to ten graphs to make it more of a feature story, for the afternoon paper. I'd do that on the road, too.

At two in the morning, you'd be walking the streets trying to find a Western Union office that was open.

In 1968, the managing editor of the *Times* called me. I think John Hall pushed it a little bit. At the Long Beach paper I was making $185 a week. I forget exactly what the *Times* offered me—I think it was about $240 a week. Then the Long Beach paper said, "We'll make you a columnist." But I just felt the increase in money, with Connie and I just getting married, along with the opportunity to write at the *Times*, was just too important.

I think of the great games I've seen. It's been pretty fabulous. Rickey Henderson's stolen base record, Pete Rose's big hit. Funny thing, I only saw one of Nolan Ryan's no-hitters. We switched around on the Angels and Dodgers beats back then, and I missed all of Ryan's no-hitters except one. I saw Bo Belinsky and Clyde Wright pitch no-hitters. I saw the Mike Witt perfect game on the last day in 1984 and the combined Mark Langston-Mike Witt no-hitter in the first week in 1990.

As for the labor stuff, the paper had been lax for quite a few years in covering it. While some of it was wearying, a lot of it was pretty challenging. The motivation was that I'm gonna get this story even if it's ten at night and I have to wake up Don Fehr, the head of the players union, and maybe get yelled at. But I knew he'd call me back the next day, too.

For a lot of that period, I challenged myself to be the equal, if not better, than Murray Chass of *The New York Times*. Murray, and rightfully so for a long period, was looked at as the guy who would have every labor story. I thought it was a challenge to try to lift myself to that level. Was it fun? No, but it had to be done.

Was I a better writer or reporter? Well, this sounds arrogant maybe, but I think I did both pretty well. I think perhaps I had a reputation as being a little better reporter than a writer, but I think, over the years, that may have changed.

I'm proud of the fact that the Mitchell Report on steroids footnoted, I believe, five stories that I wrote before the home run year of 1998 on the subject of possible steroid use. Writers got accused a lot for not being on top of that story. At least to some extent, I feel like I was aware of what was going on and tried to write about it. I might not have realized how big or widespread it was, but at least I was touching on it.

I broke a lot of trade stories. We had the 1972 winter meetings in Hawaii when the Dodgers and Angels made, like, a seven-player trade. It was the Frank Robinson trade, where Andy Messersmith and Bobby Valentine were also involved. I had all the names in the morning paper before the trade had even been announced.

I'm also proud of my work leading up to Frank McCourt buying the Dodgers. Jason Reid and I had a lot of his financial situation covered pretty well. That story was almost a done deal, and then Eli Broad, the billionaire financier and businessman, got involved. We had that, too. Eli called Bill Dwyre, the sports editor, and I think it was almost grandstanding a little bit on his part. Eli told Dwyre he wouldn't talk to anyone on the *Times* except for Ross Newhan.

When I was chapter chairman of the Baseball Writers Association, I was in charge of the off-season banquet, which we no longer have. That dinner was fabulous. We held it at the Hollywood Palladium, the Beverly Hilton, the Biltmore. A couple of times we had it in Anaheim.

One year at the Palladium, the Rat Pack came. Bud Furillo had access to Sinatra. Milton Berle was the MC, and I'm sitting next to him. He says to me, "How are you gonna introduce me?" I said, "Well, I'll go over your career and the things you've done and all." He said, "Don't forget to mention that I'm the king of television." And I did.

*   *   *

When David was drafted [by Oakland in 1995], I remember asking Dwyre how I should handle the situation. How could I write about David or his teams? Dwyre said to wait and see how David advanced before we made any decisions. There really hadn't been a precedent for it.

The only thing I did when David reached the major leagues—and he's played for five teams—was that I decided I wasn't going to write about any of his teams. We had enough people that if something had to be written about a team David played for, someone else could do it. I also made up my mind to not go into the clubhouse of any team David was with at the time.

David had been out with shoulder surgeries and was having a big year in Triple-A; then he signed with the Orioles and was in the majors for the first time in three years. Now it's his first game with the Orioles [June 18, 2004], and I'm sitting in Dodger Stadium next to Bill Shaikin, and I'm watching the play-by-play of the Orioles game on Shaikin's computer screen. They're in Colorado, and David pinch-hits in the ninth inning.

You know how, on the GameCast thing, the first thing they put up is "Ball is in play"? Well, that goes up. Then it comes up: "Home run." I kind of jumped a little and went "Heyyyy!" It's the only time I've ever done that.

It was right around Father's Day, and Connie said, "You have to write this. He's been away since 2001 and then comes back and hits a home run in his first at bat?" So I did.

It's been a great experience with David. We traveled around the major and minor leagues to watch him play. When he came back with Baltimore in '04, he hit .311 that year, and he was on fire. It was fabulous. But there was frustration along the way, not only with the injuries. In '05, they didn't play him! I wanted to shoot Lee Mazzilli, who I like a lot and who was the manager that year. I just didn't understand the thinking.

For a kid who wasn't drafted out of high school and had no Division I offers, to ultimately play in the majors and get his degree from Pepperdine, he's taught our family a lot about tenacity and determination.

As a kid, he was around the Angels a lot. He'd come down to spring training, and the Angels were great about it. They'd let David sweep out the clubhouse and be a batboy once in a while. After the games, [coach] Jimmie Reese would take these kids out—Bob Boone's kids, Doug DeCinces' kids, and David—and they'd have a phantom infield drill. Jimmie would fake hitting the ball, and they'd just run around.

When the Angels were one strike away from the pennant in 1986, I was in the press box in Anaheim. I could look down, and I saw David and his sister in the aisle, and I'm mad at my wife for letting them get in that crowd crush, ready to run on the field. But it never happened.

*   *   *

When I won the Spink, there were so many wonderful calls and letters and e-mails. Connie did a great job; she typed out all of the voice-mail messages and pasted them up. Vin Scully called, and Jaime Jarrin wrote a note that said, "It won't mean as much to you right now, but just think about your grandchildren and their grand-children." The grandkids are still too young, but they wear their Ross Newhan T-shirts that they were selling in Cooperstown that weekend. It seems like every time my name is in print, there's "Hall of Famer" next to it. It's pretty cool. I'm humbled by it.

I think it would be very hard to do the job today, and I only base that on stories I've heard from people like Jason Reid, before he left the *Times*, and Dylan Hernandez and Mike DiGiovanna, our beat writers today. The calls they get when they're on the field, and having to write right there on those, what do you call them? BlackBerrys. Who knows what they're missing down on the field when they're upstairs blogging?

The demands of the Internet combined with the demands of getting a story in the paper, I think, would have been very difficult for me.

I don't know if anybody is going to be a baseball beat writer for forty years anymore. Not without the absolute support of your family. My family was incredibly supportive. My wife always thought she was going to marry Sandy Koufax, and she wound up with me instead.

3

JOE GODDARD

The man known to all as "Young Joe" was an admitted late bloomer.

Joe Goddard was a cityside writer and editor for more than a decade, first in Indianapolis and then in Chicago, joining the Sun-Times *in 1964. Finally, in late 1973—upon the retirement of Spink winner Edgar Munzel—Goddard realized his dream when he was assigned to the paper's baseball beat.*

It was a while in coming, but Young Joe made up for lost time.

He became synonymous with Chicago baseball, covering both the White Sox and Cubs beats from 1974 through 2000, often switching teams at midseason with Jerome Holtzman and, later, with Dave van Dyck. By his own count, he covered more than five thousand major league games in nearly three decades on the beat. A two-time Spink Award finalist, equally at home in the Bard's Room at old Comiskey Park and the Pink Poodle at Wrigley Field, Goddard also served for years as the Chicago correspondent for The Sporting News.

A BBWAA member since 1974, Goddard's forty-two-year career at the Sun-Times *ended when he accepted a buyout in 2006. Today, this Civil War buff, music lover, amateur gardener, and voracious reader ("I read everything, even graffiti") lives in a Chicago suburb, still Young Joe at heart.*

The first day I was ever on the job as a newspaperman, I was taken out to dinner the night before by the editor. He said, "You remind me so much of myself when I was young and full of enthusiasm. But I have to tell you something. On cityside, murders and fires and disasters won't come to you. You have to go to them."

So the next day I report at 6 a.m. for the police beat. Then I'm walking home at two in the afternoon, and I saw a murder. Saw a guy kill another guy. It wasn't a shootout or anything, just a couple of drunks arguing.

I was all excited. I called the office and said, "I just saw a murder, I got the names of the guys involved." I remember I had to step over the body to talk to the other guy, who was handcuffed to the streetlamp. The police told me his name was Pork Chops Wilson. The first story I ever wrote was a three-graph story about Pork Chops Wilson. That's how I got started professionally. Pork Chops Wilson!

When I was in college at DePauw, a guy I knew worked at the Dodgers training camp in Vero Beach. He told me he wasn't going to work the Dodgertown Camp for Boys, and maybe I should apply. I did and they accepted me. That's really how I got into baseball. I did that for four years. Then when it came time for me to be out of college, I needed a job just to get going. I wrote to Buzzie Bavasi, the general manager, and he said that he could use me in spring training to write stories about the Dodgers' minor league teams. Back then, the minor league teams were Montreal, Atlanta, cities that eventually got major league teams. So I wrote six or seven stories a day, banging away on a typewriter. I was too busy to be scared or awed.

In Indianapolis, at the *Times*, I was on the regular desk, not baseball. In my last year, they put me into sports because I talked about sports so much. The first person I ever interviewed was Joe Louis, the great boxer. I was supposed to ask him a question about an up-and-coming boxer; Louis was in town for a charity golf tournament. I found him on the fourth green and introduced myself, and he said, "I'll meet you on the fifth hole."

So I met him there and asked him about this young boxer, and he said, "Don't like him." Now, you can imagine who he was talking about . . . Cassius Clay.

My third year in Indianapolis, I covered the Triple-A team, the Indians. That was a fun team. It was a White Sox farm team that had Dave DeBusschere (who went on to greatness in the NBA), Minnie Minoso, guys like that. I also covered the Indy 500. I was in Pit Row for the 1964 race when two of the drivers I was assigned to, Eddie

Sachs and Dave MacDonald, were killed. I hated that; I said that this was the stupidest thing I had ever covered. It's a lot safer in racing now, and the technology is so great. It's fun to listen to the guys in their cars while they're racing.

*   *   *

I wanted to get to Chicago because I grew up in the area; my friends were there and getting married and having fun. I was lonely down in Indianapolis—it's not the most exciting city in the world. I applied and was hired right away by the cityside desk at the *Sun-Times*.

One thing I covered was the space race. I did a chart with all the satellites and who was up there when. That was boring, but finally another guy from the sports section came down and said to me, "I hear you like sports." I said yeah. So he said, "Well, I don't like what I'm doing. Why don't we just trade jobs with each other?" After nine years I got moved to sports, and even then I was just writing headlines and working on the desk.

I was on the desk at the *Sun-Times* for nine years. I'm a late bloomer; I didn't get started writing baseball until I was about thirty-six.

When I finally got to sports, I had a guy in my corner named Bill Gleason. Do you remember him? He died in 2010. He came up to me with that cigar in his mouth and said, "You know, kid. You're a pretty good writer. Is this something you want to do?" And I said, "Well, yeah. I think I could, but it's really not for me to say." Then he said, "Well, I want to introduce you to your best friend."

So we walked over to his desk and it was filled with newspapers. There's a phone somewhere in there. He reached in, picked up that phone, and shook my hand with it. I've got the receiver in my hand, and he says, "This is your new best friend. Use it any time you want. Call somebody famous. Call anybody. If you have an idea, call the guy and write it. If it's any good, we'll run it, and if not, we'll tell you why it's no good."

So I did. I called George Halas of the Bears. I called Bill Veeck. I didn't know these guys, and I guess it took a lot of guts on my part to be calling them. After a year of this, they were running the stories, and I was really pleased.

Now, there was a great writer at the *Sun-Times* named Edgar Munzel. Do you know that name? Well, Edgar was nicknamed Mouse, but he was anything but mousy if he got mad. He was a force, but a nice man.

In 1973, my editor came to me and told me that Edgar Munzel was going to retire after forty-one years on the baseball beat. I knew that, I said. He said that they were probably going to hire someone from outside. I said I'd heard that, too.

He said, "Well, I'm going to try something with you. Edgar's going to Europe with his wife. The trip's in September, and the Cubs are in the pennant race. When he comes back, if they're still in the race, I'm going to put him back on the beat. But if you can show me in the three weeks he's gone that you can cover the beat, I'm going to give it to you. Don't tell anybody, because there's going to be a lot of people unhappy with this. You've got some people that don't like you." Just what I needed to hear, right? Because I was a little bit of a jerk back then, calling my friends from the office and that stuff.

So I went off to Pittsburgh to cover a doubleheader. Edgar met me at the airport. He was going to fly to New York and then to Europe. He said, "Here's the first game story for our early editions. Good luck to you," and he got in a cab and drove away. So there I was.

After three weeks of traveling with the Cubs, I came back to the desk, and they said, "You've got the job." That weekend, I threw a party for my friends, and my boss, Jim Mullen, called. He said, "Do I hear a party going on?" I said yeah. "Are you celebrating?" he asked. Well, yeah, I said. "Well, why didn't you invite me?" Oh, God. Then he said, "Well, I gotta tell you something. You're the biggest fuckup I ever had, but you've got talent coming out of your ass, and I can't keep it in your ass any longer, so go show 'em."

*   *   *

I broke in amid a great wave of Chicago writers. Dick Dozer was a wonderful man—I really enjoyed him. Thankfully, I didn't have to compete with Jerome Holtzman, because he was on the same paper and usually with the other team. Holtzman was a legend for sure, but the only time we really talked to each other was when we switched teams at midseason. I'd go to the Sox, and he'd go to the Cubs. That worked well for us.

A lot of people would ask me why I didn't just stay with one team. I'd say, "Why would you stay with one team when you had the chance to go to both leagues?" I really believed that, to this day. There were only three cities that overlapped both leagues: New York, Chicago, and Los Angeles. By switching teams, you got to know everybody, the writers especially.

It took me a few years to realize that my best sources were the writers. If the White Sox were making a trade with, say, the Angels, I'd say, "Okay, who do I know in California?" I'd call someone like Ross Newhan, and say, "Hey, our teams are talking. Let's work together on this." If we hadn't switched teams, I'd have no sources. Other guys would say, "Gee, we never thought of that."

Second, it was a good break from the intensity you feel with a team if they're not going well. Usually, if the players don't like you or you don't like them, you can't go to another team. But in Chicago, it was a breath of fresh air for us. They don't do that anymore; no one does.

After Dave van Dyck went over to the dot-com, the writer who replaced him didn't want to switch teams in midyear. We had a sports editor, Bill Adee, who didn't like it either, so he kept me on the Sox. By then I really didn't care about the switching. I was mad at first, then I realized that as long as I could keep writing, it was okay.

I was okay on deadline. My biggest problem was that I wasn't a very good writer at first, if I ever was. I'd type out a lead, then rip it up, ball it up, throw it on the floor, and get mad at myself, swearing and everything. By the end of the game, you couldn't see my shoes because they were covered with ripped-up pieces of paper. That frustrated me because they were waiting for my copy.

Finally, I'd just have to send it. I'd give it to a Western Union guy. I don't recall missing any deadlines, but I wasn't happy with some of my writing. By the time computers came in, I didn't have any paper on my shoes. It cut down on my hesitancy and criticism of myself.

Sometimes they asked me if I'd like to come off the beat and be a feature reporter or a columnist. I was opposed to that because I wanted to stay on the beat. I've never aspired to be a columnist. I'm too nice a guy, and it's difficult for me to be critical of somebody. It's a game, after all. Now, it's also a business. You can lose some guys in the clubhouse if you're critical all the time.

I didn't particularly like Bobby Murcer when the Cubs got him from the Giants in 1977, but I really didn't know him. He was so unhappy to be a Cub. Now, Murcer saw me in the clubhouse one day. He was in his rocking chair, and he said, "Joe, sit down. We gotta talk." I figured this was gonna be interesting.

He said, "You know what your trouble is? The players don't trust you. They don't trust you in here, they don't trust what you write." I said, "Is that right, Bobby? Well, I'll have to work on that, Bobby. Thank you very much for telling me, Bobby." Of course, I was sarcastic as hell. He said, "Well, I just thought you ought to know what they think."

He changed my life. He changed the way I wrote. Because I got to thinking about that, and he was *right*. I was unnecessarily mean. Just because the team wasn't going well didn't mean I should be writing stuff I shouldn't have written.

I told Bobby that story just before I retired. In 2005, I saw him in the runway at Yankee Stadium and told him. He said, "Well, I don't remember that. But if it helped you, you're welcome." Isn't that amazing? I became a kinder, gentler man because of Bobby Murcer.

Dave Kingman, who came to the Cubs in '77, was difficult for me. He was so aloof and rude. He marched to his own drummer. He got mad at me once when we passed out questionnaires to the players on the Cubs: best curve ball, best manager you've played against, best pitcher you've faced, that sort of thing. Two of the categories were best dressed player on the team and worst dressed. I got about twelve players to fill them out, and for the worst dressed, *everyone* put down Kingman.

When this thing got published, he said, "You know me. I don't like this game. I don't need this game. And when I'm done with this game, you'll never see me again." I went around the corner and went, "Yes!" I would wait for that day! I told myself that when he was done with baseball, I was gonna get drunk.

His career ran out one spring training when no one picked him up, and there was an announcement that he was going to retire. I was with my children in Tucson with the Cubs. I tucked them into bed at the hotel, which was attached to a bar. I went over, had a quick drink, and came back to make sure my kids were okay. I did get drunk the day he was released.

*   *   *

The Cub nightlife. . . . Remember, we had all day games back then. I didn't do that part of it. Other writers, they'd really enjoy it. I remember Phil Collier from San Diego. He had a briefcase he'd carry with him, and I asked him one time what was in it. He didn't want to show me, but finally he did. He opened it up, and he had a flask of gin, a comb, and deodorant, stuff like that. He'd go right from the game and enjoy the nightlife.

The Bard's Room was where everyone drank after the games at Comiskey Park. Now, of course, you don't want to do that. You don't want to liquor up your writers after games because they can drive off and get into an accident, so that all ended eventually. Bill Veeck told us, "Fellas, we can't be doing this anymore. I'm under orders from the big boss not to give you guys booze anymore."

One off-day, I spent an entire day with Bill Veeck, when he was running the White Sox in the '70s. I went to his apartment at nine in the morning and went all through the day and night with him. It was one of the most fascinating assignments I've ever had. When I first met him that day, he was in his bathtub soaking his leg stump. He was listening to jazz tapes from the Smithsonian Institute. So there I was, sitting on the toilet interviewing him and listening in on his conversations. A strange way to begin the day.

We went to banks, we went to bars, we went to restaurants. We were back in his office at four o'clock when, suddenly we heard a train whistle. He said, "Hold on a second. That's the four o'clock train." So we went outside on a little walkway he had and waved to the train, and the engineer would give him two toots back. He did that every day at four o'clock. After that, I drove Bill into Old Town, where they have a lot of bars. That's how we closed our night, at two o'clock. So I was with Bill Veeck from nine in the morning until two the next morning.

Bill was over my head. He was brilliant. Whenever he said, "Well, let's suppose . . . " or "What would you do if . . . " and I'd go,

"Bill, leave me out of this. I can't keep up with you." His peg leg had a little ashtray, a little cigarette cup. Bill was a chain smoker, and he'd tap out his cigarette on his leg.

The South Side Hitmen—the White Sox of the late '70s—were the most fun guys I've ever been around. Richie Zisk became a good friend; we'd get together at the bar most every night. He was brilliant. One time Richie took a called third strike on a beautiful night in Boston, with the moon shining down and all that. He just stood there at the plate, and everybody left the field. Richie is still there. Afterward I saw him in the bar and asked him, "Richie, what happened?" He said, "You know what the umpire said to me? He didn't say I was out, or strike three. He told me to take a fucking hike."

Now, the more we talked about this, the madder he got. So we got out a cocktail napkin and wrote a letter to the league president, protesting the way he was called out. He asked me to type it out, and I did. I took a piece of White Sox stationery and typed it out. I gave it to him in an envelope with a stamp, and he said he was going to mail it. The next day I asked him if he mailed it, and he said no. I asked him why, and he said, "Well, I took it in to [manager] Bob Lemon, and he said, 'Jesus Christ, if you send this to the league, every fucking umpire in the American League is going to call you out.'" So Richie gave me my stamp back. We laughed about that for a long time.

One story I was really proud of was a no-hitter in Oakland by a guy named Mike Warren against the White Sox, after the Sox had clinched the West in '83. Now, this was on a Thursday night, and I wanted to catch the team charter to Seattle, because I always wanted to wake up in the city I needed to be in, you know?

I went downstairs in the eighth inning. I had my running story done, and all I needed was some quotes from Warren. I got him immediately because one of the announcers did the postgame radio show with Warren. They did it in a closet that had mops, buckets, rakes, and all that stuff. I went in and listened, and while all the other writers were on their way down, I was on my way up to type up the quotes and file.

I made the team flight to Seattle. The next day I got a call from Ron Rapoport, our columnist, asking me, "How the hell did you do that? How'd you get all those quotes and the sidebar and everything filed and the other writers didn't get anything?" I said, "Just lucky, I guess." But I knew it was better than luck; I knew I had done something professional.

The job is 24/7 now. You have Twitter, you have to blog. I could do it now, but I'd be a grouch about it. A day at the park is nine or ten hours anyway, but to have to wake up and right away blog something, then Tweet during the game.

I took my Hall of Fame vote very seriously and still do. Once in a while, you'll get a guy who abuses it, who doesn't deserve a card. That happened a few years ago with the MVP voting.

I won't give you the writer's name; he was a punk guy. He refused to vote for Carlos Delgado for American League MVP. Delgado had a great season, and this guy didn't even have him in the top ten. I asked him about that, and he said, "I hate Toronto, I'll never vote for anyone who plays for Toronto." I told him he shouldn't have a card or a vote. He said, "I don't care about the card. I can tear it up and still cover this team." I told him, "Well, go ahead."

*   *   *

Like anyone else, I was awestruck by famous people. Who wouldn't be? One time in New York, there was a guy on the field to promote a movie. While he was waiting for the White Sox to come out, he wanted to know if Robin Ventura was still inside. I said he'd be out pretty soon. Then a fan lightly tossed a ball to this guy and asked for an autograph. The guy signed it, and in throwing it back to the fan, he underthrew it and hit Scott Radinsky, the pitcher, right in the nuts. The movie star got all flustered and apologized to Radinsky, who said, "Well, look out, man. You can't be doing that." Who was it? Tom Hanks.

Then there was another time in New York, talking to an older man who had been in a lot of movies. I asked him what life was like for him now, and he said, "Well, I live in Connecticut in a nice home overlooking the Long Island Sound. It's very peaceful, and every morning I go out with my dog after breakfast with a cup of coffee, and we watch the sun rise. Every night, at sunset, we do the same thing. That's how I want to go, with my dog at my side." Jason Robards! That kind of stuff really stuck with me.

It took me a while to realize that these other writers were good guys, because they were interesting people and interested *in* people. You know, when George W. Bush owned the Rangers, he liked to sit with the writers in the press room, and he'd always say, "You guys are so funny; you know more about this team than I do."

Then there was the guy in Kansas City . . . you know, the commentator who gets in trouble all the time. Rush Limbaugh! He used to work for the Royals! He'd sit in with us all the time and tell us how interesting and funny we were. He'd just pull up a chair, say, "Can I sit here?" and we'd say sure.

We all had our list of favorite bars. In New York, Runyon's was by far the best. We loved that place, a nice, dark place to get drunk. I remember I had an argument with Bruce Froemming, the umpire, in there. We were so drunk. The next day he came up to me at the ballpark and said, "What were we arguing about?" I said, "I have no idea."

Runyon's had matchbooks that said, "If he was here, he'd be here." Isn't that marvelous? God, I loved that.

4

MURRAY CHASS

Starting in the late '60s, some of the most important baseball stories played out not on the diamond but in courtrooms and law offices. Suddenly, some of the biggest players in the game didn't even wear a uniform. A new vocabulary entered the sports pages, terms like "free agency" and "reserve clause" and "Players Association," and names like Marvin Miller and Curt Flood and Peter Seitz and Messersmith-McNally.

It was, literally, a whole new ballgame. And no one, absolutely no one, covered it like Murray Chass.

In forty-one years with The New York Times *(1968–2008), Chass developed the baseball labor beat and then claimed it for his own. Through four decades of labor issues that changed the baseball landscape forever, Chass was its most dogged and accurate chronicler, with the nation's "Newspaper of Record" as his forum. In the 1980s, Chass was one of the first writers to produce a voluminous Sunday notes column. His efforts earned him the Spink Award in 2003.*

A Steel City native, Chass got his professional start at the Pittsburgh bureau of The Associated Press, earning his BBWAA card in 1962. He moved to the AP's New York bureau in 1963 and to the Times *in late 1968. He covered the* Times' *Yankees beat from 1971 through 1986 and then became the paper's baseball columnist.*

The BBWAA's New York chapter chairman in 1979–1980, Chass recovered from a brain tumor shortly before leaving the Times. *He still writes regularly—and tweaks the blogging and sabermetric world—on his website, MurrayChass.com.*

want to feel a newspaper in my hands. I want to browse around the paper. I guess the spirit is in my fingers.

My mother was fond of reminding me that when I was eight years old, I wanted to be a newspaperman. I cannot tell you why I felt that at the time, but it's what I wanted to do.

I always realized and acknowledged my limitations. I knew I couldn't be a slugger like Ralph Kiner. I loved playing baseball, but I was a tiny little kid. As a matter of fact, my favorite player when I was growing up was Ted Beard. He was a little guy and he was left-handed, and I was a little guy and left-handed.

I started with the AP in February 1960. My first out-of-office assignments were Games Six and Seven of the 1960 World Series. I don't remember much about Game Six; that's understandable because Game Seven is all you need to remember. I was assigned to do the winning clubhouse. Sometime during the eighth inning, when the Yankees were leading, I went down to their clubhouse and was standing outside. The game was on a small TV monitor with a very fuzzy picture, and I saw Bill Mazeroski hit his home run. As soon as he did that, I went to the Pirates clubhouse.

My story was supposed to be on Hal Smith, whose home run put the Pirates in a position to win on the Mazeroski homer. There's a painting on the wall of my office, which I'm looking at right now, of Hal Smith hitting that homer. It was such a significant moment in my life. I was a big Pirates fan growing up, but when I started working, I realized I couldn't be a fan. I've always done that, and I recommend it to guys that go into the business—to give up their fandom and act professionally.

*   *   *

In December of 1963, I came to New York. I had done a lot of baseball in Pittsburgh, and in late 1963 the AP sports department needed a baseball writer. When the time came for the AP to bring in somebody from another bureau, Ted Smits, the sports editor, was on his way to the general manager's office to tell him to hire a reporter from Louisville named Kelso Sturgeon, who was a horse racing guy and then became an oddsmaker. But one of the guys in New York, Jim Hackleman, who later became a sports editor in Hawaii, asked Ted who he had decided to get. Ted Smits said, "Kelso Sturgeon." And Hackleman said, "No, Murray Chass." And just that easily, Ted's mind was changed, and that's how I got to New York.

I've always been a deadline guy, I guess because of my AP training. I still work on deadline in my life. If I have to have something mailed by such-and-such a time, I'll probably wait until the last day to do it. At the AP, there was no fooling around because there was a deadline every minute. The sooner you got something on the wire, the better it was, because the idea was to beat UPI. If you beat them by a minute, that was terrific. I learned how to dictate stories off the top of my head without writing them first. It was great training.

Throughout the season, the AP collected all the night's games and did a roundup for the afternoon papers, back in the days when they had afternoon papers. I guess my stuff caught the attention of the *Times*, and in 1969 they decided to do their own nightly roundups. They had staff members writing it, and once they decided that they wanted to continue it, they decided to hire someone, and I was the guy they came after.

I wasn't certain that I wanted to go to the *Times*, which showed how stupid I was. There were a couple of reasons. One, I liked the AP and the idea of the AP, the national scope. Also, I wasn't sure I wanted to go to the *Times* and write a roundup, because I'd been doing that for the AP, and I was thinking I'd like to do something else.

But two people offered me advice. One was George Vecsey Sr., who worked in the AP Sports Radio department. George Jr. had been at the *Times* for about a year as a writer, and George Sr. told me how much he had liked it. But more important, Dave Anderson, who was one of the few *Times* sportswriters I knew, recommended that I take the job. When I told him of my reluctance, he said, "Don't worry, you won't be doing the roundup very long." That was great advice. He knew how the department worked and that if I did a good job, I would move on to something else. Dave was instrumental in my taking the job.

I did the roundups for the *Times* for the 1969 season, and then for part of 1970. Late in 1970, I went to the Yankees beat.

My first years on the beat were fairly boring, since the Yankees weren't very good. What was to come, of course, we didn't know. But it didn't take long, because George Steinbrenner bought the team at the beginning of '73, and things started happening right away. Ralph Houk resigned; Lee MacPhail went to the American League office.

When you're covering a losing team, it's not easy, because how many ways can you say, "The Yankees lost"? You have to work at it. But then, pretty quickly, we had all the Steinbrenner stuff. Billy Martin and Reggie Jackson came in, and it just went from there.

What enabled me to adjust to the beat was that I told myself that this was the job and this was what I had to do. The most difficult thing was being away from my family so much. I had three children at that point; the oldest was eight or nine. I'm not going to blame the beat for causing my divorce, but my wife and I did separate after the '73 season. It's possible that my being away contributed to that. But traveling was part of the job.

I didn't cover all the games. I always felt that covering 100 or 110 games was sufficient. The way the *Times* baseball coverage was set up, there was Leonard Koppett, Joe Durso, and me. Durso was the Mets writer, I was the Yankees writer, and Leonard basically did both on the days we had off. So if you take 320 games combined and have three guys to split it up, you're covering about 110 games. I thought that was enough for anybody. It kept you a lot fresher. Unfortunately, once Leonard moved to the West Coast, they abandoned that idea.

* * *

George Steinbrenner was very difficult. We had a hot-and-cold relationship. The first year, 1973, he wanted me to be kept out of the clubhouse. Bob Fishel, the PR guy, told him he couldn't do that. Bob told George he didn't have to talk to me, but you can't keep him out of the clubhouse. I don't even remember what I wrote that set him off like that.

There were lots of periods along the way where he wouldn't talk to me. There was a time where he told me to "save your nickel," meaning, don't bother calling me because I'm not going to talk to you.

He was bizarre, running so hot and cold. One off-season he wouldn't talk to me, and he did me a big favor, because I worked harder, determined to find out what the Yankees were doing. George is really the only guy who knew what they were doing, but that off-season I made it my business to call a lot of other teams if I heard the

Yankees were talking to them. And I wound up getting better information out of the other teams than I got out of the Yankees.

I guess George had a two-way view of me. I impressed the hell out of him on Thanksgiving Day 1976. I got a tip that the Yankees were close to signing Reggie Jackson, and the only person I could possibly think of getting to confirm it was George. So I set about trying to find him on Thanksgiving Day. George's son Hank was at Culver Military Academy at the time, and there's a restaurant there called The Shack. I tracked George down there. He came to the phone, and he was flabbergasted, couldn't believe that I found him. If I hadn't established myself earlier with him, I certainly did then.

George came to realize he couldn't ignore me. At that time, he played the *Daily News* against the *Post*. They didn't want to be beaten by the other, so they did whatever he wanted to get him to tell them things. I never did that. I never played that game.

It was a difficult relationship. I spent many hours waiting for him to call back, as we all did. If I had to do it over, knowing what it was going to be like, I'd probably do it over because it was good and fun, and there were a lot of things that went on that were fun to cover.

The reason the labor beat was so interesting was this: I've always viewed myself as a reporter who covered sports. Not a sportswriter, not a baseball writer, but a reporter who covered baseball. I could have been a reporter in any area, and I would have liked it. It just so happened that sports was something I really liked a lot, baseball especially, so I enjoyed being a reporter of sports.

I guess I was responsible for forcing writers to start doing stuff they didn't want to do. Sportswriters want no part of covering labor; all they care about is the game on the field. I hope their being forced to cover labor has made them better reporters, certainly more well-rounded reporters.

The initial thing that led me to cover baseball labor came in 1967, when Marvin Miller, as head of the Players Association, entered into his first negotiation with the owners. Mike Rathet and I covered it for the AP. Same thing happened in 1968. Then I go to the *Times* and in 1970, there's a negotiation again. Koppett was covering that stuff, and I was the second guy.

Being a reporter, I realized there's more to cover than the games on the field. There's things that happen off the field that are significant and have a great impact. That's what motivated me to cover labor. The labor negotiations were obviously at the center of everything that happened in baseball. I made it a point to get to know the people involved: Marvin Miller and Richard Moss for the union, John Gaherin and Barry Rona for the owners.

One of the early things I did that got me in trouble with the owners was that I was often viewed as the "players guy." When I started covering labor for the *Times*, I would call Marvin Miller to get his view of things, because when I was at the AP, we were taught to get both sides of the story. Because I was probably the first person the owners saw quoting Marvin Miller, I was immediately branded a players guy, a union guy. The fact that the union people never lied to me and the owners often did, that didn't matter. The point is that you had to cover the whole story. I suppose, as I went on, I realized that really no one else was doing this.

To me, labor was probably at least as important as what was happening on the field. When free agency started, I realized I had to get to know the agents, because they were going to be important to the story. I was able to have some vision of what was coming and adapted my work to it.

There was nothing I could do about being labeled the union guy. Jerry Reinsdorf, the White Sox owner, was almost vicious in his comments to me, like, "How much did the union pay you this week?" Jerry's a strong anti-union guy, but I just ignored him. I knew that I was not a pro-union guy, that I was being objective.

I basically ignored the criticism. As a matter of fact, I used to think about how funny it was that these people were accusing me of being pro-union, when I wasn't even a member of the union back when I was at the AP! As I mentioned, the union people never lied to me. To this day, Miller and Moss and their successors . . . I never caught them in a lie. The owners' people all lied. Not John Gaherin, though. John was an outstanding person. But after him, they all lied. They just couldn't acknowledge a reporter knowing something that they didn't want them to know.

When free agency came, baseball became a year-round sport. Up until then, I had done pro football as well as baseball. Sometimes I'd end the baseball season early and go right into the NFL. Now, with free agency, I wasn't going to be able to do both. I chose baseball. If I hadn't, I would have killed myself because the NFL would have been nowhere near as much fun to cover.

*   *   *

Maybe the story I most enjoyed breaking was the end of the 1981 strike. It happened late at night. I was at the hotel where they were negotiating. An owner called my house and woke up my wife. "Where's Murray?" he said. "Well, he's at the hotel, and I don't have a number for him," my wife said. Remember, this is before cell phones. "Well, you gotta get to him and tell him that the strike's over," he said. "We have an agreement."

She called the *Times* office, and whoever picked up asked her who the source was. My wife, being a good wife, wouldn't tell him. Then he demanded to know, and she still refused to tell him. "Just get a hold of him and tell him to call me," she said. Well, it worked out. I just thought that was terrific, because I have never, ever told anybody who my sources are.

People used to think they knew who my sources were, but they didn't have the slightest idea. When I started to do contract stuff, they used to think I got the information from the union. They were very wrong, because the union never gave me one contract. I used to call *them* once in a while and give them the details of a contract before they even had it.

Another one I broke was the famous Billy Martin tirade at the airport in 1978. Now, Billy was a guy who would often get upset but would blow off steam without getting in trouble. If, say, Phil Rizzuto was on a trip, Billy would talk to Rizzuto, vent his anger, and that's as far as it would go. If Phil wasn't on a trip, the next person he'd go to was Moss Klein of the *Newark Star-Ledger*. Moss had a relationship with Billy so that if Billy told him something off the record, Moss of course honored that. Billy knew that he could trust Moss. Well, Moss wasn't on this trip. I guess I was next in line.

That was the day [July 23, 1978] Reggie Jackson came back from suspension. Five days earlier, Reggie had been suspended for defying Billy. First Billy put on a bunt sign, and Reggie didn't bunt. Then he took it off, and Reggie attempted to bunt. Billy threw an empty beer bottle against the wall of his office; there were pieces of glass all over the floor when we walked in. He was just irate, and he suspended Reggie.

Reggie comes back the following Sunday in Chicago. Billy is really agitated because Reggie is back, and he has to deal with him. After the game, we're on the bus, and Billy's sitting in the front seat. The writers are sitting close to the front. Billy said to me, "Can I see you when we get to the airport?"

The bus pulls up outside the terminal, and we go inside. I walk over to Billy, and he starts venting about Reggie. Now, I understood what he was doing. I was familiar with his routine, even though this had never happened with me. I was prepared to keep it off the record, knowing that he was going to be in a lot of trouble if I wrote it. He never said it was off the record, but I sensed it was.

Anyway, while we're talking in the terminal, Jack Lang comes over. He was on the trip for the *Daily News*. Now, Jack never saw a conversation he didn't get involved in, so he came right up to us and started listening. I just let Billy go on. Soon the other writers see what's going on, and they come over, including Frank Brown of the AP, who had been sent to Chicago to cover Reggie's return. I knew Frank was going back to New York; he wasn't going on to Kansas City, which was the next stop on the trip.

So I whispered to Frank, just to protect myself more than anything, "Frank, this might be off the record." So Frank immediately says to Billy, "Is this on the record?" Billy says, "You bet it is." And he continues. That's part one.

Frank went to the phone and called AP. I went to a phone and called the *Times* and dictated the story. I had to make the plane—that's when writers made trips with the team. But there was a delay of some kind; that's why I was able to do all this before the flight. Otherwise, it would have been Frank's exclusive.

Now, Henry Hecht, who was there with the *Post*, somehow missed this first part. As I get off the phone, Billy is walking by, and he asks me, "Did you get all that in?" I said yes, and he said, "OK, good." Now Henry and I walk with Billy to the gate, and Billy starts in again. It was during that short walk that he said, "The two of them deserve each other. One's a born liar, the other's convicted." That's why Frank didn't have that part—he wasn't going on the plane to Kansas City. Henry and I were the only two who heard Billy say that.

I wasn't taking notes at this point, but from the second he said it, I repeated it in my head, over and over, to make sure I got it 100 percent accurate.

We get on the plane, and I write it down. We land in Kansas City. I go to the phone, call the office again with another new lead with that quote. The *Post* in those days was an afternoon paper, so Henry couldn't get it in the paper until later, so I guess I was the only one who initially had that, a pretty good exclusive.

I know I was later accused of quoting a drunk manager. I had seen Billy enough to know when he was totally drunk and out of it. He was not. I also heard later that, before the game, Billy was talking to a magazine writer, and he used a similar comment about Reggie and George deserving each other. I don't remember who it was or if it ever appeared, but it was something that was in his mind. He had rehearsed it, I guess.

So if Lang and the other writers hadn't come over, it very likely never would have gotten out. There would have been no "the two of them deserve each other" quote. I might have been wrong if I had done that, but as I said, that was my understanding of Billy at the time.

*   *   *

The notes column started in August 1984, during the Olympics. Joe Vecchione, the sports editor, said, "All we have in the paper is the Olympics. I'd like to get something else in there. Can you do a baseball notebook?" I said sure. I wrote the first one; he liked it, and I liked it. It continued until I left the *Times*.

I missed very few Sundays in those twenty-four years. There were a few times I went to Israel to visit my kids, and once or twice my wife got me to actually go on vacation without working. I figured out that I had done 1,155 Sunday columns, and I was looking forward to making it twenty-five years. I didn't quite make it, except on my website, where I follow the same style on the weekends that I followed in the *Times*.

I'll tell you why the column died. The *Times*, in its desperation to do something to either quit losing money or to make money, decided they had to get rid of people. I had no intention of taking a buyout until the sports editor told me that I had to give up not only the Sunday notes column but the two or three general columns I was writing a week. He said, "You have to go back to being a reporter. We have to beef up our reporting."

He knew I wouldn't go back to being a reporter. When I went back to work after I recovered from my brain tumor, my wife was afraid that if I went back to working the same way, I'd somehow have a relapse. So, I suggested I become a columnist, and they said okay. So they knew I would take the buyout.

The sports editor told me he was killing the Sunday column because it was "an anachronism. Nobody wants to read that stuff anymore." Of course, people would tell me that it was the first thing they read in the Sunday *Times*.

I worked hard at it. All my columns were based on original ideas. Peter Gammons did it too, but he started the notes network. You'd pick up papers across the country every Sunday and see the same stuff because everybody exchanged notes. I never did that; I refused to become a part of that. Every item I did was original with me.

Once [Oakland general manager] Sandy Alderson called me and said, "Look, there's something you have in the column that isn't right." He read it to me, and I said, "I never wrote that." He said, "You didn't? Well, I thought you did because everyone else did."

I just figured that if my name was going to be on it, I wanted to know what was in it and where it came from. Not that I didn't trust people, but . . . I didn't trust people. How do I know this guy's facts are right, that he's quoting someone accurately? It was just easier doing my own stuff.

When I was BBWAA's New York chapter chairman in the late '70s, I took it so seriously that I got into trouble with the *Times*. The *Times* was struck by one of the unions in 1978, and we didn't work from August to November, and during that time was the '78 World Series. At that time, I was vice chairman of the chapter. Joe Gergen of *Newsday* was chairman, but since his paper wasn't on strike and Joe was working, I figured I would police the press box to save him the problem.

Now the Yankees are in the '78 Series. I was in the press box, and I see a guy named Sidney Zion sitting in the second row, and I know Sidney Zion doesn't belong there. I asked him to leave, and he wouldn't, so I had the ushers remove him. A few days later, I got a call from the *Times* sports editor, Harold Claassen, asking what I was doing running the press box. Was I working for the Yankees now?

I explained to him that as chapter vice chairman, it was my responsibility to do the seating in the press box, and Sidney Zion didn't belong there. Sidney Zion was a well-connected political writer and complained to the executive editor of the *Times*, Abe Rosenthal, that this guy Murray Chass had him thrown out of the press box.

*   *   *

I'm very pleased with what I'm doing on my website. When I decided to take the buyout from the *Times* in 2008, I realized that I wasn't ready to quit writing. If things had remained as they were at the *Times*, I'd probably still be writing there. I wanted to continue writing, so I decided to look into starting a website.

I started on July 15, 2008. I spend more time on the website columns than I thought I would, but I work the same way. I call people, talk to them, do a lot of research. I don't spend a lot of time browsing around the Internet, but I would be surprised to find another site like mine where there are original columns actually quoting people.

The problem with blogs is that bloggers don't have to do any of that. They just write what they want off the top of their head, whatever their opinion is. They have no accountability. I read something a couple of months ago on a website, ridiculing Dan Shaughnessy of the *Boston Globe* for his views on specific pitchers. That offended me. Dan Shaughnessy is a professional writer, a good columnist, and has many years of experience. I would defend him anytime, anywhere, and I did in a column on my website. I happened to name the guy who wrote the column, and I called him "whose name is unknown to me."

Frankly, I enjoy annoying people like bloggers. I enjoy annoying stats freaks. I don't enjoy the development of baseball where everything is run by statistics.

It's a generational thing. The bloggers are all younger. The guys who read my site are older, and that's fine with me, because we live in different worlds. The younger people who are so immersed in statistics don't care that human beings play the game. This last Hall of Fame election, I got so much material that I drew the conclusion that we don't need to have people vote on the Hall of Fame anymore. We just need statistical charts drawn up, and the players who meet the minimums are the ones who get in, and the others don't.

I take my Hall of Fame vote so seriously that I'm considering giving it up. For years I couldn't vote because the *Times* didn't let us. The last few years, not working for the paper, I voted. I've never been sure the writers should be voting. I once tried to get the BBWAA to give up the voting.

When the Hall of Fame changed the rules to make sure that Pete Rose wouldn't get in by placing him on the permanently ineligible list, I was offended. While I was not prepared to vote for Pete Rose, I thought the Hall of Fame didn't trust the writers to do the right thing, and so they took it out of our hands.

Here's another thing with these silly bloggers. I did a column on my Hall of Fame vote last year, saying that an hour before the midnight deadline, I realized I hadn't yet filled out my ballot. I was going to fax it in, so I knew I had until midnight. These jerks took it to mean that I hadn't even *thought* about it until then, and they criticized me for spending less than an hour deciding who I was going to vote for. But I had spent *loads* of time on it; I just hadn't filled out the ballot. But that's how they jump to these conclusions.

The Spink Award meant a lot to me because the writers vote. Just to be nominated out of the New York chapter was pretty good because there were a lot of guys in the chapter, some fairly influential guys, who I didn't have a good relationship with. I used to annoy people in meetings with my views on things. So it was impressive enough to get nominated out of the chapter. But to be elected, it was a tremendous honor.

Years earlier, I was involved in the Spink controversy with Joe Durso, who won the award in 1995. Joe was a colleague of mine for many years. I did not have a very high regard for Joe's work ethic, for his work product. I thought Joe lacked a lot, including some of the basic fundamentals of being a reporter. It astounded me that he covered the Mets for the *Times* as long as he did. I never understood it. The kind of work I did covering the Yankees was 180 degrees from the kind of work he did covering the Mets.

Joe was in line for the Spink Award for one reason: his good friend Jerome Holtzman was the person who oversaw that. That was before we voted on three nominees, and I felt that Holtzman was railroading Durso into the Hall of Fame. I was outspoken about that, made some enemies. That didn't bother me because I felt that if we're going to take this thing seriously, the people we put in the writers' wing of the Hall of Fame have to be really top-notch people. I didn't think Durso represented a serious decision on the part of the writers for the Spink Award. As a result, Holtzman and I stopped talking to each other. Didn't bother me. I say things that I believe, and so be it how people feel about it.

Look, my induction speech in 2004 annoyed some people, some younger writers. But I said what I felt needed to be said. However anybody wants to think of me, that's okay. My wife still loves me.

I find it unfortunate that baseball writers don't last long these days. It's much more difficult because it's year-round. I'm encouraged by a guy like Tyler Kepner at the *Times*, who seems to be in it for the long haul.

One thing that disappoints me is that most of the beat guys don't even go into the opposing locker room anymore. You don't learn anything by not talking to people on the other side. Guys like Earl Weaver and Sparky Anderson would yell at the New York writers, "Hey, you didn't come in to see me!" because we made it a point to talk to them. You can't meet people if you don't go into the other clubhouse.

I wouldn't want to do the beat the way it's done today, but I would have to do it. I might not do all of the other things that beat guys do today, the blogging and the TV and radio stuff. If that's where the money is, fine. But all I wanted to do was write, to be a reporter.

5

RUSSELL SCHNEIDER

Through the various chapters of his early life—as a Quantico Ma-rine, minor league catcher, photography student, public relations man—Russell Schneider never lost sight of what he truly wanted to be: a baseball man, a baseball lifer, a baseball writer.

The native Clevelander finally got the chance in March 1964 when he took over the Indians beat for the Cleveland Plain Dealer. *Mentored by two Spink Award winners, Gordon Cobbledick and Hal Lebovitz, Schneider covered the Indians beat for next fourteen years (1964–1977) through seemingly endless stretches of mediocre base-ball and front office upheaval on the shores of Lake Erie.*

The prolific Schneider served as a correspondent for The Sporting News *for nearly two decades and was an official scorer for twenty-one years and a staggering five no-hitters, including Len Barker's 1981 perfect game. One of the hundreds of Tribe players he covered was his son-in-law, pitcher Eric Raich, in 1975–1976. Russ also han-dled the Cleveland Browns beat and investigative assignments for the* Plain Dealer *prior to his retirement from the paper in 1993.*

Schneider is enshrined in five Halls of Fame (including the Greater Cleveland Sports Hall of Fame, the Press Club of Cleveland Hall of Fame, and the Ohio Baseball Hall of Fame) and was a 2012 and 2013 Spink Award finalist. The author of thirteen books, he was described by former colleague Bob August: "[Schneider] has earned recognition as the leading historian of the Indians, the vigorous re-porting and clear, no-nonsense prose that distinguished him at the Plain Dealer *serving him well in his later-in-life role."*

Without giving up my age, I saw my first baseball game in 1936 at old League Park. My mother took me to a game between the Indians and the St. Louis Browns. Mel Harder pitched for the Indians and a guy named Elon Hogsett for the Browns. League Park was on the other side of town and we took a streetcar there.

I couldn't believe it when I walked in. League Park looked like a factory building until you opened the gates. There was this expanse of green, the grass and the seats. I mean, that's one of my most vivid memories. That's when I decided I wanted to be a major league ballplayer.

I was always a fan of the Indians, and one of the reasons was that my mother was a great fan all of her life. All I ever remembered growing up was listening to Indians games on the radio with Jack Graney, who was one of the first ex-players to go into radio. He was on the 1920 championship team and was the best friend of Ray Chapman, the shortstop who got killed by a pitch that same year.

When I was in high school, I was the sports editor of the school paper, the *West Tech Taddler*. My main interest at the time was photography; I wanted to be a professional photographer. In order to foster what I thought was going to be my career, I got a part-time job at the *Cleveland News*. I got that through Hal Lebovitz, who at that time was the scholastic sports editor of the *News* and was also a semipro umpire.

I used to go to the old *News* building at six in the morning and pass out paste pots and copy paper, sharpen pencils, deliver the mail, and do the clippings. I'd do that until 7:45, run out, jump on a streetcar, and go to the other side of town to West Tech.

As an athlete, I was a pretty good hitter, I could throw, I could catch, and I wasn't afraid. I thought I knew the game. When I graduated from high school in 1946, I joined the Marine Corps because I thought I was going to be drafted, and I didn't want to go into the army or navy. I also did some boxing when I was in boot camp. In November '46, I was sent to Quantico, Virginia.

When my enlistment ran out in July '48, I was offered a partial scholarship to Kent State, which at the time was a pretty good baseball school. I had never really thought about college. As it turned out, we found that I and three other guys on our service team had been scouted, and the four of us signed pro contracts. I signed with the Indians.

After I had signed, Hal Lebovitz said, "Now, this makes a great story," local-boy-makes-good and that kind of crap. A few months later, Hal got another brainstorm. He said, "Would you be interested in writing stories about other guys from Cleveland who are in spring training with you?" At that time, 1949, spring training for the minor leaguers was in Marianna, Florida. Hal said they'd pay me $100. Great, I said. Then I asked if it was $100 a story, and Hal said, "Oh, no, no." I really didn't care, though. I think I did fifteen or sixteen stories during that spring training. I have them all in a scrapbook downstairs. Those were the first things I ever got paid to write. They were called "Reports from a Rookie."

They gave me a Class C contract—I was going to get $250 a month. I went to spring training in March '49. A couple of guys I was in spring training with were Jim Lemon, who later became a player and a manager in the big leagues; Al Smith, who played for the Indians; [Harry] "Suitcase" Simpson; and Hal Naragon.

Frankly, I wasn't that good a player in 1949, and I was let go. Part of me was relieved because I could read the writing on the wall. On the other hand, I was also devastated because I was so determined to be a ballplayer.

I wasn't going to pump gas the rest of my life. My father was a bakery salesman, and I didn't want to peddle bread. I figured that the next best thing to playing ball was being a sportswriter.

When I was finishing up college at Baldwin-Wallace in 1955, an opening came up at the *Plain Dealer* for a scholastic sportswriter. Gordon Cobbledick was the sports editor, and I applied and got the job. I had been stringing for the *Plain Dealer* at Baldwin-Wallace; they had pretty good basketball and track teams. From February on, I was going to school and doing that job. I was also doing sports publicity at Baldwin-Wallace, and so there were times I'd be sending news releases to myself at the *Plain Dealer*.

Cobbledick asked me what my ultimate goal was, and I told him that I wanted to be a baseball writer. Cobby mentioned that they already had a young baseball writer in Harry Jones, who'd been there since 1948. I said that someday Harry had to retire. But then a few years went by, and I couldn't see any end in sight to Harry Jones's job as a baseball writer. I was getting very discouraged, and then Baldwin-Wallace offered me a full-time job as their director of public relations. I did that for a few years, but I was bored to death.

I spent some time at Dow Chemical, also in public relations. Then the guy who did our printing said, "Hey, my cousin has just bought the Cleveland Barons hockey team. They're looking for a good PR guy." So I interviewed and got the job.

My boss, Tom Roulston, couldn't understand why the *Plain Dealer* didn't give the Barons any space. Heck, the American Hockey League was the minor leagues. The Indians and the Browns, meanwhile, were going strong. One week before the hockey season ended, we had a big argument. Roulston wanted me to walk into Gordon Cobbledick's office, throw a $20 bill in front of him, and ask him to do a column on the Barons.

I said, "Let me tell you something, Tom. If I know Cobbledick, and I'm sure I do, if he doesn't pick me up and throw me out of the office, I'll be very disappointed. And if you think I'm gonna do that, you're full of crap." He said, "You're done. Don't come in tomorrow."

I've got two kids, a wife, and no job. I called a friend and got a job at Dix & Eaton, a PR agency, for $10,000 a year, which was more money than I had made anywhere. Meanwhile, Harry Jones quit the *Plain Dealer* to become an Indians broadcaster. The guy they had hired to take my place as the scholastic writer was promoted to the Indians beat. I was devastated. Then, two years later, this guy was fired. This is in September 1963.

My office was right down the street from the *Plain Dealer* building. Every single weekday, I'd go down to see Cobbledick on my lunch hour and ask him if I could come back to the paper. He said that the front office didn't like to rehire people who had quit. I reminded him that the Indians beat was the job I had always wanted. Every day, I'd go down, knock on Cobby's door, and ask if he was ready to hire me, and he'd say, "No, not yet."

Now it's almost Christmas and I make my usual visit to Cobby. This time he said, "Come on in." He told me I had the job, and I was ecstatic. But then he said, "I want to hear this from your wife. You're going to be traveling a lot, and I want to make sure it's all right with her."

Well, I think she cried for five days. She just didn't want it. But if you ask her today, she realized that it was the best thing that ever happened to us, especially to me. All the doors that opened to us and all the people we know were because of that.

*   *   *

I say this without fear of sounding like an egotist: I was a very good baseball writer. I know that people who read me would tell you that. I never shirked my job. I had a great career, made pretty good money at the end.

I knew the game. I had been a catcher, and I knew it from that point of view. I knew the game because I played it. A big factor was that I've always known what guys go through to play this wonderful game. It's not easy during the difficult times. I knew how to deal with adversity as an athlete.

Now, was I close to the players? No. I was arms-length with most of them. I never had a real close friend in baseball until after I got off the baseball beat, which was the way I wanted it. Sam McDowell may have been one of the most interesting guys I ever knew. If I had to pick out one guy who was my best friend among the players, it was Max Alvis. I also got very close to Dean Chance, who's from Wooster.

I've got to say this: I learned more inside baseball—how managers work and think on the major league level—from Alvin Dark than from anybody. There's only one other guy who I thought was as smart a baseball man as Alvin Dark, and that was Gene Mauch. He and Alvin were close friends.

The Indians finished above .500 in only three of my fourteen years on the beat. That also made me a good baseball writer. You know, it's easier to cover a losing team. Maybe easier isn't the right word. It's *more interesting* what happens, the ups and downs and travails. If you cover a winning team, you get into the habit of telling about how wonderful these guys are. You don't see the warts and the pimples until you live with guys who are struggling to hang on.

I got punched in the face in 1973 by a coach named Joe Lutz. One of the guys who was involved in that was Rocky Colavito, who was also a coach. That's when Ken Aspromonte was the manager and Warren Spahn was the pitching coach. They didn't like something that I wrote.

That incident helped me gain some respect. That's another reason I felt I was a good writer: that the players knew that I knew the game, knew what they were going through. It happened in the locker room, after a game in Anaheim. Getting punched by a coach helped me gain, what did you call it? Street cred? The players knew what I went through and how I dealt with it.

One thing that helped to establish me in the eyes of the fans was the work I did when the Indians were sold by Vernon Stouffer in 1972. They didn't have any money—they had less operating capital than they have now. The guy who bought the team was Nick Mileti, the guy who founded the Cavaliers in the NBA. Nick owned the Indians because he had fifty-four partners, each of whom kicked in something like ten grand apiece. He didn't have any money himself.

Now, you know who Bob Short was, right? He owned the Lakers and moved them to L.A., he owned the Senators and moved them to Texas. Bob owned a hotel in Minneapolis, the Leamington Hotel. Somehow, he and I became good friends. Every time we'd go into Minneapolis, I'd send my bags to my room at the Leamington and go visit Bob. He was a great source and filled me in on everything.

One day Bob said to me, "How do you like your new owner?" I said, "What? What are you talking about?" He said, "Don't you know? We're having a meeting tomorrow to approve the new ownership of the Indians. A guy named Nick Mileti."

I knew Nick's name because it had come up a few times. Short said, "I'm surprised you don't know. Hell, the goddamn team is going bankrupt. They gotta sell it, and Mileti's gonna buy it."

So I had a helluva story the next day, a big story than ran across page one. Now, that was also the time that George Steinbrenner and Al Rosen were also trying to buy the Indians. Steinbrenner was a good friend of mine because he was a Cleveland guy. George and Al had a gentleman's agreement with Vernon Stouffer, who was a lush, to buy the Indians for, I think, $10.8 million.

Everything was all set up for this big announcement at the East Ohio Gas Building. Marsh Samuel, the old Indians PR guy, was the front man for George and Al. Marsh had all the media set up to announce that the Indians were being purchased by a group headed by George Steinbrenner and Al Rosen.

Allegedly, Stouffer was upstairs with Steinbrenner and Rosen, and they would call down to Marsh and tell him, "It's done. Announce it." Then the phone rings and Marsh answers it, and then he says, "The deal is off."

Later I found out that Nick Mileti had taken Stouffer out, gotten him drunk, and convinced him to sell the team to *him* rather than Steinbrenner and Rosen, because Nick was a local guy. He wasn't even going to pay $10.8 million. Gabe Paul later said, "Nick was going to pay Stouffer in green stamps and promises."

George was devastated, of course. Rosen told me that it was Gabe Paul who told George that he could buy the Yankees because CBS wanted to bail out. And ever since then, it's been speculated here in Cleveland: Can you imagine what would have happened if Stouffer had sold the Indians to George Steinbrenner instead of Nick Mileti?

*   *   *

I'd really like to know if anybody else has ever scored five no-hitters. I also covered two additional no-hitters outside of Cleveland, Dave Morehead's in 1965 and Joel Horlen's in 1967. Get this: I also *caught* a no-hitter when I was playing with Stroudsburg in the minors.

I asked our current Indians writer, Paul Hoynes, about it. He called the guy at the Elias Sports Bureau, Seymour Siwoff. Seymour told him that they don't keep track of the guys who scored no-hitters. That's hard for me to believe. I might call the Hall of Fame next. You know, I'm not looking for any credit, but I think that's amazing. I scored a no-hitter on the day my father died, August 25, 1967—Dean Chance against the Indians. I had to leave two innings early.

I was an official scorer for twenty-one years. One day a sports editor I didn't get along with called me into the office and said, "You know, it might be a conflict of interest for you to be covering the Indians and also be the scorer." In a way, he was right. Peter Bavasi, the son of Dodgers GM Buzzie Bavasi, was running the Indians then, and he and I didn't get along. He kept harping that the Indians and the American League paid my salary. I was convinced that Peter was a double agent who was eventually going to move the Indians to St. Petersburg.

Anyway, the sports editor said it was a conflict of interest. Well, maybe it is and maybe it isn't. But I said, "Let me tell you something. I've been doing this for twenty-one years. You're telling me it took the *Plain Dealer* twenty-one fucking years to determine this?"

Eric Raich was the number one pick overall in the January free agent draft in 1972. He'd been a defensive tackle at Southern Cal under John McKay then played baseball. He was part of that run of five straight titles under Rod Dedeaux, their great coach.

The following spring, the Indians brought him to spring training. My daughter, Eileen, was a senior at Baldwin-Wallace. She was having a tough time in college, so my wife and I brought her to spring training to give her a break between semesters. Every year, the owners of the Indians had a St. Patrick's Day party in spring training. So Kay's mother (who was Irish all the way), Kay, and I took Eileen to this party.

Eric met my daughter, and two years later they were married. And on May 10, 1975, in Frank Robinson's first year as manager, they called him up from Triple-A. By the middle of the year, he was in the starting rotation and went 7-8. He wasn't a world-beater, but he was a pretty good pitcher. In Eric's second major league start, he beat Nolan Ryan for his first win. Pretty good! I threw a big party for him after the game at the hotel in Anaheim.

Most of the guys knew Eric was my son-in-law, and they didn't try to take advantage of it. Eric never told me anything, and I never asked him for anything. I just made sure I never violated that. Honest to God, I made a point of not taking advantage of our relationship. After the game, he went his way with his teammates, and I went mine.

Except for one time, in 1975. Eric hurt his arm toward the end of the season. He went to spring training in 1976, but he couldn't pitch on the major league level anymore, and it turned out he had a torn rotator cuff.

Dennis Eckersley was pitching against Texas on a rainy Friday night in '76. I liked Eck, but he was very cocky back then. Eck was working on a no-hitter, and there was a bad hop grounder hit to Buddy Bell at third base. I swear to God, although no one admitted it, Buddy threw the ball into right field because he knew it was going to be scored a hit. I'm the scorer, and I called it a hit and an error.

When Eckersley walked off the field at the end of the inning, he looked out at the scoreboard and saw the hit, then he looked up at the press box and gave me the finger. The next day I went down to the clubhouse and said, "That was a real horseshit thing you did. Don't ever do anything like that to me again." So Eckersley says, "Well, fuck you and fuck your son-in-law, too!" Well, we almost went at it, and Buddy Bell had to get between us. Eckersley apologized to me later. Eric wasn't in the clubhouse when it happened, and I said to him later, "What the hell was that all about?"

*   *   *

One thing that a lot of people ask me is, "If you love baseball so much, how come you gave up the baseball beat to cover the Browns?" Let me tell you. One day, I was grousing to Hal Lebovitz; this is in January 1978. I was complaining that I was tired of the damn travel, plus I wanted to be the lead columnist. Hal said to come downtown; he had something he wanted to talk to me about. He couldn't tell me what it was, but I would love it, just love it.

I figure I'm getting the column. So I go down to the office, and he says, "We want you to cover the Browns." I said, "What? Why?" Hal said that I had been tired of the traveling and Kay was tired of me being away all the time. I told Hal I thought I was getting the column. Hal said, "This will set you up perfectly for the next time the column opens up. You'll be the only guy who ever covered both major beats, the Indians and Browns."

He told me to go see Dave Hopcraft, the managing editor. Now, remember that name. I go to see Hopcraft, who was always a cocky SOB. He says to me, "We want you to cover the Browns." I asked him why, and here are his exact words: "I want you to cover the Browns because we want you to get [owner] Art Modell the way you got Phil Seghi." Seghi had been the Indians' general manager.

What the hell did *that* mean, I asked. He said, "You were really tough on the Indians—it was great. Art Modell has had a free ride in this town for too long." That's another exact quote. Well, I mentioned that Art and I were good friends, and then he said it would be another $100 a week, which was good money back then. I told him to give me a day to think it over.

I talked to Kay, and she's really happy because now it means I basically come off the road. We have three kids now of high school and college age. I went back the next day and said to Hopcraft, "I told my wife that she's sleeping with a football writer." So Hopcraft was all happy.

When I got to the door of Hopcraft's office, I can still see myself reaching for the knob when I heard him say, "Take that, you fucking Art Modell!"

Now, here's the payoff. After I retired, I worked for the Sun Newspapers, a weekly chain in Cleveland. In 1995, when Art Modell moved the Browns to Baltimore, you know who was doing PR for him? Dave Hopcraft! He had gotten fired at the *Plain Dealer*. That was amazing.

I left the *Plain Dealer* for two reasons. I did not get along with the third or fourth sports editors after Cobbledick. I wanted to be the columnist, and I interviewed three or four times for that. I also interviewed several times for the sports editor job. Every time, the managing editor said, "Oh, you were one of the finalists" and all that.

By that time I was nearing sixty. Two weeks after I turned sixty-five and could make the most on my benefits, I went in and gave the sports editor and the managing editor a note: "I have decided to retire effective the minute you read this." And I did; that was it. By then I had written three or four books and felt like I could do it that way.

I don't have any regrets. Maybe one in that I never got the major column, the one that Bill Livingston has today. When I read Livingston, I often think that he's one of the best sports columnists I've ever read. He and I are good friends. We weren't always; he always assumed that I resented him, which I did. I don't think I ever did anything to show that—I just kept it inside. But Bill's one of the best around.

I would like to think I could do the job today, but I'd also say I wouldn't want to. The big reason is that, at that time, the baseball beat was *the* coveted job on the newspaper. Everybody wanted to be the baseball writer because he was the big guy on the paper. And I think I was. I say that not egotistically but honestly. But it's not like that anymore. Part of it today is that you really have to work your ass off.

When I started, I had a telegraph operator at my elbow, and all I did was type my stuff and give it to him. He even corrected it! Jerry Holtzman used to say, "I have to write my lead swill for the early edition." He never worried about spelling or anything like that because his telegrapher would correct it.

From there I went to a telecopier, then a dictation machine. I once got locked in the ballpark in spring training, with my wife and three kids in the car outside, because I had to sit upstairs and dictate my story into a recorder. From there, we had the little RadioShack computers and then the big Texas Instruments computers. I'm not smart enough to do all the things on a laptop they do today.

One other thing really galls me. The first day of spring training in 1964, I go to Hi Corbett Field in Tucson, Arizona, wearing a white shirt, a tie, and a red sport coat. I walk in, and Gordon Cobbledick says, "Where the hell are you going?" He's dressed in cowboy boots, cowboy hat, jeans, and a plaid shirt. He says to me, "Get your ass back to the room. Take the tie off, take the coat off. Leave the shirt on but roll up your sleeves." Today, these guys in the press box come in looking like they just came off a truck somewhere. They're in shorts. They're all scraggly and unkempt. They look like they just rolled out of bed. I mean, geez.

Here's how great the beat was back then. Dan Coughlin, who later became a TV commentator, covered the Indians for one year at the *Plain Dealer* after I left. Dan wrote a column saying that it was the worst experience of his life, something he wouldn't wish on his worst enemy. I wrote a column in response saying that Dan Coughlin is a good friend of mine, but he's nuts; it was the best job I ever had, and I'd go back to it in a minute. Well, Bowie Kuhn, the commissioner, wrote me a letter saying, "Thank you for doing that, it was great!"

6

JIM HENNEMAN

Jim Henneman had an unforgettable debut on the major league stage: his first major assignment was the Yankees' visit to Baltimore during the climax of the Roger Maris home run chase in 1961.

It was the start of a five-decade career during which "Henny" would become a Charm City institution. A protégé of the legendary John Steadman, Henneman joined the Baltimore News-Post *out of college in 1958. Earning his BBWAA card three years later, Henneman covered the Orioles as the team blossomed into a champion, prior to a five-year stint (1968–1973) as public relations director of the NBA's Baltimore Bullets.*

Returning to the renamed News American *in 1973, the native Baltimorean became synonymous with Oriole baseball. He covered the beat for the* News American *from 1973–1980, and then for the* Baltimore Sun *from 1980 to 1993. Henny was the BBWAA's national chairman in 1984.*

Today, Henneman still covers the Baltimore sports scene for the website PressBoxOnline.com and as a regular contributor to the periodical Baltimore Sports. *He also serves as an official scorer at Oriole Park at Camden Yards, where the legends of champions past—Henny's beat, from the Robinsons to Ripken—live on.*

Anybody who tells you they were at their best on deadline, they're tricking you. This is what we all know about deadlines: we're pushed to the max. Even today if I'm writing for a magazine, if the deadline is June 10, the chances of me writing before June 6 or

7 are practically nil. With an afternoon paper, my deadline was basically to get my stuff in there by the time the early desk guy got there, which was about 5:30 or 6:00 in the morning.

Writing on deadline is a real art. It's the most difficult writing. There are legions of tales of guys just ripping up their stories and starting all over on deadline. I remember Game Six of the 1975 World Series. When Bernie Carbo hit the three-run homer to tie the game, guys all over the place were ripping their copy out of their typewriters and throwing it away. Somebody then actually went around and picked up the crumpled copy and made a column out of all the different leads that wound up on the floor.

I was more or less an accidental writer. There was really no formal training. I went to college as a business major, so I kind of stumbled into it.

My senior year at Loyola University I had a relapse of rheumatic fever, which I had as a kid. During my recovery period, I met John Steadman through a mutual friend and he offered me a job as a copy-boy, with the intention that I'd go back and finish my senior year. The All-Star Game was in Baltimore that year (1958). I had pitched against Al Kaline in high school, and they had me write a story about that; it was the first story I'd ever done.

John had two openings at the paper that fall. They offered me a job, and I figured I was in a happy place as far as a future career was concerned. So instead of going back to school, I stayed at the paper. That's how it started.

I think I was John's first hire when he became the sports editor. I should qualify that by saying that it wasn't that he was bent on hiring me, but he needed a copyboy, and he knew I'd had an interest in sports. It was a thirty-nine-hour-a-week job for a dollar an hour. I worked six-and-a-half hours for six days a week, and that came to thirty-nine hours and that made you a part-time employee.

John Steadman became a dear friend. He gave me little short things to write, three- or four-paragraph things without a byline. He'd help me with basic writing; I'd had no formal training. Technically, neither did John. He was really a self-made person. I'd look at John years later and realize that, in a lot of ways, John was an introverted person, but he always projected himself as an extrovert. He was attracted to characters, and part of that was that he would have loved to have been a character himself.

John was one of the most dynamic speakers I'd ever heard. He could mesmerize a room. After John passed away, his brother told me that John once took a Dale Carnegie course; that's what really helped him become a good speaker. That's about the best testament to Dale Carnegie you could have.

As sports editor, John was more the captain of the team than a boss. You worked with him, not for him. He was godfather to one of my children, one of the great influences on my life.

The role of sports editor now is non-writing and non-visible to a degree. But John was as visible and prominent in the city of Baltimore as a man could be. His standing in the community was such that I never knew him to turn down a speaking engagement or an appearance. I also never knew John to personally take money to do it. He'd have a favorite charity that he'd ask people to donate to. To this day, I meet people who heard John speak at a Holy Name Society or at a Kiwanis Club, things that weren't in the sports realm, and be so impressed.

People didn't always agree with what John did, but he was genuine and a community person. He spent his whole life here, as I have. That's something you don't see much in the business. My old friend, the late Charley Eckman, used to say, "An expert is somebody from out of town."

*   *   *

In 1961, one of the fellows at the *News-Post* left, and they moved me into a secondary role. I'd only been at the paper three years, and I was still a pup. My first real exposure to baseball writing was that series when the Yankees were here in '61 and Roger Maris was looking to pass Babe Ruth in 154 games, which was the edict set down by Ford Frick, the commissioner. John Steadman basically told me to just pay attention to Roger Maris, just cover him. I didn't have to worry about the game or anything like that.

You hear about how hectic it was for Roger back then, but I can tell you that the coverage for that series, compared with that we have today, wasn't nearly as great as what you would get for a normal regular-season series. It really wasn't a problem. After the game I'd be right there with Maris. There wasn't the crush you'd have now. If you had something of that magnitude today, you'd be off in an interview room the size of a locker room. It was much, much different.

Starting in '61, I was the UPI stringer along with doing sidebars for the *News-Post*, so I was at the ballpark a lot. In '66, when the Orioles clinched the pennant, I was on that road trip when they clinched in Kansas City. I was doing a lot of baseball; I just wasn't the "beat guy."

When I left for the Bullets, John didn't want me to go, but in those days there wasn't much money to be made in the newspaper business. I had a chance to increase my salary to the degree that I felt I owed it to myself to take a chance. I did it for five years, and although it wasn't baseball, it still gave me the perspective of being in the front office of a major league team, even though the NBA was in its infancy compared to today. But it was good exposure for me. I went into the job with a definite partiality toward the media. When I was a PR guy and things were written that were critical, it kind of stung me. It wasn't personal, but you wear it on your sleeve a little bit.

When the team moved to the D.C. area, it was sort of a mutual decision that it would be better for me to stay put. They didn't offer, and I didn't ask. It was a good five-year run. I was between jobs for a few months when the job that Steadman had prepared me for from the beginning suddenly opened up and I went back. I took a cut in pay and didn't regret it at all.

I got the Orioles beat in mid-season of '73. I knew I could cover a beat. I covered the Bullets for five years before I worked for them. I was excited about it. John had wanted to put me on the Orioles beat back in the early '60s, when I was very young. The publisher was worried that the ballplayers would perhaps take advantage of my youth and inexperience.

The beat was a lot different than it was today. I was an afternoon guy for most of my career, so basically, you had to outlast the other guys. You don't want to be giving away your angles to the AM guys, so you worked in a question here and there without tipping your hand. Earl Weaver would give me little bits because I was almost always the last one left in his office. There was a reason for that: the

AM guys had to ask their questions and then get a move on. Another thing was that games started at eight in those days, but they weren't as long as they are now.

On the road, I would go back to the hotel and write stories and then file by Western Union. They had Western Union operators at the ballparks, so if you got done at a reasonable time, you'd file from there. Otherwise, you had to look for a Western Union office. It was very much a time-consuming thing. I remember many times going to a Western Union office at three or four in the morning, and then it was up to those guys to get it to the office.

Gradually, that changed. We dictated our stories for a while, and then someone would come in and transcribe them. The first thing I remember transmitting electrically was something called a Teleram. It was a big, bulky machine that cost about $4,500 and weighed about forty-five pounds. You had to lug it around and keep it with you all the time.

Bob Maisel and Lou Hatter were two of the original guys on the Orioles beat. Lou was a guy who was instantly friendly. The fact that we were on opposing papers didn't enter into it. We tried to beat each other, don't get me wrong, but there was a good friendship there. I also got to know Bob Maisel's dad, Fritz, who was scouting for the Orioles at the time. Fritz was a great player, although most people today wouldn't have heard of him. Rickey Henderson broke his single-season stolen base record with the Yankees. Not a lot of people realize that.

Bob Maisel was a guy who was just steady. He didn't overreact, he didn't underreact. It seemed to me that he was able to look at things in more than one perspective. Bob wasn't terribly controversial, but he also wasn't afraid to take an unpopular stand. I always found him to be a comforting guy.

When I was on the beat, Bob was the sports editor. Many times, Bob would compliment me on a story or a column. I was scoring a game one time, and there was a ball hit in the hole, one of those plays where you don't know if he'll throw the guy out or not, and the shortstop didn't handle it cleanly. I just sat there and stared, trying to figure out what happened. I made the call, then looked over to see what Bob's reaction would be. He said, "It wasn't anything until you called it." I never forgot that.

*   *   *

I always thought that I was a pretty good reporter, but I enjoyed the writing part, the column part, the feature part. You can paint the picture a little more. The reporting part would come down to the five W's: who, what, when, where, and why. That was the old standard. I think I did have a style of writing that appealed to people; I think I could reach people emotionally if it called for it.

Al Bumbry dropped a line drive in the '79 playoffs that cost the Orioles a game against the Angels. Al was really devastated, but he was great. He answered wave after wave of reporters. I didn't even write about the play; I wrote about him and how he dealt with it. I probably got more comments about that than any of the game stuff I did during that series.

There are two kinds of reporting, too: you're reporting who won the game, and you're also reporting, "Is this guy getting fired, and if so, who's getting the job?" Trades and things like that. I was good at sniffing out some of that, and a little naïve when it came to some of the other stuff. I maybe didn't anticipate trades as much as I could have. I did break the story of Hank Bauer getting fired and Weaver getting hired. That was strictly a gut feeling thing.

Earl Weaver was hired as manager in 1968 right before I left the paper. In fact, I wrote the story on my birthday, July 10. That's how goofy it was. I didn't even know I was leaving at the time. The '68 All-Star Game was in Houston, and I realized that the front office people from the Orioles had gone home early. All of a sudden, I wondered what was going on.

Jerry Hoffberger, the owner, was gone. Harry Dalton, the GM, was gone. They both had left on a private plane. There was evidently a big owners meeting the next day. Steadman had also come to Houston for the All-Star Game, and I remember picking up the phone in the middle of the night and saying, "John, I think they're making a move here." I knew that Dalton had just taken over and that Earl was their guy. It was just one of those things that fell into place.

So I'm on the phone with Steadman at three in the morning, talking from the gut. John was able to help me a little; he got to somebody who wouldn't answer a question from me earlier. Then he called me and said, "Go with it." It's four in the morning in Houston, and I'm writing a story that's going to lead the paper the next day. Not just the sports section, but the whole paper.

Now we're flying back, and it's nervous time because nothing was happening, no one was saying anything. But then, about five in the afternoon, they confirmed it. That was pretty exciting but also a little nerve-racking. I had known Earl for a long time; he was one of the first people I had met with the Orioles. I had gone to the minor league camps a couple of times, and I knew Earl from the first time I went, back in 1959 in Thomasville, Georgia.

I was around enough in '66, '67, and '68 to get a real feel for that team. During that time, for instance, Frank Robinson started the kangaroo court. They used to do that after every winning game, and we were always allowed in there. A lot of times, it was good fodder for us, especially for an afternoon paper. Frank would put the mop wig on, and they did a lot of ridiculous things, fine guys for saying or doing something stupid.

I was there for most of it in '66 . . . Frank hitting the ball off Luis Tiant that went out of Memorial Stadium, all those things. That was a unique team, and the '79 team was a real fun team as well. You look back at Earl's tenure, and Hank Bauer's before that, and you could say that the Orioles won all the World Series they were supposed to lose and lost all the World Series they were supposed to win. It was kind of crazy.

Looking at the roster of the '66 team, you'd think that maybe there were a lot of holes there. There were a lot of role-type guys; at one point they had four catchers. What a lot of people don't realize about that team is that in May, they weren't in first place. Then Boog Powell went on a tear, from the middle of May to the middle of August. You have Frank, Brooks [Robinson], and Boog in the middle of the lineup. They had a real solid core.

I remember Hank Bauer saying at the All-Star Game, "Casey Stengel always said, get to 30 games over .500 and then play .500 ball the rest of the way." You just had a feeling. They opened the season in Boston; I was on that trip. Frank comes up, his first time as an Oriole, and gets hit by a pitch. Then Brooks hit one into the net. First half of the first inning of the first game. It just went like that.

I was with them when they clinched the pennant in Kansas City, and I'll tell you, I've seen a lot of celebrations, but that thing was crazy. Then they flew to Anaheim right after, and I did most of my writing on the plane. Now we get to Anaheim and the night's just started. There was a big Buddha in the lobby of the hotel, and they wheeled it out and put it in front of Charlie Lau's door.

That was also the time of Moe Drabowsky's rubber snakes. Charlie Lau had taken Moe's rubber snake that night and cut that thing up into a zillion pieces. So the next day Moe comes in with a *live* snake. They come off the bus in Anaheim, go into the clubhouse, and there's the desk where the pass list is kept. Right next to it is a live snake . . . harmless probably, but live. Guys were running all over the place trying to get away. Then Moe put the snake in a ball bag and covered it with baseballs, so now guys are going out on the field and reaching in when finally the snake's head pops up out of the bag. Bauer finally had to sit Moe down and said enough's enough. Luis Aparicio and Paul Blair were getting dressed in the dugout, they were so scared.

*   *   *

I enjoyed being around Frank Robinson a lot. After the Orioles clinched in '66, I went to St. Louis to pick up the Dodgers, who were fighting for the pennant. In the last game of that series, Walter Alston put the winning run on base intentionally with two out in the ninth inning to keep from pitching to Orlando Cepeda. The next batter, Mike Shannon, made out to end the game. It was the pivotal part of my story. When I came back to Baltimore, Frank called me over and said about Alston, "You know, I've seen him do that before. That's not the first time. He's not afraid to do stuff like that." It showed me that even then, Frank was thinking like a manager. And the irony of it is that Frank eventually got traded to the Dodgers and played for Alston, and the two of them didn't get along.

Earl Weaver was a piece of cake to cover. I think most people thought that. Earl had a routine: he always liked to watch the visiting team hit and then take infield practice. He'd sit in the dugout, and that would often be our time to be with him.

Today, everything is structured. The manager meets with the media at four in the afternoon for fifteen minutes, and that's it. With us, there was always a fifteen- or twenty- or even a thirty-minute span where you just sat around the dugout and shot the breeze. Usually it was when the other team was hitting. Earl was good at it. There was nothing structured, and Earl was very off-the-wall. He'd go into a city on the road, and guys would come over from the other dugout and sit down with him. If he saw somebody whose name he didn't remember, he'd try to get his name before the guy got there. That was pretty impressive.

That doesn't mean he was the easiest guy to deal with all the time. I had some go's with him; everybody did from time to time. There was always this love-hate thing with the players. The one thing about Earl was that it was always about the players. I can only remember twice, in all the years I covered, that I saw Earl on the field after the game was over. Once was when Brooks hit his last homer, to win a game against Cleveland in April '77, which to this day Earl calls one of the greatest games of his life. The other time was when John Lowenstein hit the homer to win the first game of the playoffs against the Angels in '79. Otherwise, the congratulation stuff on the field was all about the players. Today, of course, it's a ritual. But whenever that team celebrated on the field, Earl was back in his office.

Earl never kept the clubhouse closed. His philosophy was always, "Let's get 'em in, get 'em out, and then go home." With the Al Bumbry play I mentioned before, Bumbry was an emotional wreck. He was a terrific person but a very sensitive guy. After that game was over, Mark Belanger and Lee May went to Earl and asked him to keep the clubhouse closed. They didn't want the media coming in and seeing Al in that state. Earl came out of his office—I heard this story later—went over to Al, and said, "Al, we wouldn't even be here without you. Don't worry about it." Then they opened the doors, and Al sat there and talked about the play, going through wave after wave of reporters. Today they don't have to do that because everything's done in an interview room.

Earl would come up with great quotes. Like when Mike Cuellar was fading out, he said, "I gave that guy more chances than I gave my first wife." I loved his philosophies on the game: "Keep the double play in order." "Don't let the long ball beat you." "A ball in front of you won't beat you; a ball over your head will." I mean, it just makes too much sense. He started the Weaver Cards (which they kept by hand), stat cards for every pitcher against every hitter. It wasn't any printouts—just kept 'em in folders that they took on the road.

In 1983, the year before I was national chairman of the baseball writers, I was the vice chairman. Those things are nice honors, but they're done on a rotating basis so that there's a semblance of order. Baltimore's time just came up, and the chapter nominated me.

Being national chairman is an honorary thing. Back then, most of the issues dealt with access and stuff like that. The BBWAA had much more clout back then than it does now. They really don't have much control over press boxes anymore since so much of the media is electronic.

The Hall of Fame vote is really an entity they need to protect, although, to be honest with you, a lot of papers are making it more and more difficult because they're not letting active guys vote anymore. It's a little worrisome to me, but I think they'll keep it this way. There will always be some bitching; I have complaints every year. But there's a system of balances there that makes it tough to get in. It's an exclusive fraternity, and it should be.

I said this twenty years ago: we're gradually moving toward the football mentality, where it's basically mass journalism. I miss the one-on-one opportunities. For instance, yesterday I got to the ballpark at five o'clock for a seven o'clock game, and guys were all upstairs in the press box, writing. And I'm thinking, man, this is the time of day when we were just starting to collect stuff. This would be prime time. Now, if you're there at two or three in the afternoon, other than having a briefing with the manager, you probably don't have a lot of one-on-one time. It used to be fun to just hang around the batting cage. Earl was really good about that.

Today, the field is cleared an hour before the game. Hell, I'd sit in the dugout sometimes until five minutes before the national anthem. It was a different time, and in fairness to them today, there was only a handful of us. Now, where do you draw the line? You have to deal with bloggers, and how do you know who's legit and who's not?

Some of the stuff I read on the Internet bothers me because there's obviously no editing, no nothing. They just fire it out there and say whatever. You throw mud against the wall and hope some of it sticks. I see it as a real problem because these websites are going to be looking for credentials everywhere, and I know they're already having some problems in that regard. I don't know what'll happen down the road.

But I could do it today. I like the game, and I think that helps. That would be enough reason for me to say I could do it. But I don't think you're going to see guys doing it as long as we did it.

I see Brooks Robinson and Boog Powell a lot, and one thing we talk about is how you benefitted from the relationships with people you were around, much more than anybody will ever have today. I think circumstances don't even allow it, which is a shame.

The print business is such a struggle now. I'm not an advocate of the good old days, but it's not going to be the same. Everything now is gravitating toward the Internet. A good friend I worked with, Neal Eskridge, always said that someday we'll get all our news off a television set. That was forty years ago, and he never realized how good a vision he had.

7

PETER GAMMONS

Peter Gammons's 2004 Spink Award certificate hangs in the Fenway Park press box and reads in part, "Gammons . . . has in many ways defined baseball coverage . . . writing with skill and flair in a style filled with allusions to cultural icons from Robert Frost to Warren Zevon."

Today, Gammons presides over a multimedia platform that includes print, television, the Internet, and perhaps some media that hadn't even been invented when this was written. But Gammons's influence upon the game and its coverage is solidly based on his two remarkable decades at the Boston Globe.

Joining the Globe *out of the University of North Carolina in 1968 (on the same day as another Hall of Fame sportswriter, Bob Ryan), Gammons was on the Red Sox beat from 1972 through 1976 and again from 1978 through 1985. He was a centerpiece of the* Globe's *celebrated, talent-laden sports staff of the '70s and '80s. His style, wit, and unique perspective turned August home stands into soap operas, pennant races into passion plays, and World Series into epics of Shakespearian proportions. In 1972 he began what many regard as his signature: the voluminous Sunday notes column, which became the game's community bulletin board and set a standard for decades to come.*

In 1976 Gammons left the Globe *to join* Sports Illustrated, *at that time the world's number one sportswriting destination. Two years later, the lure of day-to-day newspaper work pulled him back to the* Globe, *where he served as national baseball columnist from 1982 through 1985. Gammons would return to* Sports Illustrated *for a four-year stint starting in 1986.*

Gammons's TV work began in earnest in 1988, when he first appeared regularly on ESPN. Joining the network full-time soon thereafter, he was a mainstay on ESPN's various platforms for two decades, which included a three-month period during which he recovered from a brain aneurysm in 2006. In late 2009 Gammons left ESPN to join the fledgling MLB Network and the Boston-based NESN cable outlet.

A three-time National Sportswriter of the Year, as voted upon by the National Sportscasters and Sportswriters Association, Gammons was inducted into the association's Hall of Fame in 2010. The young man who had aspirations of being a rock star now jams for charity in Boston's annual "Hot Stove, Cool Music" concert series. This self-styled "ink-stained wretch" paved the way for a generation of baseball writers to flourish in journalism's brave, and sometimes bewildering, new world.

B ob Ryan and I started as summer interns at the *Boston Globe* on the same day—the day Bobby Kennedy was assassinated. That was in '68, and I started full-time in February '69. Originally, I was going to do news. But one of the writers had been ill, and they asked me if I minded doing sports, and I said I'd love to. I'd written more sports than anything in school.

So the first day, Ryan and I go in there and they say, "Okay. Bob, you take the National League; Peter, you take the American League. Call every team and see what they're going to do about Kennedy's death." See, there was a 3:30 edition of the *Globe* because at that time, it was both AM and PM. So we had to call every team and find out what they were planning to do after the assassination. When 3:30 rolled around, Bob and I had a dual byline on the front page of the paper, on our first day. I'd say it came six-and-a-half hours after arriving.

Remember, back in the '40s and '50s, baseball was basically covered without going down and talking to the players. When we moved into the '70s, it was more of a get-to-know-the-players type of thing. Bringing the players' personalities to the public became something that was much more important. I think the whole writing style of coverage changed in the late '60s and early '70s.

I was lucky enough to come along at that time, because that's also what interested me. I wanted to know about people, and my personality is such that I really do like people. Whether it's going to minor league games or major league games or Cape Cod League games, getting to know the players is something I really look forward to.

I was interested in writing, but it wasn't something that, automatically, I thought I would do. Actually, I thought my math grades were better than my verbal grades. That may have come from doing baseball statistics when I was five years old.

I really didn't know. Maybe I wanted to go into politics. Maybe I wanted to be a rock musician. I went to college completely with an open mind.

I went to North Carolina, and in my freshman year I was at a pub in Chapel Hill. I got into a discussion with Curry Kirkpatrick, who would become a giant at *Sports Illustrated* but was then sports editor of the *Daily Tar Heel*. Curry was originally from Buffalo, and he was a big Buffalo Bills fan, and they were playing the Boston Patriots on that upcoming Sunday.

We got into a little discussion, and he convinced me to at least try sportswriting. So I did. I think I wrote it out on longhand, a piece for the *Daily Tar Heel* about a soccer game.

When I started at the *Globe*, I covered high schools, I covered colleges. I did sidebars and things like that at Red Sox games, over '69, '70, and '71. I did a lot more in '71, and I was approached by a few different papers—a couple in the U.S. and one in Montreal— about becoming a baseball beat writer. I was very interested, and so the *Globe* said, "Okay, you've got the Red Sox beat." At the *Globe*, because we were so good and ran both AM and PM editions, we had three or four beat writers in those days. So in '72 I went to spring training as the beat writer.

As luck would have it, of course, spring training ended with the first players strike. I was there at the last baseball game played before the strike . . . Red Sox vs. Tigers at Joker Marchant Stadium in Lakeland. Bud Collins was the columnist, and I was the beat writer. So my career began with a strike.

I was a lot younger than most of the beat writers. Probably the closest to me in age was Will McDonough, who did a little baseball but not much because he was so great at football. At the *Globe*, there was Clif Keane and Ray Fitzgerald and Neil Singelais, and they were all quite a bit older than I was. So were Bill Liston with the *Herald* and Fred Ciampa with the *Record*. It was a little of my being out on my own, which wasn't a bad thing.

What probably helped me was that I was basically the same age as the players. In 1972, that was the year Carlton Fisk and John Curtis and Lynn McGlothen all came up. Rick Miller, Cecil Cooper, Ben Oglivie . . . they had a whole influx of players who came up from the farm team in Louisville. It was a huge changeover in personnel. That helped me a lot in getting to know the players and relating to them, because, again, they were all essentially my age. Half the team was very young, and that's a help to somebody coming along.

I think it's much harder to get to know the players today because clubhouse access is so restricted. In my day, right up to 1985, you could just walk into the clubhouse at any time. On the road, I used to work out every day. I'd go into the clubhouse some days and throw batting practice or shag flies. I think it afforded me the opportunity to get to know the way players think. I think that's terribly important. It's not just holding up a notepad or a recorder and getting words.

*   *   *

I used to say that players are not paid to be Winston Churchill looking back at World War II. They're paid to just sort of react. I used to talk to players when they'd first come to the Red Sox. I'd sit down with them in spring training and say, "Okay, these are some of the things you have to understand about me. I'm going to come to you when you screw up, when you go 0-for-4 and strike out with the bases loaded. I'm going to come to you because I want your side of it. I'm not coming to point the finger at you. I'm going to try to do it by myself, away from the crowd, so I can get your answers because I want to know if something happened that I should know about."

Another thing I always used to talk to them about was, like, "Look, understand. I'm really interested in who you are, what you do, and why you do it. That's going to have to be a need-to-know kind of thing. It's understanding who you are and where you're coming from." Everyone is different, and players were good that way. Once they understood that, there could be a trust.

Certainly, we had people who occasionally hollered at me and so forth. But by getting to know them and understanding them, you could develop a relationship. Jim Rice once told me, "You know, you come to the ballpark every day and go out there and work out. If I'm really mad at you, I know I can find you naked in the shower."

Rice, actually, was tremendous to cover, because he hated talking about himself. He used to say to me, "Let's say I hit two home runs. You can say it a lot better than I can, that's what you get paid to do. You're supposed to be able to write it better than I can say it." But if he made an error or struck out or something, he'd usually say something like, "Hey, I screwed up. It's my fault." But he'd always answer to it; he wouldn't duck. I respected him for that.

There were a couple of times where he thought—this is in the early '80s—that I was a little unfair to him. What he'd do was take a felt-tipped marker and underline what I'd written, give it to me, and say, "Just tell me later if you don't think that maybe you went overboard here." Instead of getting mad, he'd do that. It was his rational way of dealing with thinking that I was unfair to him, which was very helpful to me.

The early Red Sox teams I covered were extremely colorful. First of all, to travel with Luis Tiant was one of the great joys of my entire career. He was one of the greatest leaders I ever met in sports. His ability to make everybody laugh when entire teams were down was astounding. Plus, he was the best money pitcher I ever covered. He was just so much fun. One day we were in Milwaukee, and we're on the field. The Red Sox were waiting to start batting practice. Gorman Thomas, who was always at the ballpark early, was sitting in the Brewers dugout. Tiant came down the runway, and as he walked by Thomas, he just threw his arms up and went "Yaaaahhhhh!!" Oh, man. He said to Gorman that he was so scary, "You could be anything in the jungle but the hunter."

Tiant was just hysterical. His diatribes on the buses about [Carl] Yastrzemski and so forth. You had Yaz, who was a distinct personality. Reggie Smith, who was going through torment because there were still a lot of racial issues in Boston, leading into the busing era. Then you had Bill Lee coming along, who was hysterical and great fun.

So it was a very colorful team, with all those young players. Fisk, Rice, Lynn, Burleson. Very few teams brought as many good players to the major leagues over a three-year period as the Red Sox did. And that was a lot of fun, because they had distinct personalities and they were extremely colorful.

They had the incredible year of 1975, with Rice and Lynn as rookies and getting to the seventh game of the World Series and all that. Red Sox Nation was spawned by '67, I think, and '75 was the year it really grew up. We used to joke that you could rob every house in the city when Luis Tiant pitched.

*   *   *

I think I was a better reporter than writer, perhaps in terms of volume of writing and working hard. I remember when we thought the Red Sox were going to sign Catfish Hunter, getting very close to New Year's Eve in 1974. Charlie Finley had allowed Hunter to become a free agent over some insurance issue in his contract.

I was trying to find Dick O'Connell, the Red Sox general manager, who was traveling with John Harrington, the team treasurer. I knew they were down in Hertford, North Carolina, at Catfish's place. I was told they had driven off but they would stop for the night in Virginia. I called 253 hotels and motels until I finally found O'Connell. And he told me, "Yeah, we're out of it. We're not going to go after him; he's going to sign with the Yankees."

I don't think of myself in terms of this scoop or that scoop. I just think in terms of the fun of being in the business and never giving up on things. I thought writing under pressure was perhaps what I did best. That time that you had . . . you wrap up the lead, go downstairs, come back up, crank out fifteen hundred words, and get it all into the desk in less than an hour. I loved that pressure, and I loved being able to write that way and being able to get that done.

Deadline writing was never easy, but I loved the competition of it. You have to understand that, if you're out on the road for the *Globe*, you're the only one out there with both an AM and PM paper to file for. You'd have to do a pre-game notebook, then your running [as the game progresses], then put a top on it when the game's over. Then you'd go downstairs, come back up, write the full game story, and rewrite the notebook. And then go back to your room, write a few stories for the PM edition, and send it on those machines that had the big drum and kept spinning. So there was a lot of angst when you got finished at three or four in the morning. But that was all part of it. I was young and I loved doing what I was doing. I loved the beat and I loved baseball and really liked covering the personalities.

I actually remember, in 1972, having to take an off-day story on the road to a Western Union office. I remember having Western Union operators in the press box for maybe a year or so. Then you had Amfax and Canfax and all these companies that had Telecopiers, and they'd send your copy one page at a time.

We'd take those things on the road and send from our room. You'd be writing for the afternoon paper, and you'd get done, and now you're sending it, and you had to send it at either four minutes or six minutes per page. You'd doze off, and then you'd hear, "beep-beep-beep," so you'd get up and put another page in there.

There were also times where they had us call up and dictate our stories into a recorder, and then it would be transcribed by one of the office boys. That led to a very funny thing that happened to Clif Keane. The fans were really booing Yastrzemski. It was a Saturday night, and they had Clif call in his story. Yaz had been taken out of the game—he'd been hurt—and he was booed. Clif quoted Eddie Kasko, the manager, as saying "Yaz is fine." It was buried way down in his story.

Well, the guy transcribing the story thought he said, "Yaz is *fined*." So they moved it up to the lead graf, and the next day in the paper there's this headline, "Yaz is fined." Poor Clif! Needless to say, Yaz wasn't happy, and the Red Sox weren't happy. Those were the perils of that thing.

I grew up as such a baseball fan on every level, down to the minor leagues. In 1970 I asked Fran Rosa, who was the AM sports editor, if I could do a thing on Sundays about the minor leagues. Call it "Majoring in the Minors"—sort of a notes column on the minors. Fran said fine, and it got a lot of popularity.

Then in 1972, when I started covering the beat, Fran and Ernie Roberts, the PM sports editor, said, "You know, you want to do that on the major leagues?" I said yes, because I had said to them earlier that there should be a notes column. I loved them. Dick Young did it in New York, not just on baseball, and I loved that kind of thing. I always thought every sport should have those kinds of notes columns.

So when I went to spring training in '72, Ernie and Fran said, "Okay, get started." And that's how it happened.

It was fun to do, and it was a tremendous help to me for my career. I was a typical reader, and readers loved it. They liked the short things, and Boston was a great city to do it in. It's a very knowledgeable baseball city; it's a very diverse city. You could write notes about the San Diego Padres and people would know who they are. You can't say that about every city.

*   *   *

When I went back to the *Globe* after being with *Sports Illustrated*, it was because I missed the day-to-day writing. The thing that was so great about it was that Mark Mulvoy, who at that point was the number two or three guy at *Sports Illustrated*—he brought me back ten years later—was a great managing editor. He always knew what the story was, and he almost always decided on the right cover. I mean, he just had the knack. He had what I call tremendous street journalistic instincts. He had started at the *Globe*, and he never stopped being a newspaper guy even though he was the managing editor of the be-all-and-end-all sports magazine.

Mark understood why I left. When I started talking to the *Globe* about coming back, Mark said to me, "Are you talking to them about maybe going back?" and I said I was. He said, "I thoroughly understand. Don't think you're going to hurt me or hurt my feelings, because I brought you here. I understand it." And he didn't have to say anything more. Mark was tremendous to me, and he was a major reason I went back to *Sports Illustrated* in '86.

Some people have been really good about constantly reminding the public about how I crossed over into television, whether it was Ken Rosenthal or Jayson Stark or Buster Olney. They've been really terrific about that. But I live in New England, and there are people who come up to me and still think I write for the *Globe*. And that's *great*. I love that, even though I haven't written for the *Globe* on a regular basis since 1985.

What I do on television is still the same. I'm trying to report, trying to be fair, trying to explain why people do what they do. I think that the reporting, the accountability, all those things that go into being a print journalist completely apply to television journalism. My favorite show on television, and I make no bones about it, is *Morning Joe* on MSNBC. In an era where supposed news channels are not that at all, it's a show where people are accountable and responsible. They report. There's a diversity of opinion.

I really believe the opportunity to report is there in television. But I am very proud that I was elected into the National Sportscasters and Sportswriters Hall of Fame this spring. It was really wonderful to be presented by Bob Ryan. I was so proud of it. That's who I am, that's how I started.

Television is something I love doing, and I've said and written this many times: the vision that John Walsh had for ESPN was really shocking to people. I know that there were people at ESPN, when I started full-time in 1990, who could not believe that John had hired some writer to be on television. But John really understood the importance of information and where all journalism was going. He was way ahead of the times.

So it was really John Walsh's doing, not mine. And whether it's Kenny or Buster or Jayson or Tim Kurkjian or whoever is talking about getting this opportunity, it was really John Walsh who did it. He's one of the greatest visionaries in journalism I've ever known. As much as I've worked with great people, John Walsh was the greatest man I ever worked for. He dramatically changed television, and he dramatically changed the lives of print journalists.

In 2000, I lost out on the Spink Award to Ross Newhan, which was an honor. Ross helped me a lot when I started, and he deserved to win. I remember being excited about the possibility. As I said, Ross was a mentor and a great friend, and he belonged there. He goes all the way back to the original Angels in 1961.

When I won it in 2004, even though my prime work at that time was in television, it was a reminder that even in television, what I do is the same as what I did when I was a beat writer. I always say that even though I have to wear a coat and tie on television, I'm still an ink-stained wretch.

8

MAURY ALLEN

One of the most prolific and wittiest writers in New York baseball history, Maury Allen was a fixture at the New York Post *from 1961 through 1988, both as a beat reporter for the Mets and Yankees and as a columnist. Following his* Post *tenure, he served for more than a decade (1988–2000) as a columnist for the* Westchester Journal News.

After newspaper stints in Indiana and Pennsylvania, the City College of New York product returned to his native New York in 1959 with Sports Illustrated. *A BBWAA member since 1963 and an early member of the Chipmunk generation, he served as New York chapter chairman in 1974–1975.*

On those rare occasions when Maury wasn't in a press box, someone would invariably joke, "Maury's out writing another book." But it was no joke. Allen was the author of forty books, including his last, a 2010 work on Brooklyn Dodgers legend Dixie Walker, written in cooperation with Walker's granddaughter.

Allen's cinematic claim to fame came when he joined a group of other legendary writers in the famous Shea Stadium press box scene in the 1968 film The Odd Couple. *He also—unknowingly—played a pivotal role in the Fritz Peterson–Mike Kekich wife-swapping story of 1973. A member of the International Jewish Sports Hall of Fame, Allen kept active in retirement as a regular contributor to the website TheColumnists.com.*

On October 3, 2010—ironically, the fifty-ninth anniversary of the fabled Bobby Thomson home run that shattered this young Brooklyn

Dodgers fan's heart—Maury Allen lost a lengthy battle with leukemia at the age of seventy-eight. This interview—his last—was conducted eight months earlier, just before he fell seriously ill for the last time. Happily, all of the wit, passion, and irreverence that marked Allen's career were in full force, one final time.

I'll tell you the definition of a New York sportswriter. He's the guy who walks into the press box in Cincinnati or Chicago or Detroit, and all the other guys in the press box hate him.

The bottom line is, we got all the attention and the standing that they dreamed about getting. Not only because I think most of us happened to be better—although there are good writers everywhere you go—but because we had *more* good writers. It's like Sinatra said, if you can make it in New York, you can make it anywhere. Our competition wasn't with the writers from Chicago or Boston; it was the guy sitting next to you.

The names that you knew if you were a newspaper reader in those days, which everybody was, were the sportswriters' names. Nobody knew who wrote about Eisenhower or the civil rights movement or the space race. But everybody knew Dick Young and Jimmy Cannon and Milton Gross and John Drebinger and the names that were in the paper every day.

In my first or second year at the *Post*, '61 or '62, I'm sitting in a press box just bullshitting with the other guys. Cannon is sitting there writing his brilliant column. Now, the mere fact that I'm sitting next to Cannon in a press box is a thrill. This one particular day, I'm talking to maybe George Vecsey and Steve Jacobson and Phil Pepe, and Cannon just turned to me and said, "Shut up and keep typing!" His point was, first of all, don't make noise in the press box. But also, that's what you're here for. You're here to create words that those kids on the subway are gonna read.

I really took that to heart, and that became my mantra. I was writing for the guy on the subway. My goal and mission in life was to entertain that blue collar guy who was riding the subway from Brooklyn to Manhattan to work in the Garment District, reading the *Post*.

I've felt that even to this day. I could write more esoterically or more romantically. I've done it in books and magazines. But when you're writing in a newspaper, the goal is to entertain that fourteen-or fifteen-year-old kid that's really a fanatic about sports.

When I got into the business in 1955, the life goal of myself and a lot of guys like me was to be a bylined sports writer in New York City. That was the pinnacle, the top of the pyramid, the mountain, the Himalaya, whatever. If you did that, there was never anything else in your life that you'd want to do.

*   *   *

When I was in the third grade, I wrote a composition, and I got an A+ on it. That composition happened to be about Lou Gehrig. It was a review of the movie *The Pride of the Yankees*. I got an A+ on the review, and I came home, showed it to my parents, and I got fussed over, and it was a big deal. And I said, "Hey, this way you get a lot of attention when you get an A+," and your ego is out there, and it's a big thing.

So at that point, at about ten years old, I'm saying that either I'm going to play shortstop for the Dodgers like my hero Pee Wee Reese, or I'm going to write about Pee Wee Reese.

I was going to be the next Dick Young. I would go to about ten games a year at Ebbets Field for fifty-five cents, and the thrill was to come home and read what Young had written in the *Daily News* and then try to imitate it. I always thought I could be Dick Young. I never thought I could be Jimmy Cannon. Cannon was very unique and eso-teric. He had been a war correspondent, and he had sort of a different standing.

How I got my job is a funny story. I had been at *Sports Illustrated* for about three years, but I really missed the daily writing which I had done in Indiana and Pennsylvania. I'm writing once a week, once every two weeks. Sometimes your articles wouldn't even run. So I decided that I'm gonna get on a daily paper, the *Post*. I wrote Ike Gel-lis, the sports editor, a couple of letters, and he'd always send me a nice form letter back, saying that there wasn't anything available but to keep in touch.

In the winter of '61, Arch Murray dies in a fire. He was a smoker and a drinker, and he started a fire in his room and died. When I see that, I decided I'm going have some balls. I called Gellis and reminded him that he'd always said that if there was an opening, we'd talk. Well, now I *know* there's an opening, and he said to come in the next day. I spent that whole night memorizing trivia, so if they asked me who played third base for the Yankees in 1910, I'd know it. I must have slept an hour or maybe two that night.

I went down to the *Post* on 75 West Street on the docks. I walked in, and it's like the Nuremberg jury. There were about ten guys at this long table—Gellis; Sid Friedlander, the assistant sports editor; Paul Sann, the editor; and Jimmy Wechsler, the great columnist. I'm nervous as hell, but I figured that whatever they ask me, I'm gonna know. So Gellis said, "I've got one question for you, kid: do you smoke?" And I said no. He said, "You're hired, go to personnel!" So the bottom line to get into journalism is don't smoke.

In '62 I went to the first Mets spring training. Len Shecter and Lenny Koppett were already there from the *Post*, so I wrote sidebars every day and little features. Within a few years, both Shecter and Koppett left the paper, and they made me the number one baseball writer.

My very first road trip was to Chicago, when the Cubs didn't have a manager. Instead, they had a rotating band of coaches. The coach this day was Elvin Tappe, who was also the backup catcher. I ask myself, what can I write that'll be interesting, that people will get a kick out of? So I wrote a fictional story that, in order to compete with the Cubs, the Mets would start *their* manager in center field tomorrow. The manager of the Mets is Casey Stengel, who's seventy-two years old. I wrote the story, tongue-in-cheek. Well, the *Post* put it on the front page, not the sports page, with a big picture of Casey as a player with the Dodgers in 1914.

I thought Casey Stengel was the smartest and most entertaining person I had ever met in my life. He would have been a great success in business, art, theater, whatever it was. He just had a very unique mind. I used to spend a lot of time with him on the road and in the hotel bar. I'm not a drinker, but he'd have six or eight scotches and I'd have a beer, and he would just ramble on.

Stengel was eighty-five when he died. At the end of his life, he was totally ignored. I made it a personal mission to call Casey in California once every two weeks or so just to keep him up to date on the gossip that was going on with the Mets. One of the things we love about this business is gossip about the games and the players. Most of it you can't write, but you love to sit around and talk about it. Casey missed that because he was in California and a lot of attention wasn't paid to him. I called him and filled him in from about 1969 up until he died in 1975. It turned out I spoke to him the day before he died.

* * *

There was really a revolution in sportswriting in the early '60s, and we were the foundation of it. Myself, Phil Pepe, George Vecsey, Steve Jacobson, Stan Isaacs, Vic Ziegel. There were about six or seven guys that came in at the same time, all around the same age. The writers didn't write the game—they wrote the people. That was the change. People have seen the game on television, and *The New York Times* is gonna give you the details of the game. So if you're on any paper besides the *Times*, tell them something they don't know.

Well, with the early Mets, they don't know that Rod Kanehl worked on the back of a truck, or that Joe Christopher was from the Virgin Islands and worked as a farmer, or that Larry Bearnarth had gone to St. John's on a basketball scholarship. You got into the lives of the players, what they did on their off time or with their families. Humanizing them became a real centerpiece of Chipmunkia, if you want to call it that. The point was that these players are just the same as we are, except they have that unique skill that allows them to do what they do for a living. They have families, they have kids, and they struggle to make a living.

You have to keep in mind the comparison of the salaries of the players to the salaries of the sportswriters at this time. I was making $36,000 then. Well, I was making more money than maybe twenty guys on the Yankees when I started covering them. The major league minimum was maybe $6,000 at that time, and maybe only Mickey Mantle, Whitey Ford, and Roger Maris were making any real money.

We got total resistance, 100 percent, from the older writers at that time. There was a lot of sarcasm. I remember Dan Daniel. There was one game that the Mets won on what you'd call a walk-off homer, a silly term they use now. I think Jim Hickman hit it. I went downstairs, and I said I'm gonna get stuff on Hickman's background and about the fact that he's from Tennessee and he's a shy guy. As I got up, Dan

Daniel said, "Where are you going?" I said, "I'm going to the clubhouse." He said, "You saw what happened. You don't have to talk to these idiots." The attitude was that we were wasting our time talking to the players.

There was a hard core of older reporters. Dick Young was caught in the middle at that time. He was maybe in his fifties by then, so he wasn't old enough to be totally crotchety, but he wasn't young enough to be a Chipmunk. But he had gone down to the clubhouse to talk to the players, so he was a transitional guy. But the other guys, like John Drebinger, Dan Daniel, Barney Kremenko, they were all against the idea of going into the clubhouse. That's where the line was really drawn. They were sarcastic, and a lot of them were unfriendly to the young guys.

Getting back to Dick Young, I decided this is the guy I want to imitate. But he wasn't particularly nice to young guys. He had a little insecurity. As big as he was, he was worried about the young guys coming along, especially the Chipmunks, who were changing the game and maybe his standing within it. He had an abrasive, sarcastic personality that I found difficult. I'm pretty much an easy-going guy. Young's ego and aggressiveness made him overwhelming, so I developed an antagonism toward him.

Then, for whatever reason, he saw me as a threat because I was young and a competitor, writing for a great sports paper. It was just one of those things where we couldn't be in the same room together.

There were two incidents that became the focus of our antagonism. One, of course, was the Tom Seaver trade in 1977. Seaver had been the first great hero of the Mets, and he got into a contract dispute, just as the doors were being opened for free agency. Young wrote a couple of columns that were very personal about Seaver, including the one at the very end where he said Seaver was jealous of Nolan Ryan and that their wives were also jealous of each other.

So I wrote a story for the front page that was bannered, "Dick Young Ran Tom Seaver Out of Town." Up to that time, I had never written a word about another newspaperman by name. But I thought it was so important for the readers and fans to know about Young's fight with Seaver, and Seaver saying to me that he was leaving because he couldn't play in a town where Dick Young was so powerful. That was the beginning of a relationship that was as bitter as any.

Within that story, I had mentioned that Young's son-in-law [Thornton Geary] had worked for the Mets, and that was one reason he was so sympathetic to the team and to [board chairman] M. Donald Grant. Young got really, really angry. He went on radio and TV badmouthing me and wrote terrible things about me and the *Post*.

About two weeks later, we go to Chicago. Jennifer, my daughter, was nine at the time and a red-hot baseball fan. I had always taken my kids to spring training but never on a trip during the season. This time, I decided I'm gonna be a hotshot father and take her on the road. I took her to Chicago, and we had a great time. She went to all the games, sat in a front row seat, really being fussed over.

I come back from the trip, and the next day, Young writes something like, "Maury Allen freeloaded on the Mets charter, taking his daughter to Chicago and not paying any attention to his job" and stuff like that. Now, when I wrote about Thornton Geary, he was a thirty-five-year old man who could take care of himself. But my daughter comes home the day after this article runs, and she's hysterical because all the kids have seen it and made a big deal out of it. Family is number one with me, and the job is number two, and if my family is attacked, it's pretty tough. I spent pretty much the rest of my life not speaking to Young. It's the only relationship I ever had in this business where I couldn't stand the guy, and he couldn't stand me.

What happened to Dick Young was that he got old and couldn't handle it. A lot of people get old and they go through their aging process in a smooth way. They accept that their glory days, their importance and impact, are in the past. He could not stand that. He went crazy over my presence and the attention I was getting, and then later on, it shifted to Mike Lupica, whom he hated just because he came to the *Post* and then to the *News*, and he saw him as a threat.

Jerry Holtzman may have been my closest friend in the business. I met him in 1959. We were very close pals. He was a brilliant student of the game.

As much as I loved writing, I loved the idea of turning a phrase or coming up with a word and using it in a very unique way. Holtzman was kind of my inspiration for that. Young, on the other hand, was a straight nuts-and-bolts guy. Young wrote the way people talked in New York. Holtzman had the capacity to take a few words and use them in a very unique way, to make people sit up and notice.

Holtzman was brilliant at the end of his life. He created the save rule and made Mariano Rivera and all these other relief pitchers millionaires. It was all part of his sense of baseball history being so connected with the culture of the country.

*   *   *

I was the fastest writer in the press box for two reasons. One, I knew my story as soon as I got to the clubhouse. I knew what I wanted to write before I even talked to the players. And I would ask the players questions that I knew would fit into my idea of what was the big story of the game. I did a lot of research, so I knew a lot of personal background on the players. So if a guy hit a big home run or was the hero of the game, I'd ask a personal question. That was part of my skill.

The second thing was, unlike Red Smith, who had the famous line about sitting behind the typewriter and having it slowly bleed out, I was exactly the opposite. I sat at the typewriter and wrote the whole story and then I was gone. I never felt that anything I wrote would get better if I stared at it or drank beer or bullshitted with the other guys. The idea was to do my work and go home and share it with my family.

I wasn't the greatest writer, I wasn't the best reporter like Holtzman. But I think I wrote the most entertaining stories that were written in those days. All my stories were, basically, to make people smile. I always had one line or one little anecdote in a story that was geared to that. Joe Falls from Detroit once wrote that I was the best anecdote writer on the beat.

The funny thing was the *Post* was an afternoon paper, and I had the latest deadlines of anyone. When Leonard Koppett was on the *Post*, he was famous for going out after every game and having dinner. Chinese food, nine times out of ten. He would go out, have his Chinese food, then come back to his room and write. His thinking was, "Well, my deadline is six in the morning. Why do I have to get it in by eleven at night?"

Here I am in 1963 or so, and as soon as I'm done in the clubhouse, I'm sitting down and writing, and after I've filed, *then* I'll go out to eat. I also think my mind worked sort of rapidly, and getting it all out while it was still fresh in my mind was the best way I knew.

The idea of having it hanging over my head for two or three hours wasn't something I wanted to deal with.

*   *   *

The Peterson-Kekich story was the only story I had that I refused to write. When Peterson called me and asked me to write it, I refused. I didn't think he should make this public.

When I was covering the Yankees, every year I used to have a barbecue at my house. I would invite two or three players and some more couples, friends of mine. So there'd be twelve, fourteen people in our backyard, and my wife, Janet, would put out a beautiful spread with hot dogs and hamburgers. We'd sit around and bullshit and have a good time.

In August of 1972, we have our annual barbecue. The three players we invited were Fritz Peterson, Ron Swoboda, and Bobby Murcer, who were the guys I was closest to on the team. The day before the party, Peterson called me and asked me if he could bring Mike Kekich to the party. Sure, I said. What's a few more hot dogs? So they all come to the party at my home in Westchester.

Now, what was interesting about it was that Peterson's wife, Marilyn, always had this beautiful blonde hair in the five or so years we had known them. So now she comes to the party with long *brown* hair down to her shoulders. She explained that she had always worn a wig, believe it or not, because she wanted to look sophisticated, like the other players' wives, and the blonde wig made her look that way. That particular day, she decided to "be herself" and have long brown hair. When she walked into the house, we were sort of taken aback. That sort of began it.

We have dinner and then have some beers, and I don't notice anything particularly romantic going on. Now, my house was up on a hill and had a long driveway. They leave the house, and now it's an hour later, and Janet and I have done the dishes, and we're getting ready to go to sleep. I'm closing the curtains of the front window and see the car that Peterson and Kekich had come in. It's still there in the driveway, and the four of them are standing by the car, talking, about two hundred feet from the house. I couldn't hear what they were talking about.

A few days later, Peterson calls me and says that, after our dinner was over, they went to a motel and switched wives that evening. He said that he was gonna marry Kekich's wife, Susan. I was shocked, and then he said to me, "I want you to write it so it sounds clean." I said, "Fritz, you don't have to say anything about this. It's your business. I have no business writing it."

I told him this was personal and to just go about his business. It's 1972, and writers weren't writing that stuff in those days. I told him he should just go to spring training and it wasn't anyone's business that he was going to marry his teammate's wife.

Now it's January 1973, and Peterson calls me at the Baseball Writers Dinner. He tracks me down—I'm paged—and I get all concerned. Who could be pulling me out of the writers' dinner? It's Peterson, and we go through this whole story again. He decided that he wanted it out, and I told him to call Milton Richman at UPI, who would handle it in a very objective way. Milton had none of the jazzy writing style that would make it a gossipy kind of story. He wrote a very straight column about these two players swapping wives, and that was it.

Of course, then Young jumped on it because he was beaten on the story, and then Bowie Kuhn issued some statements, and it became a worldwide controversy. But I never wrote about it because I felt it wasn't my place. I did write a magazine piece about it for *Ladies Home Journal*, but that was six months later.

And remember, this was the first spring training for George Steinbrenner as owner of the Yankees! So he comes in, and the big story in spring training isn't the new owner. It's these two pitchers who have swapped wives.

The Odd Couple is my movie claim to fame, with the scene we shot at Shea Stadium. Me, Young, Koppett, Jack Lang, and Milt Gross are in it, and we each got $100. Haywood Hale Broun got $200 because he had some lines.

No one knew anything about it. Some flunky came around in the morning and asked Harold Weissman, the Mets PR guy, who was covering the game that day. As each of us came to the press box, the guy asked us if we wanted to be in a movie they're filming with Walter Matthau. And we'll pay you! Oh, my God.

This is two hours before the game. They sat us down in our regular seats in the press box and did it. Matthau is on the phone with

Jack Lemmon and missed a triple play that the Pirates hit into. They wanted Roberto Clemente to hit into the triple play for $100. Clemente told the producer, "I don't hit into a triple play no matter what the price is." He wouldn't do it, and Bill Mazeroski said, "I'll hit into a triple play for $100!" So Mazeroski hit into the triple play, we're all excited and jumping up and down, and Matthau's back was to the play and he missed it.

*   *   *

We knew that the standing of the Baseball Writers Association revolved around New York, and most of the credit for that goes to Jack Lang. Lang was never a good writer, but he cared about the organization and the baseball writers' standing. He protected his turf like a bulldog. You had to pay your dues before you were accepted into the club.

The main connection in baseball was among the writers who traveled with the team. If you were a fringe guy, a sidebar guy, you had no standing at all. But if you were one of the writers on the road, then you were one of the guys. And it took a long time for guys to get into that sort of exalted club, and part of that was Lang protecting the franchise.

We once went to this fancy restaurant in San Francisco called The Blue Fox. During the meal, the waiter brought over the largest peppermill anyone had ever seen. It was about two feet tall. Lang looked at it and said, "I gotta take that thing home." We're all in the bag by then, and we asked him, "How are you gonna steal a peppermill that big?"

Lang said, "Well, Tommy Holmes is here. I'll just put it through his empty sleeve." Tommy, you remember, had lost an arm. Now, he never did take it, he was just goofing. But his tag line was, "I'll put it up Tommy's sleeve and we'll just walk out holding hands. We won't have to worry, this is San Francisco."

Lang came up with the idea of the writers' World Series charter plane. He decided it would be cheaper to get a charter than it would to have everyone hustling for flights. My favorite story about the charter was when Lang sat with Jimmy Cannon. I was about two rows behind. Cannon kept telling Lang what he was going to write, and near the end of the flight, Lang said in a big, loud voice that everybody heard, "Jimmy, I don't read you!" That was an emotional blow to Cannon, whose ego was gigantic.

While it lasted, the charter was great fun. The idea of a hundred writers on the flight . . . you got to talk to them in a social way. I was always interested in talking to the out-of-town guys and getting a sense of what they did.

For the first five years I was in the business, before I got married, I was in Toots Shor's maybe once a week. I wasn't a big drinker, but the idea of sitting at a table with Joe DiMaggio or Jack Dempsey or Toots himself was unreal.

One of my biggest thrills, and I don't know the exact year, was when I walked in there and Toots was at the door, and he said to me, "Come over here, you crumb bum, I want you to say hello to . . ." Once he called you a crumb bum, you had made the big time. You were a big shot. You belonged to the club, and you couldn't get any higher.

Back in the '60s, it was the goal of every player to make the New York Baseball Writers Dinner. It was the only time these big stars would appear, in tuxedos, out of their uniforms. You weren't asking them about the games, you were asking about their wives and families.

The writers show was Broadway quality. I've got to give credit to Young—he wrote a lot of the great lyrics. Koppett was sort of the father of the dinner for a lot of years, and Lang did the business end. Everyone performed and took it very seriously. In those days, the baseball writers didn't work in January. Now, they work just as much in January as they do in July. But then you got up, had your breakfast, and went to the Hotel Americana to work on the show. This went on for three weeks.

The ultimate was that, every night after you rehearsed, you went to Shor's and had free dinner and a few drinks. The night of the dinner was an all-nighter. Even a guy like me, who didn't drink a lot, stayed there all night because the stories and the tales and the fraternity were so overwhelming you couldn't walk away from it.

As a retired guy, I consider my Hall of Fame vote the most important thing I do connected with baseball. I have my own standards and vote for the guys who I think will measure up. There are some guys who are not in there who I think should be. Tommy John is one. Jim Kaat is another.

Then there are guys who are in that shouldn't be. The Veterans Committee has become a complete political fiasco. The idea that Marvin Miller, one of the most significant guys in twentieth century baseball, isn't in the Hall of Fame is a joke. He changed the game more than Babe Ruth, more than anybody.

I've been to about fifty Hall of Fame inductions, and I think I cried at every one. There's always something emotional and sentimental that one of the players will say that brings tears to my eyes.

You could do the job today because you had to. But I wouldn't want to do it, let's say that. It isn't fun anymore. When I go to the ballpark and sit in the press box, which is once or twice a year now, I hate to be one of those guys that say, "It was better in the old days." But the bottom line is, it *was* better in the old days. It's not fun anymore.

It's too much mechanical work. The writers write from the minute they get to the park until the minute they get home. There's no time for the banter or the fun or the fraternalism of being a sportswriter.

And nobody wants it anymore. There isn't one guy in the press box in his 20s or 30s who's saying, "I want to be doing this when I'm seventy." It's never going to be like what it was in our time: the fun, the entertainment, the joy, the thrill. I got up every morning of my professional life with a smile on my face, thinking, "I'm gonna watch Willie Mays play baseball and get paid for it." I don't think they feel that way today.

It's a little sad today in that kids use newspapers as an instrument for something else. The goal today is twofold: one, to get on television; two, to make a lot of money. In my day, television and money were so immaterial and so unimportant in your career decisions that it never really played a role. The whole idea was to get a byline in a New York City paper and then sit in the subway and see some kid reading your story. That was the emotional kick, the orgasm that every guy like myself dreamed of having.

9

HAL McCOY

Hal McCoy may be the quintessential Keeper of the Game.

For a staggering thirty-seven years—from 1973 through 2009—McCoy did not so much cover the Cincinnati Reds beat for the Dayton Daily News *as he defined it, setting a standard for consistent, day-to-day baseball coverage which may never be seen again.*

McCoy's crisp writing—his paper estimated that he covered more than seven thousand games and wrote more than twenty-five thousand stories—served as gospel for generations of Reds fans, and his integrity, professionalism, and thoroughness made him a legend throughout Reds Country. He chronicled the deeds of the legendary Big Red Machine of the '70s, the lifetime banishment of his close friend Pete Rose in 1989, the tragicomic reign of Marge Schott (who tried to bar him from Riverfront Stadium), and the team's twenty-first century resurgence.

Through it all, McCoy earned the respect of the entire baseball community. (What other beat writer was given a "Day," as Hal was at Great American Ballpark in 2009?) The esteem in which he is held has been the trademark of a career that began for the Kent State product on the Dayton Journal-Herald *in 1962, included a 1967 stop at the* Detroit Free Press, *and then moved, finally, to the* Dayton Daily News *in 1968. In Dayton, McCoy worked under two Spink winners: Ritter Collett at the* Journal-Herald *and Si Burick at the* Daily News. *He was the BBWAA's national chairman in 1997.*

McCoy himself was the 2002 Spink Award winner, but the honor was a bittersweet one, coming just weeks before he lost most of his

eyesight due to ischemic optic neuropathy. The disease attacked Mc-
Coy's right eye in 2002 and his left eye early the following year. He
has been legally blind ever since.

Undaunted, McCoy continued on the beat until the end of the
2009 season, when the Daily News *ceased its daily Reds coverage.*
The self-styled "dinosaur" found a new home at Fox Sports Ohio,
where he blogs daily, conducts interactive chats with fans, and
contributes to the Reds pre- and postgame television coverage. He
also reestablished his online presence at the Daily News *with his*
blog, "The Real McCoy," and in print with his weekly "Ask Hal"
column.

It is doubtful that anyone in this new age of baseball journalism
will handle a beat as long as Hal McCoy. It is even more doubtful that
anyone will handle it nearly as well.

I went thirty-six years without missing a road trip. Life on the road
never got to be a grind for me. Never did. I always say there are
three things in my life that I love. I love baseball, I love to write, and
I love to travel. And I got to do all three and I got paid for it. I always
told my wife that someday I would get a real job, but I never had to.

Mostly what I miss now is the camaraderie in the press box and
all the friends I've made in all the cities over the years. Not just the
writers, but the press box attendants and the PR people. It's such a
pleasure to see all who've become friends and acquaintances. I miss
that right now, I miss it a whole lot.

Most writers say the travel is what gets 'em. That's why most
writers only do it two or three years, but I always enjoyed it. The only
thing about the travel, and it didn't bother me until I lost most of my
eyesight, was going through airport security. That was a total hassle.
Once I got through security, it was like somebody took an anvil off
my shoulders. Now we're home free, you know?

When I read other writers, one thing I always look for is how they
wrote their leads, what seemed to work and what grabbed the reader's attention. As the game goes along, I'm always thinking about
the lead. I think that when someone reads a good lead on your story,
they're going to keep reading. I always tried to strive for something
different. I always felt good when people would say to me, "We love
your leads."

Ever since I got out of college, I wanted to be a baseball writer. I went to Kent State on a baseball scholarship and played with Gene Michael, whom I went to high school with and who later became a player, manager, and executive.

The little taste I had of a truly big city was when I was in Detroit. I loved the *Free Press*, I loved what I covered, but at the time I did not like Detroit, so that kind of soured my taste a little bit.

In Detroit, I was covering the Big Ten, football and basketball, and it so happened that it was 1967, the year of the riots. I stood on the top of the *Free Press* building and watched Detroit burn for three days, I couldn't get home because they kept us at the paper. Shortly after that, Si Burick called me and asked me if I'd like to come back to Dayton. I said, "I'll be there tomorrow."

Talk about mentors. Earl Lawson took care of me on the beat, Si Burick had hired me, and early on in my career I worked for Ritter Collett. And the one year I spent in Detroit, I worked under Joe Falls. All Hall of Famers. I had pretty good tutoring!

When I came back to Dayton, I covered the University of Dayton basketball team and, believe it or not, auto racing. I covered four Indianapolis 500s and four Daytona 500s. I also covered the Dayton basketball team when they won the National Invitation Tournament in 1968 with Donnie May and Bill Hosket, two great guys I'm still close to. I actually covered them both in high school for the *Journal-Herald*, when they were on the Dayton Belmont High School team in 1964 and won the state championship. I covered every game but one . . . the one game they lost!

About 1969 I started covering the Reds as Jim Ferguson's backup. The first major league baseball game I ever covered, Dave Bristol was managing the Reds and Gary Nolan had a sore arm. That night, Nolan was supposed to throw in the bullpen before the game, and Fergie told me, "Whatever you do, ask Bristol how Nolan did."

So, after the game which the Reds won something like 2–1, me being the bright, young reporter, the first question I asked Bristol was, "How did Gary Nolan do before the game?" And Bristol lit into me: "How in the hell can you ask me a question like that after we just saw a great game?" It scared the hell out of me, and I don't think I asked another question for about four games. Later, when Bristol came back as a coach with the Reds, I related that story to him. He

laughed and said, "I always loved to intimidate young reporters."
And he certainly did.

*   *   *

In 1973, Fergie left the paper to become publicity director of the
Reds. Si Burick called me into his office. Now, just before that, Bob
Hertzel had been working at our paper covering the Bengals, and
then he left to cover the Reds for the *Enquirer*. Si said to me, "We
have two beats available: the Bengals and the Reds. Which one do
you want?" It took about a half a second for me to say, "I'll take the
Reds." So when I took over the beat for the *Daily News*, Hertzel was
at the *Enquirer* and Earl Lawson was at the *Post*.

Earl was my mentor. He always told me that when he was first
coming on the beat, Si Burick took him under his wing and took care
of him. He said he was returning the favor for Si, and that's exactly
what he did. One of the first days, Earl said to me, "Kid, follow me
around. Keep your mouth shut. Watch, listen, and observe." And for
about two years, I was Earl's shadow. If he went into the visitors'
locker room, I went there. If he went into the visiting manager's office, I went with him. I made a whole lot of connections, people I still
know to this day because Earl introduced them to me.

When I started out, we all carried little portable Olivettis [type-
writers] everywhere we went, and we had Western Union operators
in the press box. I used to have a little trick: when we were on deadline at big events with a lot of writers, I'd hand my story over to the
Teletype operator along with a $10 bill, and it would go right on top
of the pile.

Being a PM paper, sometimes Earl and I would go to the clubhouse after the games, get our quotes, and then get on the team bus
back to the hotel. We'd write our stories at the hotel, then grab a cab
and go to the Western Union office downtown and send our stories
there.

Then I went to Portabubbles and RadioShacks, kicking and screaming every step of the way. I'm not one who likes change. Si Burick
went to his grave using a typewriter; he was the last one. They'd have
to hire a woman in the office to take dictation from him. I wasn't that
bad. Every advance was better, but I fought it every step of the way.

Earl Lawson used to carry a Telecopier with him. It had this roll on it; you'd put your copy on it, and it rolled around and around and sent the copy via telephone. It was very sensitive; you'd get halfway through your story, and any little bit of crowd noise or press box noise would knock it off, and you'd have to start all over. I remember one time I went into Earl's room after I had sent my story, and his room was just destroyed—curtains torn, tables overturned. He had gone nuts because he couldn't get his Telecopier to work.

One day, I believe it was in St. Louis, we're going to the ballpark. Earl was in the cab, and his Telecopier was on the front seat. The cab made a sudden stop, and the Telecopier went flying, hit the floor, and broke. Earl called his office and said, "The monster is dead."

I was always a very fast writer, and I probably should have been on an AM paper all along because I've never missed a deadline in my life. I'm so fast that I hardly do any rewriting; what comes out of my head goes on paper or into the computer, and it stays that way. I go through and check for typos and factual errors, but I hardly ever rewrite.

I always thought of myself as a better writer than a reporter. I was always proud of my writing, and I always loved to write. I like to entertain. Earl Lawson had the nickname of Scoops, and when he retired, I picked up that name because I was very seldom beat on a story. So I guess I can probably say I was a combination of both.

*   *   *

When I started on the beat in 1973, the Reds had already been to the World Series a couple of times, but it was still the infancy of the Big Red Machine. In my first year, they were in the playoff series against the Mets where they lost but should have won. Then in 1975 and 1976 . . . well, it's the best team I've ever seen and probably the best team in the history of the game as far as I'm concerned.

I was just starting out as a baseball beat writer, and I thought that this was the way it was always going to be. I really didn't appreciate it until about 1982, when the Reds lost 101 games and I saw the other end of it. I didn't stop to smell the coffee along the way. I saw something very, very special and really didn't appreciate what I was seeing at the time.

What made it so easy for me, along with having Earl Lawson at my side, was that this team had Pete Rose and Joe Morgan and Johnny Bench and Tony Perez and George Foster. All those guys were so easy to cover. They made writing easy.

They were cocky and arrogant, no doubt about that, but they had a right to be. As far as dealing with the media, they were just fabulous. Pete Rose alone. You'd go in, stand in front of his locker, open your notebook, ask one question, and he'd fill your notebook for you. That's another thing that made me think that this was the way it always would be.

Most managers will tell you that you have twenty-five players, and you've gotta treat them all the same way. That's not the way Sparky Anderson worked. Sparky would say, "I've got some superstars here, the Benches and Morgans and Perezes and Roses. They're special. They get treated special; they have different rules." He called the rest of the team his "Turds." Darrel Chaney even had T-shirts made up that had "Turds" on the front, and all the extra guys wore them. Sparky would say, "When you guys accomplish what these guys have accomplished, then you'll be treated as superstars. But until then, these guys play by their own rules."

Sparky was fabulous with the media. These days, everything is structured. Everybody meets with the manager at once—it's a set time where all the media go in. It didn't work that way when Sparky was managing. Sparky had time for everybody. I'd go in there by myself, sit down, and talk, and he'd talk as long as you wanted and give you everything you needed.

Sparky always wanted to please. During the 1975 World Series, I'm sitting with Sparky in his office, and a wave of writers comes in. One writer asked him a question, and Sparky answers it, gives him all these good quotes and all that. Then another wave comes in, and another writer asks Sparky the exact same question. Sparky answers it in totally the opposite way he answered the previous writer. So when everyone left, I said, "Sparky, two different writers asked you the same question, and you answered it totally differently." He said, "Well, you can't give all the writers the same story."

The biggest scoop I ever had was probably Sparky's firing. I'm pretty proud of that one. Nobody else had it, and we had it in the paper the day it happened. The team was on a Japanese tour and they had just returned. He was at the airport in Los Angeles. Sparky was told he would have to fire two of his coaches, and Sparky, being the loyal guy that he was, told Dick Wagner, the general manager, that if you're going to fire two of my coaches, you might as well fire me, too.

*   *   *

Probably the toughest year of my baseball career was 1989. When the Pete Rose story first broke, my sports editor at the time, Ralph Morrow, called me in and said, "This stuff is starting to hit the fan on Pete. I know how close you are to him. Do we need to take you off the beat for now and put someone else on, or can you handle this?"

I said, "I know it's going to be tough, but I consider myself a professional, and I'll do what it takes. I don't want to be taken off the beat." That was a very tough year, because I not only covered every game, but, every day, I had to ask Pete something about the investigation. It was very difficult, knowing that he had been a friend both on and off the field.

We had three or four investigative reporters working on the story, too, but they never saw Pete. I saw him *every day*, and they'd feed me information, and I'd have to go to Pete and say, "How about this? How about this?" It became a kind of kill-the-messenger type of thing. After it all ended and he got banished, Pete didn't speak to me for about fourteen years. That became very tough.

But now here's a great story. About three years ago, my wife and I and another couple were in Las Vegas, and we were walking in the mall at Caesars Palace, where Pete appears all the time to sign autographs. He was in there signing, and my wife said, "Go in there and say hello." I said, "Are you kidding? You want to start a brawl? The guy hates my guts." But, again, she said, "Go in there and say hello."

So I go in, and he had his head down, signing away. I said, "What do you say, old timer?" He looked up, and his face turned red, blue, purple. . . . He jumped up, shook my hand, took me behind the table, had one of his people go back to get me one of his game jerseys, signed it, had a picture taken, signed it, and handed it to me in a leather folder. He wrote, "To a great Hall of Famer, from the Hit King, Pete Rose."

Now, it gets better. This whole thing was during the All-Star break, and the next day we're in New York to start playing again. The team doctor, Dr. Tim Kremchek, was on the trip. He's very close to Pete, and he said to me, "So, I heard you saw Pete yesterday!" I said, "How in the hell did you know? I haven't told anybody." He said, "Pete called me and said, 'Doc, you'll never guess who stopped in to see me. Hal McCoy! And I thought he hated my guts!'"

So now when Pete's in Cincinnati, he stops up to see me. About a week after the Las Vegas thing happened, he was in Cincinnati at the ballpark. Of course, he's not allowed in the press box. He was outside at the door and asked to see me. I came out, and Marty Brennaman, the announcer, came along. The three of us are standing there talking, and a fan sees us and says, "Can I take a picture of you three guys?" We said sure, and as the guy is taking the picture, he says, "Look at this . . . three Hall of Famers!" And Pete says, "Well, two-and-a-half, anyway."

*   *   *

I had opportunities to go elsewhere, and I'm glad I never did. I love Dayton. I love the city and loved the newspaper because, even though it wasn't in a big-league city, it was a big-league newspaper. We covered everything. I covered the playoffs and the World Series whether the Reds were in it or not.

At the time I was getting a lot of job offers; they were all from PM papers. The *Cleveland Press*, the *Kansas City Times*, the *Washington Star*, the *Houston Post*, the *Philadelphia Bulletin*. Most, if not all, of the major PM papers in the country came after me, and I turned them all down, and all of those papers are dead now. They're all gone.

The closest I came was with the *Columbus Dispatch*. They offered me a columnist job, and I almost took that, but my oldest son was a junior in high school, and he was a big basketball star, and I didn't want to uproot him.

The *Philadelphia Inquirer* also offered me a job, and I went for the interview, thinking it was going to be baseball. They said, "We want you to cover the Flyers." I said, "To tell you the truth, I've never seen a hockey game in my life, and I don't know a blue line from a red line!" Tim Kelly was the sports editor, and he said, "Well, we've read your stories, and you write about people. We love your game stories, and you would adjust quickly." I said, "Nah, I'm a baseball guy. No thanks."

The *Cincinnati Enquirer* came after me a few times, and then when the Devil Rays were formed, the *Tampa Tribune* asked me if I wanted to be the beat writer. I considered that, thinking that maybe a change would be good. But every time I considered another job, the *Daily News* came up with a nice raise for me. So I kept thanking all these papers for coming after me and getting me nice raises. But I really did want to stay in Dayton. I'd established myself here, and I'm glad I did. Now, everywhere I go, people recognize me. If I had left Dayton, I probably wouldn't be where I am now.

Fortunately, I won the Spink Award before my eyesight went bad. If I had won the award afterward, I would have thought it was a sympathy vote. The vote was announced in December in Nashville, and then my sight left in January, so that was after the fact.

To win the Spink Award was the highlight of my professional life. People always ask me what it's like to be in the Hall of Fame. I'm supposed to be a man of words, and that's one thing that I cannot describe. It's just on a higher plateau, to be with all those immortals. When I was called up to make my acceptance speech, I looked behind me and saw thirty-seven Hall of Famers sitting on that stage, the icons of baseball, and I thought, "What the hell am I doing here?"

*   *   *

In 2002, in St. Louis, I was walking to my seat in the press box, and my right eye felt funny, and all of a sudden it got real blurry. It felt like I had something in my eye, but I couldn't get it out. That was the last day of the road trip. When I came home, my right eye was still blurry.

My wife, Nadine, made me go to the eye doctor, and he's a very humorous, effusive guy. But as he examined my eye, he got real quiet. He told me I'd had a stroke of my optic nerve, and he had good news and bad news. The good news was that whatever happened in my right eye probably won't get any worse and that only 15 percent of the people who get this also get it in the other eye.

So for the next year, I adjusted. My left eye took over, and I didn't even notice. I still played tennis, I still drove my car. Well, on January 27, 2003, I got out of bed, started down the steps, and I could not see. Everything was blurry and dark, and I knew what had happened. I told my wife, "I just hit the big 15 percent lottery." She said, "What do you mean?" I said, "It's happened in my other eye."

Amazingly, that was three days before the paper had a big event for me at the University of Dayton to celebrate my winning the Spink Award. I went to my sports editor, Frank Corsoe, and told him that I was done, that I'd have to retire. He said, "Why?" I whipped out my eye charts and showed him, and we both had a good cry. Nadine was standing there watching two grown men cry.

Finally, Frank said, "You're not quitting. You're going to spring training." I said, "I can't go to spring training, *I can't see*." Frank said to go to spring training and at least try it. If I can't do it, well, okay.

So I went down to spring training. I flew into the Sarasota airport and stood at the luggage carousel, and I couldn't pick out my luggage. I had to wait until everybody got their luggage so that my bag was the only one left. I took it to my condo in Siesta Key then went out to the ballpark.

I walked into the clubhouse and stopped as I walked in the door. I looked around, and it was dark and blurry. I couldn't recognize the players. Aaron Boone was sitting at his locker, and I guess he saw the perplexed look on my face. Now, I've told this story over and over, and Aaron says he doesn't recall it. He doesn't realize that he gave me seven more years of my career.

Aaron got up from his seat, came over, and said, "What's wrong?" I said, "You're probably seeing me for the last time." He said, "What do you mean?" I told him what happened, and then he grabbed me by the elbow, pulled me to his locker, pointed to his chair, and said, "Now, you sit down. I don't *ever* want to hear you say the word 'quit' again. You're too good at your job, you love what you're doing, and everybody in this room will do everything they can to help you."

That turned me around. When I walked into that clubhouse and couldn't see anything, I was about to turn on my heels, go home, and quit. For a ballplayer to do that for a writer. . . . You know, we don't always have the best of relationships, and I had written some things that Aaron didn't like. But for him to do that just meant the world to me. I stuck it out the rest of the spring and said to myself that maybe I can do this. I've just got to be very careful. With a lot of help from a lot of people, I was able to keep doing it.

I had some good crying sessions in my condo that spring because I was so frustrated that I couldn't see. I was tripping over things and not recognizing people unless I got right up in their face. That's the toughest thing about what I have now. I don't recognize people, and maybe they think, "Geez, what's wrong with that guy? I've known him for years and now he doesn't even say hello."

Bob Nightengale from *USA Today* came to camp about two weeks later and wrote a story about what had happened to me, and the story went national. I got over a thousand e-mails after it came out. One serviceman who was serving in Iraq e-mailed me and said, "You're my hero." I e-mailed him back and wrote, "That's not possible. You're *my* hero."

*   *   *

The recognition from the fans really started when I won the Spink Award. I get cards and baseballs sent to me from all over to autograph. Almost every day, when I go to the ballpark in Cincinnati, there's a group of autograph seekers who'll stop me and have me sign balls and pose for pictures. I'm really gratified, and I've never refused one. If they think enough to want my autograph, that's fine with me. But it does amaze me. When I was a kid, I idolized Jim Schlemmer of the *Akron Beacon Journal*. I saw him a couple of times, but I never thought of asking him or another writer for an autograph. It just amazes me.

My wife and I were in Las Vegas about a month ago, and three times people wanted to come up to me and shake my hand. We have some close friends with whom we often go out to eat, and they always call themselves "chopped liver." You know, people will come up to say hello to Hal, but they won't talk to us. What are we, chopped liver?

After my retirement date came up, the editor of the paper came in and said, "You're eligible to retire, but you have a job here as long as you want it." I said, "Well, as long as you cover the Reds, I'll be here as long as I can. I love what I'm doing, and I don't want to retire."

Well, things changed in August of 2009. The way the economy was, the corporate offices decided they could no longer do much of anything. They quit covering Ohio State home games, they quit covering the Bengals. They still covered the Reds for a year after that. But in August '09, they called me in and said they would no longer be able to cover the Reds. I said, "Road games?" and they said no, the home games, too.

I looked at the editor and said, "I guess I'm done." He said, "You still have a job here if you want it." I said, "What would I do, cover high schools? I'll just retire." They finally offered me a quarter of my salary to do four blogs a week and my Sunday "Ask Hal" column, which fans seem to like a lot. So I still do that.

Then Fox Sports Ohio came along and said, "Would you like to reinvent yourself?" I said, "Does it mean covering baseball?" They said yes, and I said, "I'm there."

I covered all the home games [in 2010] and wrote stories for the website and also did online chats the entire game with fans. I set it all up myself and answer all the questions, post 'em, and it's become very popular. Makes the games go fast. People ask me how I can do it, and I say that's the beauty of baseball—I can do it all between pitches. I also do some of the postgame shows on TV.

Now, if someone had told me ten years ago that this is what I'd be doing now, I'd have asked them what they were smoking. I'm seventy years old now, with all this new technology. In fact, during the [2010] playoffs, Fox came to my house, and I did the postgame show via Skype. Hell, a year ago, I didn't even know what Skype meant.

I don't think anybody's going to cover a baseball beat for thirty-seven years. That's not going to happen. I'm a dinosaur, and I refer to myself as a dinosaur all the time. The reason I'm still doing this is because I love baseball, and I love writing so much.

To me, this is the only way you're going to be able to continue. Newspapers are dying, and the coverage of baseball by newspapers is dying. It shrivels every year. I just don't see anybody doing it the way I did, because of the business. Not because there isn't anyone else that could do it, because there are many, many who could, if they want to. And I want to, very badly.

10

HAL BOCK

Over two full decades, across the nation and around the world, more people read the words of Hal Bock than of any other baseball writer.

As baseball editor (1968–1980), baseball columnist (1980–1984) and then as general sports columnist (1984–2004) for The Associated Press, Bock's readership spanned the globe, although, ironically, he was sometimes anonymous in his home base of New York. He gave the AP years of concise, crisp, and dogged baseball reporting, in the same tradition as his predecessor, the legendary Joe Reichler, the 1980 Spink winner alongside his (and Bock's) rival, UPI's Milton Richman.

For the AP—then, as now, the world's largest news-gathering organization—Bock covered every World Series from 1968 through 1988, and again from 1993 through 2003. He wrote the critical first lead story on every Series game from 1972 through 1979. For the AP's worldwide membership, he broke the stories of the umpires' strike settlement in 1979 and the reinstatements of Mickey Mantle and Willie Mays in 1985 after their initial bannings due to their work as greeters and autograph signers at casinos in Atlantic City, New Jersey.

The author of thirteen books, Bock is still an occasional AP contributor in retirement. A BBWAA member since 1966, he currently teaches journalism at Long Island University's Brooklyn campus.

Jerome Holtzman once told me that when he was a kid, he was fascinated by the writers more than he was by the players. And in many ways, that describes me. To see a byline in the paper was a magical thing. I would think, "Wow. This guy's name is in the paper every day." Whoever the hero of the game was, his name was in the paper. But the next day, it wasn't. But Dick Young was in the paper *every* day.

I'm eight years old, and my father decides it's time for me to go to a baseball game. So he takes me to the Polo Grounds for the Mayor's Trophy Game between the Yankees and the Giants in 1947. When you're eight years old, the ballpark is bigger than the world; you don't know where to look first. You walk into this shrine with grass greener than you've ever seen and stands up to the sky where fifty thousand people can sit, and you're looking around, trying to absorb all this.

My eyes are going all around, and I see this structure hanging off the lip of the second deck. I ask my father, "What is that?" He said, "That's the press box. That's where the writers sit." I said, "The writers? Do they come here every day?" He said yes. I said, "That's their job?" He said yes.

Well, now I go, "Ho-ho, now wait a minute." I've discovered something very important. I decided right there, at the age of eight, that that's what I'm going to do.

Now it's time for me to go to college, and I have to find a school that offers journalism as a major. Today, that's not difficult. But in 1956, it was *very* difficult. I went to New York University because I was kind of intrigued by Greenwich Village, and it was also a little bit easier commute.

I joined the school newspaper and met a guy named Hy Kurzner, the sports information director. One day in 1956 he said, "Would you be interested in working at the *World-Telegram and Sun*?" I looked at him like he was crazy. That was my dream! He said, "Phil Pepe is the new schoolboy editor, and he's looking for an assistant."

So I call Pepe up. In those days I was in the Air Force ROTC, so I show up at the office looking like a flyboy. I walk in, Pepe interviews me, and we're set to go.

I used to come to work every day at about five in the evening, and I would work until about nine at night. I would take all the scores in; coaches, managers, they would all call in. I would get to write every day, and I was in heaven. I'm a freshman at NYU, and I'm being published in a major New York daily. No byline, but I'm in the paper. One of the managers who used to call in, from Lincoln High School, was named Marvin Aufrichtig. You know him as Marv Albert.

In 1960, the AP needed someone to work the Olympic desk. I guess they called all the schools, because my professor said, "Would you like to work for the summer at the AP?" I worked for six weeks in the summer of 1960 on the Olympic desk, which was composed of four people in New York: Don Weiss, Jim Kensil, Jack Hand—all of whom would later go to the NFL—and me. We compiled all the scores and statistics from all the events. To watch these three guys, who would become giants in the business, I was just in awe of the three of them.

Then I went into the service, six months active duty. When I came back, I got hired by Herbie Goren as an assistant in the Rangers publicity department. I didn't know up from down about hockey. I was vaguely familiar with the name Andy Bathgate, but that was it. I was getting married, and I needed a job.

So I went up to the Garden on 49th Street. Herbie sat in Muzz Patrick's chair in the general manager's office, since Muzz was away at training camp. He said, "Well, what players do you know?" I said, "Well, I know Andy Bathgate." He said, "OK, you're hired." I'm hired at the rate of $75 a week. I worked that season with the Rangers, then at the AP as a summer relief guy, then back with the Rangers, after I convinced them to give me a raise of $15 a week. In November 1963, the AP offered me a full-time job.

My hero in those days was Jack Hand, because he always wrote the breaking news lead on the big games. I was in awe of how he was able to handle that. He was cool as a cucumber. Nothing rattled him. And he never took his jacket off. *Never.* It could be a hundred degrees and you'd want to say, "Jack, take your jacket off!" Then he'd start to write, sometimes a paragraph at a time, take it out, and give it to the Western Union operator.

I thought to myself, *that's* what I want to do. I want to be able to be the first lead on the wire. The first news of the game will have my name on it. That's what I want.

* * *

If you were a prominent AP writer, your name was known all over the country, but you were an unknown in New York. Everybody knew

Dick Young or Jack Lang. Their bylines were in the papers every day. Our bylines were never in a New York paper. The players didn't know us, the executives didn't know us. We were just a face in the crowd.

So you worked very hard; you made sure you introduced yourself. Whenever I talked to a player or executive, I'd say, "I'm Hal Bock of The Associated Press." That was a given, you had to do that. Dick Young didn't have to. But that was the start of every conversation.

You work for a wire service, and you have thirty teams to cover, or however many there are. You go to a game, and you've got to know everything about both teams. Regardless of the outcome, the New York papers are going to write the Mets and Yankees. Well, I wasn't privileged to do that. I had to write the winning team. But that's okay, I didn't mind that. I wanted to know about all these guys.

In February 1966, Joe Reichler left the AP to become the special assistant to the new commissioner, Spike Eckert, because Eckert didn't know the way to get into the front door at baseball. They hired the wrong guy, as you know. He needed someone to sit at his right hand, and they brought in Reichler. Now the AP needed a baseball writer, so they promoted me. Then Mike Rathet left to work for the AFL, and they promoted me into Rathet's spot.

Reichler had left enormous shoes to fill. For many, many years it was Reichler for the AP and Milton Richman for UPI. They went head-to-head, and it was a fierce competition. Now, all of a sudden, it's Hal Bock for the AP and Milton Richman for UPI. Hal *who*? I was pretty much left on my own. Fly, baby, fly . . . and try to beat Milton Richman.

Milton was a very warm guy, a sweetheart. I remember at the first winter meetings I covered, in 1969, I introduce myself. He says, "Great, let's take a walk."

Now, Milton Richman, whom I've known for about thirty seconds, says, "Hally . . ." Milton used to call everyone by their first name, and he put an "-ly" on the end. He said, "Hally, I gotta ask you a question." I'm thinking this is pretty good, Milton Richman is gonna ask me a question. He says, "I've got an offer from the Pittsburgh Pirates to work in their front office. What do you think? Think I should take it?"

I thought, "This is the craziest thing that's ever happened to me." What am I supposed to tell him? Am I his career counselor? What do

I know? I said, "Well, you gotta think it over, Milton." I thought it was very odd. I could have gotten rid of my number-one competitor right there. Believe me, the thought crossed my mind.

I went up against Milton at those winter meetings in '69, and he just cleaned my clock. Every trade he had on the wire well before me. I sat down and wrote a letter the following year to all the teams, saying, look, could you please make your announcements in the press room instead of surreptitiously? I got no response. I mean, who's this guy and who cares what he wants? I remember Buzzie Bavasi of the Padres coming into the press room to announce some trade, and I asked him a question. He looked at me and said, "You're not one of my writers."

There was one time Milton beat me, and it really got to me. At the meetings in 1974, the Expos are going to trade Willie Davis to the Rangers. We're waiting for the announcement in the press room, but the announcement is delayed because they can't find Billy Martin, the Rangers manager. Until they find Martin, we're not going to have an announcement. Dick Joyce and I are covering for AP, and Dick is on the phone to the office back in New York. Billy Madden, who's covering for UPI with Milton, is on the phone to *his* office. Milton's typing his column, and I'm just standing there.

Now, into the room walks Jim Fanning, who was an executive with the Expos and later their manager. Jim Fanning had played shortstop in Class C during the war, and his second baseman was Milton Richman, so they were buddies. Fanning walks over to Richman, bends over, and whispers in his ear. Milton turns around, gives the high sign to Madden, and says, "Let it go!"

I go berserk. I know that they're on the wire with all the names and details of the trade, and I have nothing. I just stormed out of the room, saying "This is bullshit!" People are looking at me and everything. Down the hall I go. In another room, the city of Toronto is holding a press conference to attract major league baseball; this is before the Blue Jays. There's no one there except the mayor, a few dignitaries, and me. I'm the only journalist there. Come right in! Now, I don't drink. But I was so pissed that I said, "Give me a vodka martini!" I knew that was a drink of some kind. I had two vodka martinis, and nothing bothered me. I didn't feel any pain after that.

That was the second time I had done that. The first time was during the American League playoffs in 1970. Dick Couch and I are covering the series for the AP, starting in Minnesota. I'm very excited about this. It was one of my first prime assignments, and I'm nervous. Well, I screwed it up. I don't remember exactly what happened, but it wasn't good. It was just a mess, and I was pissed at myself.

We get on the baseball writers' charter to fly to Baltimore, and I'm seated behind Russ Schneider from Cleveland. This was the year that Denny McLain had gone crazy with the Tigers, when he dumped the ice water on Watson Spoelstra and Jim Hawkins in the locker room. On the plane, Hawkins is schmoozing with Schneider, and behind them is a pissed-off Hal Bock. Schneider is talking about the ice water episode, and he says to Hawkins, "Well, I read on the wires that such-and-such happened." And Hawkins says, "Well, you know how the wires always fuck things up."

I couldn't believe it. I said, "That little fuck, I'm gonna break him in half!" I'm gonna commit murder at thirty thousand feet. He's a little shit, and I'm twice his size; I'll kill him! I'm getting out of the seat and Couch says, "No, no. Just relax." I go, "No, fuck him! The wire service people work thirty times harder than he'll ever work!" Couch says no, no.

Here comes the stewardess. Couch says to her, "He'll have a vodka martini." I look at Dick and say, "You know I don't drink. And besides, I have to kill Jim Hawkins!" Couch says, "Just have this and you'll feel better." I had the vodka martini and I was, like, catatonic. Nothing bothered me! So those are my experiences with vodka martinis.

*   *   *

The thing I'm proudest of is that when I retired in 2004, I had covered more World Series games than any other AP sportswriter in history. In the old days, before World War II, they didn't send writers to the World Series. If the Series was in Pittsburgh, the Pittsburgh guy wrote it. When it moved to Yankee Stadium, the New York guy wrote it. It wasn't until Reichler started covering the Series in the '50s that he went to all the games. Well, he was gone by 1967. I covered the World Series for thirty years, '68 through '88 and again from '93 through 2003. I was clever enough, though, to avoid the Earthquake Series in '89.

The first World Series that I wrote the lead on was in 1972 between Oakland and Cincinnati. That series went seven games; six of them were decided by one run, and a couple of them got flipped in the ninth inning, so all of a sudden my story is out the window and I have to start over, under deadline pressure. And the adrenaline that's pumped . . . it's just the greatest feeling in the world. Because I *knew* I could do it. After the Series I said to my wife, "I've just been through hell, and now I know in my heart that there's nothing that can happen, nothing I'm going to cover, that will throw me. I know I can handle anything."

That World Series, in 1972, convinced me that I could do that job. I loved being on deadline. It was the reason I stayed there for forty years. I absolutely loved writing deadline copy.

One day I'm sent to cover a game at Yankee Stadium. Ralph Houk had become Yankees manager for the second time; this was when all the players got old on him and they couldn't win any more. Now, when you arrived at the ballpark, the first thing you did was call the desk to find out if anything was up or if they needed anything special. The late, great Ted Meier was on the desk, and he said, "Yeah, I got a request from a member in Springfield, Massachusetts. You gotta ask Ralph Houk why he hasn't been able to turn the Yankees around." Well, gee, that'll be good. That'll be a *great* conversation starter.

But you gotta do what you gotta do. Fortunately the Yankees win, which might make it a little easier. Now we trek down to Ralph's office, and there's maybe a dozen writers. We go in, and we're asking about the game, this play and that play. One by one, the writers leave his office and go into the clubhouse, leaving just me and him. Me, who's about twenty-five years old, and him, who fought at the Battle of the Bulge.

I said, "Ralph, I'm Hal Bock of the AP, and I want you to know that this isn't a question from me, but I was told to ask you this." I asked him the question, and he went berserk. He really went nuts. He said, "Are you kidding? How could you ask a question like that?" Then he stands up, and I figure he's gonna kill me. He moves toward me, and I move toward the door that leads to the clubhouse, figuring that he's not going to carry on in front of the players and the other writers.

But he *follows* me into the clubhouse, and now he's got me be-cause he's going to make an example of me. "You've got some fuck-ing nerve asking me. . . . Who do you think you are?" If I could only dig a hole and disappear, right? The players are looking at me like, who is this guy who got the Major, this World War II hero, all upset? Finally he calms down and goes into his office, and I go about my business, whatever it is.

The next day I come back to Yankee Stadium, because that's my job. You know how the writers stand around the batting cage before the game, right? I'm standing there, and Houk comes up to me, and I'm thinking he's going to kill me. He says, "Hey, kid. I'm sorry about last night." I said, "That's okay." He said, "That's it, good-bye," and just moved on. That was a baptism of fire.

*   *   *

The umpires had gone on strike in 1979. They brought in replace-ment umpires, and it was a disaster. Now, my birthday is in the mid-dle of May, and it happens to coincide with the birthday, within a day or two, of Bob Fishel, the great PR man. The baseball writers decide to throw Fishel a birthday party in Manhattan, and I'm invited.

Now, Bob Fishel's closest friend in the world was Lee MacPhail, who at that time was the president of the American League and was negotiating with the umpires. I got to the restaurant, and everyone was there except MacPhail. I thought, "That's awfully odd. He wouldn't miss this . . . unless something's going on." So when I got back to the office, I started making phone calls. Someone told me—I won't men-tion who—that the strike is over, that they negotiated all night and reached a settlement.

I called both sides in this dispute, and they both denied it. Then I go to Wick Temple, the sports editor, and tell him that I have this guy who's in a position to know, telling me that the strike is going to end. But I also have other people denying it. What do you want me to do? He said, "Do you believe your guy?" I said, "He's always been straight with me, and I believe him." I was still thinking about MacPhail not being at Fishel's party.

So Wick said to go with it, and I did: "The Associated Press learned today . . ." What an exciting thing that is! The adrenaline is pumping, baby, and it's on the wire. Then I went home and turned on the Yankees game, and Frank Messer said on TV, "The AP is reporting that the umpires strike is over. UPI is denying it." And I'm thinking, "Oh, shit. Milton's killing me again."

Next day I get to work. The late Dick Joyce says, "Read up, Mersch." I grab the daily report and start reading. We had various quotes from various umpires saying they didn't know anything. But then Jim Evans was quoted out of Dallas saying, "Yes, that's what I understand." If Jim Evans had been in the room, I would have kissed him. This confirmed what I had written, but until I read it, I'm thinking that I'm out here on a limb, and it's a very shaky limb.

Another good one I had was when Peter Ueberroth reinstated Mickey Mantle and Willie Mays in 1985. Bob Wirz from the commissioner's office had called a press conference. What's it about, Bob? "I can't say." Well, we suspected what could be up, because there had been some rumblings. We had Willie Mays's phone number. . . . I call, and his housekeeper answers the phone. I said, "Is Willie there?" She said, "No, he's on his way to the press conference at the commissioner's office." Well, thank you very much!

*   *   *

Last summer I was at Citi Field doing a story, and I ran into John Jeansonne from *Newsday*. He had been dropped in there at the last minute, and he said to me, "You know what I find around here? It's very, very much like a fraternity." I said, "That's exactly what it is, and you're not a member. And if you're not a member, you're out of luck." It takes a long time before they embrace you as a member of the fraternity. They don't welcome outsiders very readily, and if you're a new guy on the beat, it's going to take you time before you become one of the boys.

Don't forget, the beat guys traveled together and ate together every night. They're on the road, they're doing whatever they're doing. We were not part of that society. Wire service guys were on the outside looking in. I was not a member of the inner circle, so to speak.

I grew up loving baseball and caring about baseball. Some critics decided in the '60s and '70s that baseball had become stodgy and football was the game of modern era, and I considered that to be so much bullshit. Red Smith put it best when he said that baseball is dull only to people with dull minds. There's nothing like baseball. You gotta be thinking, baby. It's not all blocking and tackling, or who's bigger and stronger. There's a lot of brainpower that enters into every play.

I always thought baseball should be the number one sport. I love the game and still do. It's the game of my childhood and my adulthood.

I see that enthusiasm for baseball and writing in some of the kids I teach, not all of them. Some of them take journalism because they don't want to take chemistry. But some of them have a real passion for it. I have one kid who's decided that he's either going to be a beat writer or the general manager of the Knicks. That's his passion, and it's great. Follow your passion. But a lot of the kids are taking journalism just because they need three credits.

11

TRACY RINGOLSBY

A proud son of Wyoming, Tracy Ringolsby's reputation as one of the most prolific baseball writers of the past half-century is grounded in an unstinting frontier work ethic.

Known throughout baseball as the Cowboy, Ringolsby, the 2005 Spink Award winner, has traveled the nation as a beat man, first with UPI in Kansas City and then to the Long Beach Independent and Press-Telegram *(1977–1980), the* Seattle Post-Intelligencer *(1980– 1983), the* Kansas City Star *(1983–1986), the* Dallas Morning News *(1986–1991), and finally to Denver's* Rocky Mountain News *(1991– 2009). The BBWAA's national president in 1986, he holds the unprecedented distinction of serving as chapter chairman in five different cities (Los Angeles–Anaheim, Seattle, Kansas City, Dallas–Fort Worth, and Denver). He is also a cofounder of the national periodical* Baseball America.

Just four years after receiving baseball writing's highest honor at Cooperstown, Ringolsby found himself a man without a paper when the Rocky Mountain News *shockingly folded in February 2009. (One of his earlier stops, the* Seattle Post-Intelligencer, *folded one month later.) In short time, the Cowboy resurfaced as a pre- and postgame analyst on Rockies telecasts. He serves in that role today for ROOT Sports as well as contributing a regular blog—appropriately titled "Write 'Em, Cowboy"—to the network's website.*

A 2009 inductee into the Wyoming Sports Hall of Fame, Ringolsby is a member of the executive committee of the National Western Stock Show and a member at the benefactor level of the Professional Rodeo

Cowboys Association. His sprawling horse farm near Cheyenne is less than a two-hour drive from Coors Field.

I don't buy in national stores. I've never been inside a Walmart. I like local merchants. My appliance guy just went out of business in Cheyenne. My dad bought every piece of equipment he ever had from this guy's father-in-law when he opened his business, Automatic Electric. Then I bought everything I could from Automatic Electric.

When my daughter was living in Cheyenne, she said that she needed a washer and dryer for her apartment. I said, okay, go down and talk to Dick at Automatic Electric. She said, "Dick wants $600 for the washer and dryer. I can go to Walmart and get it for $550." I said, "Okay, how are you gonna get it to the apartment?" "Well, Walmart will do it for $60," she said. Dick, of course, will deliver it for nothing.

"So, you're going to spend $610 at Walmart?" I said. "And another thing. If something goes wrong, Dick will have someone right there to take care of it." She went to Dick and said, "I only have $200 now. Can it put it on layaway?" He said, "If it sits here in the basement, no one's going to use it. Just take it home and pay me $200, and then $200 over the next two months."

Those are the types of relationships I have. Those types of businesses aren't around anymore. Well, the newspaper business isn't any different. People's habits have changed. Our business is shrinking, but so are other businesses. I think we have to realize we're not on an island. We did a very poor job of seeing the future and adapting to it, and now the business struggles to survive. That's the reality of it.

A lot of it goes back to a work ethic I picked up from my dad. I was taught, let's call it, the Wyoming Work Ethic. That's how my dad was raised. If you say you're going to produce something for somebody, you better make sure you produce it and do it well, because you've given the man your word that you'll take care of him. Your word is worth more than anything. You don't do something just to get by; you do it because the way you handle a job is a reflection on you as a person and your character.

That was my dad's attitude with everything he did. He had lost a leg, but it was never an excuse for why he couldn't do things. He wouldn't use handicapped parking or anything like that because he felt there were people who needed it more.

I want to provide as much information as I can about the team I cover. I want people to have a reason to pick up the paper. I always enjoyed what I did. I have a half-brother who worked underground all of his working life; he was a miner. My mother's father was a coal miner. My dad was a bookkeeper, and his dad was a telegrapher for the railroad. I was doing something that was fun, and I could look at green grass and go to ballgames. What was not to like about it?

We lived in Southern California when I was in grade school, and my dad would arrange his vacation over a week where there would be two scheduled doubleheaders. My mom would wrap a bunch of chicken gizzards, and we'd take some iced tea, and me and my dad would sit in the left field bleachers at Dodger Stadium, right by the bullpen.

My favorite player as a kid was Fred Kipp, because that was the first baseball card I ever got. I also really liked Tracy Stallard, because his name was Tracy. I was lucky because I could grow up listening to Vin Scully and Jerry Doggett doing the Dodger games. What a great education. Then when we came back to Cheyenne, at nighttime, we could get KFI from Los Angeles, KSFO from San Francisco, KMOX from St. Louis, WCCO from Minneapolis, and KPRC from Houston. My dad and I would just sit and listen to games every night.

In 1959, when the Dodgers played the Braves in the playoff, my mom took me to the second game at the Coliseum. She wrote to my teacher, "This will be an excused absence for my son, because when he grows up he's going to be a baseball writer."

*   *   *

I was working for a taxidermist in Cheyenne in my junior year of high school. There was an afternoon paper in Cheyenne, and their sports section would hire a high school senior to go out and cover whatever was going on. Basically, it was a one-man sports staff. A guy I knew in high school was supposed to be the sports editor his senior year, 1968–1969. But our school started having male cheerleaders that year, and he decided he wanted to be a male cheerleader instead.

He said to me, "I know you really like sports. Would you like to be the sports editor?" I was making $1.50 an hour, and the paper paid $1.25. In my old job, I had to be at work at 4:00, and at the paper I wouldn't have to get there until 5:30. So I decided the newspaper would be a better deal. Plus, I wasn't going to poke holes in my fingers with needles, trying to sew bullet holes or torn eyelids.

When I worked at the *Tribune* in high school, we had a great man named Jim Flinchum as the editor. He'd been head of European operations for UPI and wanted to come to a town and raise his family, and he got this job in Cheyenne that didn't pay anything. He wasn't always the most diplomatic guy on earth. He covered anything political, wrote editorials, a very professional man. He was an ultraconservative in a state that's 72 percent Republican, but the Democrats really liked and respected him, too.

Mr. Flinchum taught me a lot of basic things based on wire service reporting, like to try to keep a simple approach to what you write. As a young kid, I was hands-on. He'd take things I'd done and break them down.

When I was the sports editor in Cheyenne, the UPI office was right next to my desk. Pete Kelly was the bureau chief at the time, and when I went to Colorado State, he arranged for me to string for UPI. In my sophomore year, I was named editor of the paper at CSU. That summer, I was a vacation relief writer for UPI.

Mike Kennedy, who wound up being a feature writer for the *Los Angeles Times*, was working for UPI in Cheyenne. When he took his vacation—he had a bloodhound named Blue—he just took off. We never heard back from him. He was a free spirit and he went to Alaska.

They were scrambling to hire somebody, so I went to work for UPI. When Pete Kelly went to Denver, he got me transferred there to write sports. Then UPI transferred me to Kansas City to be the regional sports editor. That was in December of 1975, when I was twenty-four. The next year, I got hired to write baseball by the Long Beach *Independent Press-Telegram*, covering the Angels.

At UPI, you learned a lot of basic principles about how to get your information and where you wanted it go in the story, because you had no idea how much was going to run in a particular newspaper. You learned the inverted pyramid, and if you didn't do it that way, you might not get the facts in the paper because they would only take four grafs, or eight, or ten.

You always wanted to win the logs. Every day, if you were in, say, a two-newspaper market, you'd have to go through the papers and message New York about which paper used the AP story and which used the UPI story. If I was covering a Wyoming or Colorado football game, I wanted to win the logs, and one of the key things was to be quick. The guy back on the desk didn't want to wait an extra hour for your story to show up.

I had people who were good editors. One thing they stressed to me was, "You're writing about your subject. You're not writing about yourself. You're not the story." Personal pronouns don't need to be there. I don't think I could have stayed forever at a wire service, but the seven years I spent there taught me some really strong principles.

I had been at UPI in Kansas City for seven-and-a-half years. Then the sports editor for the Long Beach paper, John Dixon, called me and said they had an opening, and that "Jim Cour said I should hire you." I had gotten to be good friends with Jim, who worked for UPI in Los Angeles and later went to the AP. They were going to offer me a job, and I asked if I should come for an interview. He said, "No, Cour said I should hire you. Be here by February."

I don't want this to sound wrong, okay? But I was kind of at that stage where I had to make my mind up. Did I want to be a wire service guy for the rest of my life, or would I like to work for a newspaper? I just felt that if I didn't take advantage of the opportunity, I might not get another one.

After a few years in Long Beach, I got offered the job in Seattle. I had worked at a suburban paper, and that's nice, but I thought I'd like to work at a paper where there's a little more accountability. So I went to the *Post-Intelligencer*. About a year after I arrived, I had chances to cover other things. But a friend and I had just started *Baseball America*, and I realized that I had developed a lot of sources in baseball. If I went to another sport, I'll lose all that and have to start over again. So I stayed doing baseball.

Then, when the *Kansas City Star* needed a writer in the middle of the '83 season, Tom Whitfield, who had known me from UPI, was working there and recommended me. I was offered the job covering the Royals. In Seattle, the soccer team got more coverage than the Mariners. The main interest in the Mariners at that time was whether they were going to move. I liked the people, and I loved Seattle, but I thought it would be neat to go to Kansas City because I'd been there in '76 when they won their first division title. I also figured that in Kansas City, people really, really care about the team, and I'm going to have to challenge myself more because you can't mail it in when people care that much.

Then came Dallas. Randy Galloway and I had become good friends. When Tim Kurkjian left the *Morning News* to go to *Sports Illustrated*, Galloway convinced Dave Smith, the editor, to hire me. Now, this is funny. Earlier that year I traveled with a buddy of mine, a professional wrestler named Bruiser Brody. He made most of his money in Japan, but in the winter, he'd work a Midwest circuit to stay in shape. I spent most the winter traveling with him. We were going through the Dallas airport, and I said, "If I ever leave Kansas City, this is one place I could come." Three weeks later, Dave Smith called, and I had an offer to go to Dallas.

That was when the newspaper war in Dallas was at its height. The basic mentality was, if we can't overcover it, we won't cover it. We'd have, say, twenty-four pages on a Monday or Tuesday in the sports section. We did everything and anything, and money was no object. That was another great challenge. It was arguably one of the three or four best papers in the country at that time.

It was different than, say, *The New York Times* or the *Los Angeles Times*, and maybe I'm wrong about this. Our emphasis in Dallas wasn't really on long takeout features. Instead, it was that you had to have the news. Back then, they'd send you everywhere. Murray Chass, Hal Bodley, and I would be the only three writers at the GM meetings, and you'd maybe write once or twice the whole time you were there. Smith didn't care. He wanted you there to meet the general managers and make contacts so when things came up, you could call them and talk to them. It was a whole different philosophy than what you were used to.

When the Denver thing came up, I figured that now I can go home, because downtown Denver is only about ninety miles from downtown Cheyenne. When I was growing up, Denver was always the big city. It was where you bought your school supplies and your clothes. Whatever TV we had came from Denver. Denver's not so much a state capital as it is the capital of an entire region. It was the first time I ever made a move because, personally, that's where I really wanted to be.

In '99, things had progressed so well that I could say to my wife, "Let's buy eighty acres outside of Cheyenne and build up a horse property and live there." So we went to Cheyenne, built indoor and outdoor riding arenas and a barn, and we've got five horses. And it's only an hour and a half to the ballpark.

I was hired in Denver before the Rockies had even played a game, and I thought it would be fun to follow a team right from the start. But the most important thing was this: I had taken the national baseball job in Dallas in 1990. Part of the deal in Denver was that I could be the beat writer again.

I really wanted to get back to being the day-to-day beat writer—I just really liked that. I didn't like the national beat. I didn't like having to be the seventh guy in two weeks to interview Barry Bonds. I liked having to understand what went into a team. The two years I was doing the national stuff, I really missed the day-to-day aspect of the beat. Maybe it's the wire service guy in me. I always felt guilty that I was writing only two or three things a week.

I'm a better reporter than writer, easily. I read guys that just blow me away with what they're able to do with words. I think I'm a real good game story writer, and a real good deadline writer. But as far as writing, just in terms of sheer writing, it's probably why I didn't like the national beat. I'm not going to say I didn't want to make it readable and do a nice writing job. I think guys at times get too bogged down wanting to be too poetic.

*   *   *

Before the *Rocky Mountain News* went under, I turned down a couple of Internet jobs because I wanted the security of a newspaper! When they announced during the 2008 winter meetings that the newspaper was going to be put up for sale for a six-week period, I felt they weren't too serious about selling, otherwise the six-week period wouldn't include the Christmas holidays. So when the *Rocky* folded, there were feelings of betrayal, because you felt you had given everything you had to it. My focus at that point was, how do I patch things together and try and find out how to maintain a living and not have to move?

On top of everything else, my sports editor, Barry Forbis, was by far the greatest person I ever worked for in my life. I didn't want to leave him. I had started doing one column a week for FoxSports.com a few years earlier. Then when things were getting shaky at the paper, they suggested making it two columns a week, and I said yes.

I knew I could take care of things financially until I could figure out what to do. I'd done two-minute hits on the Rockies' pregame shows for about ten years. FSN Colorado came to me and said that if they could get me X amount of money, could I do the pre- and post-game? I said sure.

It wasn't a real good financial time for anybody. They came back to me and said they couldn't add a body. I said, I'll make you a deal. I'll go to all the road games and most of the home games, and instead of doing a two-minute segment like I had been doing, I want to do the whole pregame and the whole postgame. They said, "Tracy, we can't give you any more money than what we're already giving you." I said, "That's not the issue. This is an opportunity to find out if I can do it and if I enjoy it. I'll make the investment in trying to re-create myself if you're willing to let me do it."

Now I have a whole new deal where they're paying my expenses and more money to do the pre- and postgame. And it was all, basically, because I had gotten a severance package when the paper folded and I could afford to take a gamble to reinvent what I do. I was able to piece something together, and I've had fun doing it.

*   *   *

When I was first coming up, I'd hear guys talking about the good old days, and I'd say that I didn't want to be an old guy talking about how great it used to be. Things change. If we allow things to change around us, we have to adapt and try to change with 'em, move forward, and try to deal with whatever's going on.

Now I'm one of those old-timers, and I do think we had more fun back then. But if I spend too much time worrying about what I don't have anymore, then I won't have anything to enjoy in the future. You adapt. And I have to admit, I didn't realize how much I was going to enjoy the change, doing the pre- and postgame.

The Spink Award means the world to me because it's voted on by your peers. It's not something that you go out and campaign for. It's recognition that people doing the same job you do respected the way you did it. It's the ultimate compliment. Peter Gammons won it the year before me, and Peter was on the ballot for something like six times before he got elected.

The unfortunate thing is, there's not a lot of people in the business who realize what Peter did for the newspaper guy in the media. There's too many people who see Peter as the guy on TV, who don't realize that this guy created a lot of the opportunities that we now have for survival. He gave us credibility in the electronic media, and he was a driving force behind the creation of the notes column. I don't know how you could have been around this business for any length of time and not seen the way Peter impacted it.

Remember, I go back to the days of the Olivetti typewriter and Western Union. If you really want to be a beat writer and you're not just doing it to pad your resume and then go on to something else— which I think happens a lot—I tell people that you have to learn how to talk to somebody with your notebook closed. You're not going into a bank to make a withdrawal or deposit. If you want to create a relationship, a trust and a confidence, you have to be able to talk to someone without having your notebook open.

As a writer, if I can cover a guy and allow him to know that I'm a human being and I understand that *he's* a human being, maybe I can find something in his life that I can relate to and strike up a conversation. Maybe I can have a respect, back and forth, that allows me to understand his background just as he can understand mine. That's how people develop a confidence in you, that they know they can sit down with you and everything they say doesn't have to be guarded. It can't be where the only time you talk to them is when you need something. That's why you don't like the IRS; the only time you hear from them is on April 15.

What has always mattered to me is that most people, when they picked me up, felt that it would be a correct version of whatever happened. That it wouldn't just be a wild rumor that I was throwing up there to grab attention; that there would be a basis to it. I've been in this business since May 1, 1968, the day after my 17th birthday. I would hate to think there would be one thing that I wrote that distinguished my career, as opposed to the way I handled myself and did my job. I think that would be much more distinguished than any one thing I did.

Let's face it. Nothing I wrote ever changed the world or saved somebody's life. We're an entertainment medium. I would like to think that even people that didn't necessarily like me at least respected the way I did my job. That's more important to me than any particular story.

One from the Dallas years—we're in the old press box one night in Baltimore. We had those old machines where you typed right on thermal paper. You'd write the story into the computer, it would print out, and then you'd plug a phone into it. Texas Instruments made them. Phil Rogers, who's one of my best friends, is at the *Times Herald*, and I'm at the *Morning News*. Phil knocked a beer right into my Portabubble on deadline.

I just looked down, picked up the phone, and called the desk. I said, "You know, I've just had a machine go out on me," and I calmly dictated the story. Then I hung up the phone and said to Phil, "You know, you're a real fucking idiot." He said, "You're getting mad at me *now*? It's the first time a guy ever took an hour and a half before he blew up and motherfucked me." I said, "I didn't have time to get mad about it earlier."

12

BOB ELLIOTT

*Possessed with an unmatched sporting pedigree, Bob Elliott is base-
ball's leading advocate not for a city or a region, but for an entire
nation.*

*Elliott's grandfather, pioneer athlete and referee Chaucer Elliott,
was one of the first inductees into the Hockey Hall of Fame in Toronto. Bob's father excelled at curling and is a member of both the
Kingston (Ontario) Hall of Fame and the Queen's University Football Hall of Fame. The legacy of the third-generation Elliott may well
surpass them both.*

*Staunchly and uniquely Canadian, "Boxer"—the 2012 Spink
Award winner—is perhaps the most prestigious and influential baseball writer the country has ever produced. The Kingston native started
his sportswriting career as a teenager in 1965 with the* Kingston
Whig-Standard. *He moved to the* Ottawa Journal *in 1973 and to the*
Ottawa Citizen *in 1977, handling the Montreal Expos beat from 1979
through 1986.*

Since 1987, Elliott has been the lead baseball writer for the Toronto Sun, *both as Blue Jays beat writer and as a national baseball
columnist. In addition to his coverage of the major leagues, Elliott
carries the Canadian baseball banner with his exhaustive coverage
the nation's college and amateur game. For the last two decades, his
rankings of Canada's top amateur prospects are eagerly awaited by
the game's scouts and executives, in addition to his rabid north-of-
the-border readership.*

A four-time Spink Award finalist prior to his 2012 win, Elliott is one of the game's most prolific writers. (His byline appeared on a staggering 675 stories in 1989 and 638 in 1991.) A member of the Baseball Hall of Fame's Historical Overview Committee, Bob is the author of three books, including his definitive 2005 work, The Northern Game: Baseball the Canadian Way.

Elliott, who was on hand for the birth and death of the Expos and for the soaring heights of the back-to-back world champion Blue Jays, is that rarest of Canadians: one who, admittedly, does not watch hockey. His efforts have helped make Canada's fans—and athletes—just as passionate for that "other" sport.

I wouldn't say writing came easy to me. I learned a valuable lesson from my boss in Ottawa, a man named Eddie MacCabe. We're an afternoon paper, and I'm sitting there at the typewriter, and Eddie said, "How's it coming?" I said, "Terrible, terrible." You know, where you'd rip the paper out and throw it away and all that.

So Eddie said, "Write with your eyes," and then he'd stomp out. That was a very, very valuable lesson for any time you're stuck, especially on deadline. Write with your eyes. Tell the people what you saw.

I never met my grandfather; he passed away when, I think, my father was only three. My love of sports was certainly ingrained from my father. He'd go outside and say, "Come and get me when Dizzy and Pee Wee come on," and we'd watch the Game of the Week with Dizzy Dean and Pee Wee Reese. Then I got old enough so that he'd get some old, beat-up baseballs and hit me ground balls. He'd say, "I gotta figure out a way for you to keep your rear end down." We went and got some rubber balls that you'd use at a batting cage, so if you didn't get your bum down to field it, the ball would roll for like two blocks. So I learned how to field.

*   *   *

When I started writing part-time at the Kingston paper, I used to get the janitor to allow me to go into the editorial office. They'd have the Detroit papers, and I'd go down there and read Watson Spoelstra. Man, did he turn it out. There'd be a game story, a notebook, a sidebar, maybe two sidebars. And the detail! There wasn't any baseball in Canada then, but I thought, "Oh, my. *That's* the guy I want to be like." I guess later on, it would have been Dan Jenkins who inspired me, although I could never capture the flavor of a story the way he could, with his sense of humor.

Peter Gammons was also a big influence on me. I remember when I started doing the Expos, I forget the year, but I found this place in Ottawa that sold the *Boston Globe*. You could get the Sunday *Globe* on a Monday; it was about $4.50. It would come in on the train, and sometimes it would be there on Monday and sometimes not. I'd get the guy to leave it next door at this little restaurant, and I'd pick it up at night and just sit there and read that notes column.

The first time I ever saw it, I didn't know those pages even existed. Oh, my goodness. I'd read it like a kid on Christmas morning. Then I'd read the whole sports section, and then I'd read it again. I used to go out for beers in those days, but never on a Monday or Tuesday night when I could pick up the Sunday *Globe*. What you saw in Peter's work was *hard* work and the importance of knowing people, the thoroughness and all.

You read Peter, and it was like, "Wow. Is there anybody in baseball he doesn't know?" Being a National League guy, I never got a chance to meet him. I finally met him in the spring of '87, in the press box on the roof of Fenway Park. He was sitting there with three or four scouts at a table—I don't remember exactly who was there, but Bob Gebhard was one of them—and I said hello to the scouts and nodded at Peter. Then I went outside on the roof, and he came out and introduced himself to me. I'm sounding like a kid who met his idol, but that's what it kind of was.

I got the Expos beat full-time in '79, but before that, I'll tell you that the first major leaguer I ever interviewed was Hank Aaron of the Braves in '69. It went like this: "M-m-m-m-m-m-mister Aaron. How do you think you guys will do against the M-m-m-m-m-Mets in the playoffs?" He looked at me and said, "Well, they've beaten us eight out of twelve, son." That was it. I'm thinking, geez, how stupid of me. I don't even think I wrote anything that first time, I was so in awe.

When I got on the Expos beat, Ian MacDonald was the senior beat writer. The second year I had my writers' card, Ian was the chapter chairman, and I said, "Hey, Ian, look at this! I went down eleven numbers," or whatever it was. He said, "Jesus Christ, don't you know what that means? It means four guys died and somebody else's paper closed. So if you want to be happy with that, go ahead!" I have not discussed my number since then.

*   *   *

Growing up the way I did, I had perhaps some knowledge of sports that some of the other guys at the paper didn't. But when I got the beat, I was scared witless. I remember my first road trip was to Shea Stadium in July 1980. It was the second game of a doubleheader and Bill Gullickson knocked down Mike Jorgensen of the Mets.

Jorgensen took a couple of steps to the mound, pointed his bat at Gullickson, and yelled, "I don't need that crap!" because he'd been hit in the head earlier in his career. John Tamargo is the catcher, Jorgensen's in the box, and Gullickson's on the mound, and then I heard the guy to my right yell, "Holy shit!" and here came John Stearns out of the Mets dugout like a blitzing linebacker, straight at Gullickson, and the brawl started.

Afterward, I go to the Mets' room. Now, you wouldn't have these kinds of conversations nowadays. Jorgensen says, "You're damn right he threw at me!" Then we go to Gullickson, and he says, "Yeah, I threw at him. I didn't get out of the fourth inning in my last start, and I've got to establish myself in this league."

Then I go see Dick Williams in the manager's office, and I said, "I've just got to ask you about the beanball there, sir." Well, he just came up from behind the table and blasted me. There was Norm Sherry, Pat Mullin, Ozzie Virgil, and Vern Rapp, the coaches, all there. At Shea they didn't have a separate room for the coaches. So I turned and walked away, and if that door had been shut, I still could have slipped through the crack underneath it, I was so low.

Now, we're staying at the Sheraton. A lot of the players took the subway back. I took the bus. I let all the coaches get off first, and when I got off, there's Vern Rapp. He asked me, "What are you going to do tomorrow?" I said, "I'm going to apologize to him."

He said, "No, don't you ever do that. Then he's got you. You made a mistake, but you're young and you'll learn from your mistakes. You can't ask that question—that he threw at him—because you're implying that Dick ordered it. Just go up to him tomorrow like nothing happened and everything will be fine, I guarantee it. Get there early."

I get there early and I'm sitting on the bench. Dick Williams is on one side of me, and Bobby Del Greco, an old ballplayer who was just visiting, is on the other. I pointed to Del Greco, and I said, "Dick, you ever play against him?" And Williams went, "Oh, yeah. I'll never forget one night in Pitttsburgh . . ." and away he went. And then we were fine.

I was there on the Expos' final night. I grew up halfway between Toronto and Montreal. My father had lost an eye playing football, and we'd make the three-hour drive to Montreal. It would be cloudy, and he'd have one eye on the clouds and one eye on the road, which was tough to do when you only have one eye. We'd get to Jarry Park, and the game would be rained out. We'd get a bite to eat and then turn around and drive back.

My father had a big-time attachment to the Expos, and I remember telling him, "Well, they aren't very good." He'd say, "They will be. They're just starting out; you've got to give them time." I thought of him that time at Shea when Wallace Johnson hit the triple off Neil Allen to get them into the playoffs in '81. And I was there on the final night at Olympic Stadium.

I saw Michael Farber, the great *Sports Illustrated* writer who used to sit next to me in the press box. Michael and I were at the press conference before the game, and I said, "Michael, I think I'm gonna cry tonight. This is the team I grew up with." He said, "Well, you're from a different era. You rode the charters. I'll probably cry too. You'll be true to yourself if you have that reaction."

They did a final ceremony where the players spoke, and everyone's all emotional. Meanwhile, you've got Tony Tavares, the team president, saying moving to Washington would be a wonderful adventure. All the front office people in Montreal didn't get jobs, didn't move to Washington. It was so sad from that aspect. The little people—the assistant PR people, the scorekeepers, the custodians in the press box—they're gone, boom. You remember Monique Giroux, the PR lady, don't you? She was there on the first day in 1969, and she was there on the final night.

The thing is that a lot of people say baseball is dead in Quebec. Well, Russell Martin is an All-Star, and he came up after the Expos had left. There's an independent team in Quebec City, and they've set attendance records. So it is a good baseball area. I don't think it was the fans. It was Claude Brochu trying to sell the team and move it to Virginia, and then Major League Baseball stepped in when that failed. Short answer, it was very, very sad.

* * *

We used to do stories on Canadian guys who were going to be drafted; that would have been in the early '90s. I'd talk to scouts and player personnel guys and rank the Canadian prospects. I think my first draft list was in '95, and it ran in the paper for a couple of years. Then we put it on Canoe (the website), and the thing took off. We used to have our own chat room on the site, one of seventeen sports chat rooms. The Maple Leafs had the biggest one, of course. Pro wrestling was second, and Canadian amateur baseball was third.

About four years ago they told me they didn't have room for the list anymore. So I got together with two other guys. We put in fifteen grand each and put together a site called Canadian Baseball Network, which does the same sort of thing. Now, the top guy on my list for next year, he doesn't need any help in getting recognized, because he's in *Baseball America* and all that. But there's guys I'm ranking eighth, ninth, and tenth who people find out about through the draft list.

Logan White, the Dodger scout who signed Russell Martin and converted him into a catcher, once said, "I've seen a Canadian not make it because maybe he's too slow or doesn't have the bat speed or has a lack of ability. But I've *never* seen one not make it because of a bad attitude. I've seen that from other areas, I'm not telling you where."

When Dick Groch, the guy who signed Derek Jeter, set up his scouting system for Milwaukee, he told his bosses, "You want to go after guys and see if they've got a little bit of a hockey background, because it helps." Some Canadian guys, like Jeff Francis, never played hockey at all. But it's a tougher grind, playing hockey. Justin Morneau, Larry Walker, and Corey Koskie were all failed goalies. Walker's great line was, "I didn't find baseball. Baseball found me."

There was some frustration at one point in that perhaps baseball wasn't getting the play in the *Sun* that it deserved, compared to hockey. But we got a new boss that took over this past February. It was the night the Leafs made a big trade, and we had ten pages on the Leafs the next day.

But when he got settled, we talked before I went to spring training, and I asked him, "What's your stance on Canadian baseball? For instance, can I throw in something about a local kid getting a scholarship to the University of Illinois, which has had five straight Canadian catchers?" He said, "*I'm* going to tell *you* what to write about baseball?" It was a sign of respect, in other words. If it's worthy to write about, he said, I'll find room in the paper for it. He's the best boss I've had in about twelve years.

I once said that baseball is the fairest game in the world. I'll give you an example. You remember Yvan Cournoyer? Okay. I didn't like the Montreal Canadiens growing up, but I admired this guy. He could skate through the whole team. I'm sitting there watching TV on Saturday night. It's the first game of the playoffs, and the Canadiens are losing. I said to my father, "Where's Cournoyer? Is he not playing?" My dad said no, he's playing. Well, I said, where is he? He said, "Well, they have a shadow on him. He's going to follow Cournoyer all over the ice, right over to the bench."

I said, "You mean that guy's job is not to try to score, it's to prevent Cournoyer from scoring?" My dad said, yep, that's the way it is in the playoffs.

And the thought occurred to me. When Ted Williams is hitting, nobody's holding his bat as he goes to swing. When a Nolan Ryan or a Roger Clemens gets to his balance point, you don't have somebody pushing him off balance. No. It's just, say, Juan Marichal against Hank Aaron. There's no outside interference. There isn't any shadow.

Honest, it's not, not with all the steroid mess that's pervaded every big league sport. But that's what I meant by *fairest*. It's just you against me. I'm going to go against you. Jim Abbott can pitch a no-hitter, born without a hand. Curtis Pride can be deaf. I don't know if those guys could play the other sports. Maybe they could, I don't know. But baseball's an equal-opportunity game-player.

*   *   *

There's an old newspaper line that says, "It's better to be in sloppy and early than to send in a Pulitzer story after the deadline's gone." I would honestly answer that I've missed maybe one or two deadlines, and they were due to machine problems. But they might need a mine-sweeper to get through my copy. I'm very sloppy, and I still make the same spelling mistakes. Sometimes I don't even get close enough to a word for it to be wrong on spellcheck. My stuff needs a fine-toothed comb and a hairbrush and everything else to go through it.

I'm not a very good writer at all. I'm a better reporter. I think the story I did that I really liked was when Charlie Lea pitched a no-hitter for the Expos in 1981. At the time, I was just a goofball from a sub-urban paper. I'm waiting and waiting for him after the game. Finally I said to him, "Charles, I need your mother's phone number." He said sure, so I phoned her. She lived in Memphis.

It couldn't have worked out any better. She said, "Well, my daughter gave me this, and my other son gave me this, but Charles gave me the nicest Mother's Day gift of all." Nobody else from Mon-treal had spoken to her—it didn't even occur to them. So it became a big second-day story, where they're all phoning the mother. I had it first.

The next time I walked into the park, whether it was in my head or not, I felt like, "Okay, now I belong here." I'm very shy. I can yap and yammer and go off on tangents. But at that point, it was an older group of writers and I was just a young goofball, a newcomer.

When I was starting out in Kingston, I was the fifth guy on a four-man staff, working weekends and part-time. A full-time job came open, and my boss asked me if I wanted the job, and I said sure, I'd take it as soon as school was over. I was in grade 12. He said no, we're not going to hold the job open for you. To take it, I'd have to quit school.

I go home and tell my mother, and she starts crying. My father went to Queen's University, my grandfather went to Queen's, the Harvard of the north, or so they say. Anyway, she's very upset. Then my father comes home, and I tell him the whole story.

He said, "Well, you don't work hard enough in school. You don't want to apply yourself. You like this sportswriting job, don't you?" I said yes. He said, "Well, I'll let you do it on one condition. You can't be like those writers in Boston, like the guy who left Ted Williams off the MVP ballot because he hated him. You can't be like that."

I'm going to cover horse racing and high school sports, so I fig-ure that's no problem. There's no Expos or Blue Jays at the time, no major league baseball at all. Years go by. Then, in 1993, I'm filling out my MVP vote, and I thought about Albert Belle. I said to myself that I really didn't like the guy, the one time I tried to talk to him in Cleveland, so I bumped him down on my ballot.

And then the light went on! It was almost as if my father was speaking to me. Here I was going to be just like the Boston guy. So I redid the ballot and sent it in, and I truly believe that you should judge the player that way, because the guy sitting in section 123 doesn't know what happens downstairs after a game. I think the fans care about who's the best player, the best pitcher, the best manager, and not, "Oh, he's my pal, so I'm voting for him." I've always tried to adhere to that. I don't think everybody does; it's human nature. But the point of the whole story is that fathers know best.

13

PHIL PEPE

If you were a New York baseball fan at any time from the 1960s through the 1990s, Phil Pepe was part of your life. It's that simple.

A fixture for three decades on the sports pages of the New York Daily News, *Pepe began his professional career on the now-defunct* World-Telegram and Sun. *He earned his BBWAA card in 1960, learned at the feet of the likes of Jimmy Cannon and Dan Daniel, and became a prime player in the early Chipmunk era. Joining the* Daily News *in 1968, Pepe covered every World Series from 1969 through 1988. He was promoted to general columnist in 1988, a post he held through 1992.*

The BBWAA's 1989 national chairman, Pepe became synonymous with the New York Yankees beat, starting in the Mantle-Maris days and continuing through the turmoil of the George Steinbrenner era. He was also the News*'s beat writer on the 1969 Miracle Mets and, for good measure, the 1970 world champion Knicks. Still one of the driving forces behind the New York chapter of the BBWAA, Pepe has handled the ever-challenging logistics of its annual dinner for the past decade. He is the author of more than fifty books, including the recent "Few and Chosen" series and the 1991 bestseller* My Favorite Summer, 1956 *with Mickey Mantle.*

I made my first trip with the Yankees in 1959. The Yankees had a traveling secretary, Bill McCorry, who hated to fly, so we did that whole trip by train. I'd never been on a sleeper before.

First day of the trip, I'm standing in the lobby of the hotel in Cleveland. Now, I had been a sidebar guy, so the Yankee players were used to seeing me around. I'm standing there, and a guy comes up to me and says, "Whattyadoin', kid?" "Nothing," I said, "I'm just hanging out until it's time to go to the ballpark." "Well, take a walk with me. I gotta buy my wife a birthday present." So on my first road trip, I'm going lingerie shopping with Yogi Berra.

*   *   *

I was the sports editor of the *St. John's News*, at the St. John's University campus in downtown Brooklyn. I was dealing with the sports information director, a fellow named Bob Adams. He told me one day that Zander Hollander of the *World-Telegram and Sun* was looking for an assistant to help out with high school sports. He gave them my name, and I'm to call Zander and set up an appointment. I got into my best Sunday clothes and met with him. Now, I'm waiting to hear how I made out. A week went by, then ten days, two weeks, and nothing. Finally a phone call came, and it's Zander telling me I got the job.

I remember telling my mother, "Can you imagine that? Of all the people he could have chosen, he chose me!" Then, thirty-five years later, when I was roasted as outgoing chairman of the New York chapter of the baseball writers, Zander got up and said I was the *only* applicant.

So I go work for Zander. I'd leave school at two o'clock, get into the office at about 2:30 or 3, work for about three or four hours. Zander would leave me a list of coaches to call, to get notes, story ideas, things like that. There was one, Harry Kane, who was the baseball coach at Boys High, and one of his players was Tommy Davis. I found out that, prior to that, he'd been the baseball coach at Commerce High and coached Lou Gehrig. Can you imagine a guy coaching both Lou Gehrig and Tommy Davis?

I was about to graduate, and I thought that I'd really like to get into this business, but there were no openings. People kept telling me to go out of town and work my way back to New York. I didn't want to do that, I was already here! I wound up taking a job with the NCAA Statistics Bureau, working for a guy named Homer Cooke out of his apartment in Forest Hills. I said that I would give myself one year, and then, if there's no job, I'll go out of town.

Just before my year was up, Bill Wallace left the *World-Telegram*, Zander was bumped up to his position, and the opening came up for schoolboy editor. Zander pushed me, and I got the job. I remember the first thing I covered, my first byline, was the Penn Relays. Later, when it was my turn to take over for Zander, Hal Bock replaced me. The guy who preceded me as Zander's assistant was the brother of Martin Balsam, the actor. Warren Balsam, the guy's name was.

Now it's the summer of 1957. School is over, it's late August, so what are they gonna do with me? The Giants are going nowhere, they're terrible. Bill Rigney's the manager. Willie Mays is there, but the team is horrible. Joe King was the Giants beat writer, and I'll always believe that his first love was pro football. He never admitted it, but I always thought he had a vision about the future of the NFL. Joe convinced Joe Val, the sports editor, that he should go on a preseason tour of the NFL teams and write preview articles for the upcoming season. To do that, he needed someone to cover the Giants at home.

To make a short story long, Joe Val called me into his office and told me that he needed someone to cover the Giants, and I'm going to cover this home stand. But since I had no experience, he told me, I was going to write the game stories but without a byline. Can you imagine telling a kid that now? Today, they're there fifteen minutes and they want to write a column. What could I do? I was just thrilled to do it.

Now, this story gets better. The home stand ended, and now the Giants and Dodgers are going to play a Labor Day series in Ebbets Field. Bill Roeder, who was the Dodgers writer, told Joe Val he wanted that weekend off. We have no paper on Sunday and no paper on the holiday, so for that series, only one game is actually going to get into the paper. Joe Val said to me, "You've been covering the Giants. Bill wants to take this weekend off, and we'll need you to cover the game on Friday night. Now, it's the Dodgers against the Giants, and we can't have this story without a byline. So you're going to write this story and put Bill Roeder's name on it!"

I swear to God! Now, as disappointed as I must have been about this, Bill Roeder must have been pissed. Bill was a very finicky, meticulous perfectionist. He was the slowest writer I'd ever seen. I'd be in the office doing stuff for Zander, and he'd be in there slaving away. He used to smoke a pipe and type with one finger. And slow! He'd get up, he'd get a drink of water, he'd be there for hours. Later on, when the Dodgers left New York, they assigned him to do long, off-beat features, and he had a terrific, light touch. He was my idol. But if you imagine a guy who was that much of a perfectionist, it had to have killed him to think that this kid was using his name in the paper!

During that weekend, Don Drysdale, who was maybe nineteen at the time, pitched a shutout. I went into the clubhouse at Ebbets Field for the first time. There were TV sets on top of the lockers. I'm looking for Drysdale, and I saw this tall, good-looking, swarthy kind of kid with a towel around his waist looking up at the TV. I went up to him and said, "Don—" and just as I said it, Jack Mann from *Newsday* grabbed me by the arm, pulled me aside, and said, "That's not Drysdale. That's Gino Cimoli." That was my first experience in Ebbets Field, and Jack Mann saved me.

Willard Mullin, the great cartoonist, used to sit two desks away from me. He didn't come into the office every day. He'd do his drawings at home and send them in, by train. One time I said, "Willard, my cousin saw your cartoon the other day, and he'd really like to have the original. Is it available?' He said, "See this cabinet here? Anything in there means I no longer have any use for it. You can take anything that's in there." The day the paper folded, that cabinet must have had three hundred originals in there, and I just walked past it, never took anything. Who knew?

Mullin's work was fabulous. Dan Daniel used to get these questions he'd answer in the column, and the most famous question was always, "Has a fair ball ever been hit out of Yankee Stadium?" He'd go, "No, no," a thousand times no. Now, Mantle hits the ball off Bill Fischer that almost goes out of the stadium. Mullin's cartoon the next day showed the section where the ball went out, and from a distance, there's a little tiny figure there—Daniel—and he's got boards, nails, and a hammer, and he's saying, "Nobody's gonna make a liar out of me!"

We once went twenty years without making a new hire in the sports department. The older guys accepted me because I was there, I wasn't in anybody's way, and I wasn't a threat to them. Dan Daniel was one of the nicest people I ever knew. He had this reputation of being a curmudgeon, but what a sweetheart he was, down deep. Bill Roeder and I got to be buddies even though he was ten years older than me. Joe King used to come in on Sunday nights and do a lot of writing. He'd write for *The Sporting News*, and I'd spend time with him.

I spent a lot of time with Jimmy Cannon. Jimmy was a strange guy, with such a big ego. But I got to be friendly with him. I used to cover boxing. Now, Jimmy didn't drive. He never drove a car. He lived in midtown, and at boxing matches, he'd write his column, and then he'd wait for me to finish writing and then ask me to drive him home. I was newly married at the time, and I wasn't getting home to my wife until one or two in the morning, but I'd drive him home.

But you couldn't just drop him off—you had to come upstairs. He was lonely, he lived alone, and he'd tell me these stories, and I'd just be fascinated. Every time there'd be a fight, I knew I'd have to drive him home. One time he took me into his bedroom, and there was this huge painting of the New York skyline. He said, "Look who painted it." I go over and look, and it's signed, "Frank Sinatra."

As I recall, Cannon named us the Chipmunks. There are two schools of thought. One was that, before I had my teeth straightened, I had protruding teeth. Maury Allen had a similar problem. Supposedly, we looked like chipmunks.

The other story, which I think is valid, is that those of us who were Chipmunks liked to sit around and chatter away. We were afternoon writers, so we had late deadlines. Either Joe King or Jimmy Cannon overheard us and said, "Listen to those guys, they sound like a bunch of chipmunks!" This was the time of Alvin and the Chipmunks, so maybe that had something to do with it.

I never felt any antagonism with the older writers. They didn't exactly agree with the way we approached things. I was very conservative anyway. I'd be as likely to run with the old guys as with the young guys. Steve Jacobson and I hung out together because we both liked jazz. But I spent a lot of time with Barney Kremenko, Til Ferdenzi, Jim Ogle, those older guys. I felt I could learn from them.

*   *   *

When they first put me on the Yankee beat, I'll admit I was intimidated. It wasn't easy to plunge into that. Mickey Mantle was tough, not always accessible. I went through a lot of stages with Mickey. I got to be pretty friendly with him, wrote a book with him, got to know him pretty well. At the beginning he was a turnoff, rude and obscene, all of those things. Then as I matured and looked back after his career was over, I realized that maybe the reason he was like that was because he was in pain a lot. He was hurting and didn't have the patience to talk about what happened on the field.

Then I took another look and realized he was very humble. He didn't like talking about himself. It was his humility that prevented him from sitting there and boasting about the home run he'd just hit. You'd watch Mickey Mantle hit a home run, and he never had his head up; he always had his head down. That was the way it was in those days; you don't want to embarrass the pitcher. No high-fives or chest bumps.

After the *World-Telegram*, I was with the Widget, the merged *World-Journal-Tribune*. Jimmy Cannon had the great line about that. He said that the Widget's sports department was like Noah's Ark in that it had two of everything: two Mets writers, two Yankees writers. Three papers merging into one. It lasted about nine months.

The Widget folded in 1967, so I started doing freelance. It was tough; I had a growing family. Then I got a phone call from a guy named John Chanin, a radio producer. He was doing an ABC radio sports show hosted by Lou Boda. The executive producer was Howard Cosell. I was hired to be one of three writers, and Howard was my boss, in essence.

Howard was great to work for. He'd do a five-minute show, one on Saturday and one on Sunday. He'd be playing gin rummy in the studio until the time came, then he'd say, "Okay, let's go," and he'd do it all off the top of his head.

I also started doing books. One of the first I did was *From Ghetto to Glory* with Bob Gibson, during the height of his Hall of Fame career with the Cardinals. Would you believe that Marty Glickman, the announcer, represented Bob Gibson on that book? Marty got Prentice Hall to publish it, and the author was going to be John Lake. John Lake was a sportswriter for the *Herald Tribune* briefly and the sports editor of *Newsweek*. A few months before the book was to be turned in, they couldn't find John Lake. He interviewed Gibson, then no one could find the tapes. He just disappeared . . . to this day! I've had communications with his son, who lives in upstate New York. They're still looking for him! I think they've come to the realization that he killed himself.

So now Gibson has been paid, and they have to get this book out. Zander called me. Sure, I can do it. I was there to bail out Gibson and everyone else. Gibson would come to town, and we'd go over the same ground that he went over with Lake.

Now the book comes out, but meanwhile, I want to be back in newspapers. It's World Series time in 1968—Cardinals vs. Tigers— and I get a brilliant idea. I contact as many newspapers as I can think of and offer a ghostwritten Bob Gibson column every day of the Series. I'll write it, Bob's name'll go on it, and we'll split the money. I got the Omaha paper (because Bob was from Omaha), a few other papers, and the *New York Daily News*. It's about $500 each, so it was $2,500 total.

In the first game against Detroit, he struck out seventeen. Afterward, he got a call from Hubert Humphrey, the vice president. He told me, but no one else. I've got an exclusive, and the *Daily News* used it on page one!

The Series ended, and the *Daily News* sent me my money with a little note, "Call Mike O'Neill," the editor. O'Neill wanted to talk to me about a job as the sports editor of a trial paper the *News* was experimenting with. They never went ahead with the paper, but Mike O'Neill liked what I did and offered me a job in the sports section.

*   *   *

The *Daily News* built much of its reputation on its baseball coverage. When I was a kid growing up, it was routine in the summertime to get the *News* and the *Mirror*. I started reading Dick Young in the *News* and Gus Steiger, Dan Parker, and Arthur Richman in the *Mirror*. Now I'm part of it.

Larry Merchant once said that the problem I had as a writer was that it was too important for me to be liked. Is that a criticism? He felt that was the reason I wasn't tough enough, I wasn't hard, I wasn't acerbic.

Here's how you covered baseball then. First of all, all the games are at night, just about. You had to do an early story that had to be in by three. Then you go to the ballpark, and you write running. When the game is over, you write a lead. Then you sub it out, and you write another story, and then you go to the clubhouse and write *another* story. And the next day, you repeat the process. Meanwhile, Dick Young is not only doing that, he's writing a column as well, every day! And I'm not the only one. Jack Lang is doing it, and everyone else. All by myself! How many words was I putting out? Not good ones, but how many words? The volume was unbelievable.

Plus, this was before computers. You had to type it then give it to Western Union, and then came the old Telecopiers. Doing it all yourself! If the team was at home, maybe you had some help, but not on the road.

Now, the writers don't travel with the teams anymore. You don't fly with them, you don't stay at their hotel, you don't take the bus with them. That was one advantage we had. When we went on the road, I never touched my luggage until it got to my room in the next city. They'd wait for us on the planes and buses, within reason.

On deadline, I was as good as I had to be. When I was working for the *World-Telegram*, an afternoon paper, I was like Bill Roeder. I would take hours and waste time. Now, suddenly, I'm working for the *Daily News*, and I wind up writing the AM lead on every World Series game from 1969 to, I think, 1988. It got to the point where I didn't even bother going to the clubhouse after a Series game because speed was so important. Guys who were down in the clubhouse would come up and give me quotes.

There was a specific dichotomy between the AM papers and the PM papers. I started on an afternoon paper, and you had a different responsibility than the AM paper. Young broke the barrier in that he was the first AM guy to go into the clubhouse to get quotes. I remember reading stories by guys like Dan Daniel and John Drebinger, and there wouldn't be a single quote. But as a PM guy, you didn't have to do play-by-play. You'd wait then go down to the clubhouse. When I was with the *World-Telegram*, it was a snap: one story and you're done. The toughest part was finding a Western Union office that was open that late when you were on the road.

I wasn't big on scoops. There was one I had, and then I didn't have it. I found out that Bill Virdon was going to get fired, and Billy Martin was going to take over as Yankees manager. I had the story and wrote it. Now, one of the printers at the *Daily News* used to go to a bar around the corner from the News Building on 42nd Street. The printer who plated my story was in there drinking and started talking about the new Yankees manager. Someone from UPI was also in there, and we got beat on the story because Milton Richman got it from him. My story was already written, but UPI beat us because they put it right on the wire, all because this printer shot his mouth off.

*   *   *

The line I used to use about covering the Yankees in the Reggie Jackson–George Steinbrenner era was that you had to sleep with your eyes open. You'd be afraid to go to sleep because you never knew what you were going to miss. I didn't want to cover fights or what was going on off the field, but there's stress because you're afraid of getting beat. Billy Martin is fighting with George, George is fighting with Reggie, Reggie is fighting with Billy. And I'm all alone! If I had three other people with me like they do now, it wouldn't have been so bad.

The best characterization I can give of George Steinbrenner is this. When you go into a bakery, you take a number off the wall, right? Then you wait for your number to come up, and then you get served. When you covered the Yankees with Steinbrenner, sooner or later you're going to say something or write something that he's not going to like. So what you have to do is take a number off the wall and wait for your turn to come up again, because everyone who's ahead of you is going to screw up, and he'll come back to serving you, to talking to you.

Same thing! He got mad at you all the time and forgot it a few days later because now he'd be mad at someone else. He was always very generous, flattering. I was part of the inner circle back then. I was invited to things others weren't. When one of my kids was born, he sent a gift, that sort of thing.

When the Yankees won the World Series in 1977, he called me and asked, "Would the writers accept World Series rings?" I told him that I can't speak for all the writers, but I won't. He said, "Why not?" I said I didn't think I deserved one. I didn't do anything to help the team win. I noticed that when the Mets won in '69, they gave the writers rings, and Young and Lang wore them. I got the sense that the players may have resented that. I don't need the players to resent me wearing the ring.

There'll never be another Dick Young. He was a trailblazer, a pioneer, a leader. With all the negative things, there's much more positive than negative. I knew him as a rival, a colleague, and a boss. His influence in the business is still felt today. He had the foresight to see the transition and what was happening with television, how people were getting their information. A lot of the jargon that we use in baseball came from him. Ribbies, for RBI, for instance. The way players talked, he'd write it that way.

As a boss, he was great. When he was sports editor of the *News*, he was more interested in the good of the paper than the good of Dick Young. One time, at the World Series, I came up with a tip on something big. I forget exactly what it was, but I went to Dick because he had better contacts than I did. I said, "Dick, I just heard about such-and-such." He said, "Good, I'll look into it."

He went out, dug out the story, came back to the press box, wrote the story, showed it to me, and my name's on it! I said, "Dick! I didn't write that." He said, "But you gave me the story. I wouldn't have had it without you." That's the way he was.

As sports editor, Young wanted his style on the pages, but he didn't want the administrative stuff, and he had somebody inside to do it for him. He wanted to be the voice of the paper, which he was, and wanted to dictate policy. One of the things he kept pounding away on was that he wanted more stories—shorter stories, but more of them. Which is basically what we have today; instead of lengthy stories where people are going to get bored, you want it short and to the point.

*   *   *

I was national chairman of the BBWAA when the Pete Rose situation came up. The Hall of Fame Board of Directors had a meeting in New York, and we were invited to speak at the meeting. It was Jack Lang, as secretary-treasurer, and me. We tried to convince them that they should allow Rose's name on the ballot, and don't worry about the baseball writers. We will do the right thing. I'm not saying we'll vote for him, I'm not saying we'll vote against him. But whatever we'll do, will be the right thing. Give us that opportunity to prove that to you. They listened to us. They were cordial; some of them were sympathetic. They voted us down and put Pete on the ineligible list.

I think the writers are still the best judge of the Hall of Fame, but there are also some individuals who are not members who would be good voters. But how do you filter it out? Let's say you write a blog, you write for a dot-com, and you're very conscientious. But the guy who's sitting next to you is not. So how do you differentiate? I think it's important that you be a member for ten years. Every once in a while, someone will vote for a favorite son, but that one vote isn't enough to get him elected. So what's the big deal? The big deal is that someone should have enough pride not to minimize their vote, not to throw their vote away.

For example, there was one year I didn't vote for anybody. I was one of nine guys who didn't vote for anybody. It was the year Willie Stargell got elected [1988]. There were nine of us who sent in blank ballots. Why would you send in a blank ballot? Well, a blank ballot is a vote, because it's a percentage deal. I wanted to register my vote that I didn't feel anyone deserved to be elected that year. If you're gonna get elected, you're gonna need three votes to counteract my blank.

But I still think it's the best system. I can't think of a better one. Seventy-five percent is very hard. We've elected presidents with less than fifty percent!

*   *   *

I could probably do the job today. Could I be a beat writer? Sure. I wouldn't have to worry about getting beat on stories; I'd have people watching my back. I wouldn't have to worry about the volume of words that I had to worry about back in my day. If I were writing a column, I wouldn't even have to worry about deadlines. I'd wait until the game was over and then write the column and not worry about missing editions. Do they even have editions these days? I don't know if I could blog. I don't know how I'd deal with that. You don't know if anyone's reading it.

What makes covering the Yankees easier today is that there's so many guys to help you out. Most of the time, I was alone. I pick up the *News* right now, and they have six guys in Florida! And they're climbing all over each other!

I don't think they have as much fun today, but I used to hear the same thing from the old guys. They were traveling on the trains, and there was a lot more social time with the players. We were on the same planes and hotels, which they don't do today. It seemed like we talked about the game a lot more.

My friendships with Lang, Young, Koppett, and those guys ingrained a responsibility to the profession in me. Today, why am I doing what I'm doing with the dinner? Because somebody has to. Part of why I do it is loyalty to the job and the profession. But also, it gives me a connection. I worry about what's going to happen when I can't do it anymore, and that time is coming. I tell them that I need a young guy to step forward and who I can turn the job over to. You can't imagine all the work it entails. I was lucky; I learned about the dinner from Lang. He turned all of his information over to me. But nobody's learning from me.

Guys today, for the most part, have no idea how big the dinner was. Sometime guys with a real sense of history, like Marty Noble or Pete Caldera, will ask about the old dinners and shows. God, I wish I still had the scripts. For a while I was saving them, and then I threw them out!

Koppett was fantastic at that. I can still remember lyrics to songs that Leonard used to tell me about. Like the song about Mickey Cochrane, "Goodbye, Mickey," from back in the '30s. I wrote a song about Ron Blomberg not being able to hit left-handers called "Bye Bye Blomberg." a takeoff on "Bye Bye Birdie." [Singing], "*Vida Blue . . . makes such a schmuck of you . . . Bye bye Blomberg!*"

One song I wrote didn't make it to the show. I came up with it on the bus ride from San Francisco to Fresno during the 1962 Series when it rained and the Yankees had to go to Fresno to work out. It was about Joe Trimble of the *Daily News*, called "Trimble's Pants," to the tune of "My Romance." [Singing], "*Trimble's pants. Da, da, da, da, da, da, DEE, da . . . Trimble's pants . . .*"

14

DAVE van DYCK

The young Chicago writer was establishing himself on his first major beat—the pre–Michael Jordan Bulls—when his boss asked him about a possible new assignment . . . one that entailed, the boss said matter-of-factly, "You know . . . going against Jerome Holtzman."

Competing for space and prestige next to the standard-bearer for Chicago baseball writing was a daunting task. But thirty years after he reluctantly said yes, Dave van Dyck had written his own chapter in the city's storied newspaper history.

Originally joining the Chicago Sun-Times *in 1976, van Dyck anchored the paper's baseball coverage for two decades. From 1980 through 1994, he handled both the Cubs and White Sox beats (frequently switching teams at midseason with Joe Goddard) and then served as the* Sun-Times's *national baseball columnist for six additional years.*

In 2000, he became one of the first mainstream sportswriters to go digital, joining the fledgling FoxSports.com. Four years later, he returned to newspaper work with the Chicago Tribune, *covering both teams.*

A two-time Spink Award finalist, van Dyck served for fifteen straight years as chairman of the Chicago chapter of the BBWAA. The University of Illinois product also serves on the Baseball Hall of Fame's Historical Overview Committee. A historian in the Holtzman tradition, van Dyck—as we learn here—found a novel way to pay tribute, in print, to the Windy City legend known as the Dean.

Chicago has always been a terrific baseball writers town. You'd walk into the old Pink Poodle, the press room at Wrigley Field, and feel the presence of all those guys. Jerome Holtzman. Dave Nightingale. Dick Dozer.

Jerome must have said a million times that, "The baseball beat job is the *best* job on the paper." I'd say, "But, Jerome, what about the columnists?" He'd go, "Oh, no, no, no. This is ten times better than being a columnist." His reasoning was that you're well read. You're in the paper every day. You were read by hundreds of thousands of people, and you were *the* expert on what was going on. He was right, I guess.

You don't think of yourself as part of that great legacy. When you start out, you say, "Man, those old guys. They were doing this for fifteen, twenty, twenty-five, thirty years. I'll be dead by then. There's no way I'll be doing this beat for that long. I give it maybe five years."

When you take the job, you don't ever think that people will say, "That era of baseball in Chicago was chronicled by Joe Goddard and Dave van Dyck and Jerome Holtzman. Those were the guys who were entrusted with telling us exactly what went on." When you start out, you never think you're going to be that good or do it that long.

And then it just happens! It just keeps going, and you never think of how long you've done it. It just becomes a daily job and then a yearly job. Then we realize it's a very important job, in its own way.

I'll tell you three things that influenced my life and where I am now. One was in high school, at the beginning of my junior year. The basketball coach came to me and said, "You know, there's a job opening at the local weekly paper, and they need somebody to write stories about our high school." I said, "Coach, I don't know if I have time to both play and write stories." He says, "Well, that's what I'm tryin' to tell ya." Oh. That was his way of cutting me from the team, probably the nicest way to do it. I was a little bit crushed, but it started me on my career.

The second thing was when I graduated from college. I was an advertising minor. I had an instructor who had just retired from Foote, Cone & Belding, the huge ad agency in Chicago. He'd come to the University of Illinois to teach, and he took a liking to me and thought I had some talent. He got me an interview at Foote, Cone & Belding just as I was about to graduate. I didn't realize at the time that this was almost impossible for a kid like me.

I bought a suit, went to Chicago, and walked into Foote, Cone & Belding. I spend the whole day with the executives, eating in the executive dining room and all that. I walked out of there a nervous mess. I took off my tie, took off my coat, walked up Michigan Avenue, and said to myself, "I will *never* take a job where I have to sit in an office with a tie and coat on in a pressure situation." I think most of us in the newspaper business feel that way, especially beat writers. We want to be out there doing things, and we don't want to be stuck in a cubicle.

Of course, the third thing was the day in January 1980 where I'm staying at the Bellevue-Stratford in Philadelphia when Marty Kaiser, the sports editor, called me and said, "Would you like to cover baseball, cover spring training, and, you know, go up against Jerome Holtzman?"

I said, "Marty, I don't know. I'm pretty comfortable where I'm at. I think I do a good job on the NBA." He said, "Oh, you do a great job on the NBA. We just need someone to do baseball." I said, "Well, I'll think about it, but I know what my answer's gonna be. I don't think so."

Well, Marty basically told me what my high school coach told me. He said, "Well, I think it's a good idea if you do it." That was his way of telling me I was *going* to do it. That's how I went into the baseball beat, kicking and stomping.

*   *   *

I was comfortable with the Bulls—I was already on the inside. I knew everybody. Beat writing is sort of like being in a fraternity. I was going to say family, but it's more like a fraternity. It's kind of a closed society almost, where once you're on the inside, you really feel good and feel comfortable. And if you're not on the inside, you don't feel comfortable.

The NBA in the '70s was our own private thing, if you know what I mean. It was like our own little niche in the world. I'm trying to think of something similar in the regular work world, and I'm not sure I can. That's why I didn't want to do baseball.

But yet, once you *start* it, once you meet people, you're okay. Luckily, I had done the NBA and knew how to handle a beat. I think the most important thing back then was that you knew the other writers. It wasn't that you knew the other coaches or the players, but you knew the other *writers*. That was in an era where we didn't have MLBtraderumors.com or ESPN.com.

If there was a trade happening, you better know the writer in St. Louis or New York or Cleveland or Detroit, where you could call and say, "Hey, I heard some rumblings from my team that they might be trading Joe Schmoe. Run it by your guys." Then an hour or two later he'd call back and say, "You might be on to something. My guy says it's pretty hot." That's how you did stuff back then.

Once you got to know the other writers and your way around ballparks and cities, it was like anything else. It's not a simple beat, because it's huge and important. And you never quit learning on it. That's the other thing. You *never* quit learning. The games themselves are always new, which is the fascinating part of it. Once I got to doing it, it was challenging and fun. I've always had a great time doing it.

Jerome was at the *Sun-Times* covering baseball when I was there. He went to the *Tribune* in 1981, so now he's my competitor. That was part of the reason I didn't want to do baseball. I was going up against a legend, even back then, before he became a *super*-legend. It's really a daunting thing. You just go in saying, "I'm going to do the best I can."

Jerome was wonderful. There'll never be a better guy to break into a beat with. He introduced me to everybody, saying, "We got this kid here on the beat. Treat him right, and tell that to everybody." I thought the world of Jerome for that, and I told him a million times.

I also learned a few things from him. One night we're in New York, and we're coming back into Manhattan from Yankee Stadium in a cab. Jerome said to me, "Hey, let's get a bite to eat. I know a spot that's not too expensive. We can grab a bite to eat, and I'll buy." So off we go to eat.

I get back to my room about two o'clock, and the phone is flashing. I pick it up, and the guy on the other end says, "Hey, Jerome's got a story about such-and-such." I forget what it was about, but it was an exclusive. Jerome was trying to get me out of the hotel so I wouldn't get the call from my desk before deadline! Boy, did I learn something. I saw him the next day and said, "You wise old fox. That will *never* happen to me again!"

Right when I started on the beat, the Cubs hired Dallas Green to be their president. Jerome not only had that they were gonna hire Dallas Green but that they had eaten in a restaurant at O'Hare Airport, and he had what they ate. He had what they had for lunch that day! I just thought that was marvelous. About four years ago the same type of thing came up where there was a signing of some sort, and it was done over dinner. I asked someone at the restaurant what they ate, and the guy said, "Well, they made their proposal right when the lobster bisque was coming." I put that in the story as a little salute to Jerome.

*   *   *

At the *Sun-Times*, Joe Goddard and I used to switch teams at the All-Star break every year. That was one of the two things that helped me stay on the beat as long as I did. It was so refreshing, you wouldn't believe it. We covered a lot of bad Chicago teams back then; neither team had won a World Series since before 1920. That showed how bad it was, and you were just dying to get out of there by the All-Star break. You couldn't wait to get to the other team. Then, a year later, it was the same way, but the *other* way. You were dying to get off that team again. It was a breath of fresh air, but I think it kept both of us going longer than maybe we wanted to.

The other thing was that I did the Indy 500 every year, for five or six years. I'd be gone from baseball for three or four weekends a year, plus the whole race week. So that was a break for me, and it was something I loved, probably more than writing baseball.

Those things kept it fresh. I don't know how guys cover one team all the time, bad teams especially. It would such a grind. It would be a job instead of a passion. It would be like going into that cubicle every day.

I've always written for AM papers. I still get edgy on deadline because I want the game to be over, especially tie games running late, things like that. Deadlines are awful, and they're getting worse even as we get more technologically advanced. But that's part of the excitement of it. That's what keeps you on your toes and keeps you going. I'd hate to take my blood pressure an hour or so before deadline. The juices are flowing.

One speech I give to young writers is that you're not going to win any Pulitzer Prizes from this job. You write your best stories on the off days or in the off-season. Deadline work is grunt work. It's just as important as writing great, flowing, wonderful feature stuff, but it's probably harder because you have to write a story that makes sense. It's really a challenging accomplishment, and of course we've done it so long that it becomes sort of second nature. But I'll tell you honestly that my heart beats a little faster as deadline comes up. That's the excitement of it.

And the other part of it is, you're done. You know that even if you didn't write the greatest story in the world, there's nothing you can do about it. It's gone, it's in type, it's rolling on the presses right now, and there's no getting it back. It's like taking an 0-for-4 sometimes; you just say that tomorrow you'll come back and go 4-for-4. There are not many jobs that are like that, where you have the daily deadline pressure.

This may sound funny, but I've never written a story for a fan. I write stories for my job and my bosses, because if my boss isn't happy I don't have a job. You don't write for the fans. The story has to have certain things in it, obviously, and you can include "long-suffering Cub fans" and all that stuff, and you realize what the fans are feeling. But you aren't writing the story, per se, for a fan, or even for a non-fan. You try to write it for everybody.

I had been a baseball writer for more than twenty years when the FoxSports.com thing happened. There was a fascination of doing something new and different, like opening up a new frontier. I've always wanted to be an astronaut or break a speed record in an airplane. It was a chance to get in on the ground floor of something I thought was going to become *the* way of life.

If anything, I guess I did it a little before my time, because Fox gave up on it three years later. Now they're back into it real heavy again. Of course, we all do dot-com stuff now. I do as much, if not more, for the *Tribune* website as I do for the newspaper.

The Fox thing was fun. I wouldn't change it for the world. I made my final decision to take the job while driving to Cooperstown. You know that drive from Albany to Cooperstown? I rolled down the windows, headed out on the interstate, and said, "It's time to do it. Either you're going to do it or not." So I made my mind up while driving to the induction ceremony in 2000.

*   *   *

I tell most aspiring young writers I meet to get out of the business, first of all [laughs]. Second thing is, if they're still in college, make sure you take a lot of radio and television courses. The person who's the most versatile in this business is the one who's going to succeed. As a writer, they want you to do radio and TV; they want you to speak in front of groups. So that's important.

There aren't a lot of people who say that they want to be a baseball beat writer. There are a few, and I don't try to discourage them, because nobody wants to be a baseball writer that's older than twenty-five, I don't think! When you're young you have stars in your eyes, and you think it's the coolest job in the world. You get a little older, you realize it's not a perfect job.

Once they get the beat job, they don't stay very long anymore. It's okay. Things change. I've never been one to say, "Boy, it's awful the way things are changing." You may feel that way about some things, but you don't say it. If we always had that attitude, we wouldn't have airplanes or cars now, or have gone to the moon. There's nothing wrong with change.

I think that if you were out of the business for five years and then tried to come back right now, I don't think you could do it. Our workload now is five times what it was fifteen or twenty years ago, and ten times what it was thirty years ago.

It's not as fun as it used to be, I'll say that. You don't have as much time to watch the game and enjoy it, be around it, or take in the sights, as it were. There used to be days where I'd go out, especially in spring training but also during the season, where I'd go out into the stands and sit in the upper deck. Just sit and look at things.

The beat guys I worked with spanned a great era. We've gone from handing copy over to a Western Union operator, which I did when I started, all the way to Tweeting. We've gone from almost the days of flannel uniforms to the Pittsburgh drug trials, the steroid era, the strikes, the labor strife. We really went through a neat era; we're really the last of that group. We took the game from what had been so long into and through an entire era of complete change. I don't think the game has ever changed as much as it has over the last thirty years.

There was a bond and camaraderie among writers. You're brothers more than in some things, because not only do you do the same things, you also go through the same hardships. We talked to each other before divorces and career decisions, things like that. Who would you call? You'd call the guys you know best as baseball writers.

I think ours was a very important group of writers. To take on the tradition of Jerome Holtzman and Dick Young, who used to yell at each other in the meetings, and then take it into the modern world . . . and try to figure out how we do stuff without very many newspapers around.

Now, is it still the best job? I don't know. It's an important job, and of course newspapers have changed so much. I'm not sure we can say that anymore, but in some ways maybe it's still the most important beat because nobody wants to do it. There's so few that can really do it now, do it well and *want* to do it. If it isn't the most important beat on the paper, certainly it's the hardest, the most grueling. Your fingers get worn down, and so does your brain.

I once had a friend who said to me, "Now, you *do* dictate your stories to your secretary, right? Exactly how many words per minute does she type?" He really thought that.

15

JIM FERGUSON

For more than three decades, Jim Ferguson was known through-out baseball as one of the game's foremost publicists. He served as the director/vice president of publicity for the Cincinnati Reds from 1973 through 1990, a span that earned him three world champion-ship rings with the famed Big Red Machine of 1975–1976 and Lou Piniella's wire-to-wire squad of 1990. After a brief stint with the San Diego Padres, he was director of media relations for Minor League Baseball from 1995 through 2008. His longstanding efforts earned him the coveted Robert O. Fishel Award—the baseball PR industry's highest honor—in 1985.

But long before Fergie wrote his first press release or coordi-nated his first live shot, he had carved out a distinguished newspaper career as the Reds' beat writer for the Dayton Daily News. *Hired and mentored by Spink Award–winner Si Burick, Ferguson joined the* Daily News *out of Ohio State in 1955 and was on the Reds' beat for fourteen seasons, from 1959 through 1972. He shared the beat with the* Cincinnati Post's *Earl Lawson, the 1985 Spink winner. Fergie's tenure at the* Daily News *spanned the Reds eras from Crosley Field to Riverfront Stadium, from Fred Hutchinson to Sparky Anderson, from Gus Bell to Johnny Bench.*

When Ferguson left the Daily News, *he was succeeded on the Reds beat by yet another Spink winner, Hal McCoy. Consider this statistic: during a full half-century—from 1959 through 2009, when it discontinued its daily coverage—the* Dayton Daily News *had ex-actly two Reds beat writers: Jim Ferguson and Hal McCoy.*

Jim splits his time between homes in Ohio and St. Petersburg, Florida. Fergie's retirement from the minor leagues marked the end of fifty years of daily involvement in baseball. Following his retirement, he was still a vital press box presence as an official scorer for the Tampa Bay Rays until 2010.

There was a Western Union chief in every ballpark, and usually it was someone who'd been around a long time. He'd have different people there sending the stories. St. Louis was one place where they were always in a hurry to get out of there; they didn't want to stay around for the PM guys. So you had to go downtown and find a place. In St. Louis, it was up the back stairs, knock on the door, like you were going to a speakeasy or an after-hours club . . . "Joe sent me."

You had that in a few cities. Basically, the AM guys had their own dedicated Western Union machines, so they had an operator assigned to them. Then when they were done and had filed, they'd take the stuff from the PM guys like me.

The Western Union chiefs were very helpful. There was a guy in Pittsburgh named Rod who had been working at Forbes Field for years. I mean, he was like a copyreader for you. He'd take your story and come back to you and say, "You didn't really mean to say this, did you?" He'd save you from something embarrassing or making a bad mistake.

Writing always came easy to me. I grew up in a little town of about twelve hundred people just east of Dayton—Jamestown, Ohio—and they had an outstanding softball team that traveled all over the southern half of Ohio. When I was about fourteen or fifteen I started covering the team for a weekly newspaper. When I went to Ohio State, it was a natural thing for me to go right into journalism. I was sports editor of the college newspaper my senior year.

When I graduated in December '54, I was basically just sitting around waiting to be drafted. After a couple of months, I felt that it was ridiculous to wait for the draft. I volunteered and was all set to serve the two years, but my eyes were so bad that I flunked my physical! So I started looking for a newspaper job.

A couple of my friends from Ohio State were on the staff at the *Daily News,* and they told me there was an opening in the sports department. They helped set up an interview for me, and I went in, talked to Si Burick and the managing editor, and was offered the job. I started in the spring of '55.

I had had a couple of other offers, but the chance to go to Dayton was too appealing not to jump at. I had grown up reading Si Burick, who I still believe was one of the greatest columnists in America. He was recognized and known all over the country. Working under Si, I felt, was a chance to continue my education as a sportswriter.

Getting the Reds beat in 1959 was somewhat of a surprise. Most baseball writers in those days didn't get the beat as young as I did. You had to be around to prove yourself; you had to work as a backup writer, things like that. I was covering high schools for a couple of years and was in the process of covering Miami of Ohio as well. The guy who was our baseball writer, Ed O'Neill, was there for about four years and basically started the beat.

Beginning with the 1956 season, when the Reds had all those great home run hitters, the *Daily News* started covering the team as a regular beat. Dayton is about fifty, fifty-five miles away from Cincinnati, and in those days papers from cities that far may cover a few home games but never really treat it like a beat. Starting in '56, the *Daily News* started treating the Reds like a home team, covering them home and road.

The *Daily News* was a Cox paper, and they wanted to move Ed O'Neill to their Miami [Florida] paper as a columnist. That opened up the baseball beat. I'd only been on the paper for four years and was twenty-six years old, and probably the hardest part of my whole career as a baseball writer was sweating it out that winter. I analyzed everyone on the staff in my own mind—will they give it to this guy? Nah. Could I get it? Well, maybe. It was something I really, really craved. My parents were both big baseball fans. We'd go down six or seven times to Crosley Field every season, so the baseball thing was deep inside me. One of the biggest days of my life was when Si Burick told me I got the baseball beat.

Si was a tremendous influence in my life. I'd grown up reading him, and I worked under him for seventeen years at the *Daily News*. He kept giving me great assignments. I figured I had three of the best beats on the paper over the course of the year—I had the Reds in the summer, Ohio State football in the fall, and Ohio State basketball with John Havlicek and Jerry Lucas in the winter.

Si was the first Spink Award winner from a non-major league city, which tells you something about his national reputation. He could have worked anywhere, but he chose to stay in Dayton. Whenever there was something important going on in Dayton that wasn't sports-related—for instance, a big school meeting or something big politically—he was part of it. He was never involved in politics, but they always wanted his name to be connected with anything big going on in Dayton.

I was probably unique among baseball writers in that I never covered spring training in fourteen years on the beat. Spring training belonged to Si Burick. He had convinced the paper that it would be a good idea to go to Florida to cover spring training. By the time I got the beat, he'd been doing that for twenty years or more. Si based himself in Tampa because the Reds trained there, but really wrote about every team in Florida, staying there for a month or five weeks like all the beat writers.

I had mixed feelings about that. I wanted to be in spring training, and at the same time I had these other beats that were great. But in the back of my mind I still wondered what was going on down in Florida. The worst part was Si would call early in the morning to dictate a story, and he always stayed right on the beach. I usually had to take his dictation, hearing the surf pounding in the background.

One bonus was that it made the start of the season really special. When you got to Opening Day, it was like, "Man, I can't wait for this." You were fresh and ready to really jump into things.

*   *   *

The Reds beat was like anything when it's something new. There's a certain amount of nervousness and a little self-doubt until you prove yourself at a different level. I had proven myself covering the colleges, but this was a very big jump for me. There was definitely an intimidation factor.

The man who made the transition workable for me, made it easy and fun, was Earl Lawson. Earl took me under his wing and made it a point that, anyplace we went on the road, he would introduce me to people on the other clubs. It gave me a credibility from the beginning that would have been hard to get any other way.

In those days, there were two AM papers and two PM papers covering the Reds on a daily basis . . . two Cincinnati papers, the *Enquirer* and the *Post and Times-Star*, and two Dayton papers, the *Daily News* and the *Journal-Herald*. At the ballpark, the AM guys and the PM guys all tend to hang out together. Also, Dayton and Cincinnati were so far apart that they weren't really considered to be competing with each other.

My first year, 1959, the Reds opened at home like they always did in those days. Then they went to Philadelphia for one game, and then it rained for three straight days. I'm brand new on the beat, so I didn't know the players, had nothing to fall back on. It was a real scramble. My first trip as a baseball writer, and I'm dying.

The Reds were a very ordinary team when I took over. Then they hired Fred Hutchinson as manager. Hutch had been the manager at Seattle in the Pacific Coast League. He was a great guy to be around, a very strong man. He was tough as nails at times and soft as marshmallow at others. He put basic baseball into the team and got people to start playing the right way.

It was slow catching on, and 1960 was not a good season. But they came from out of nowhere in '61 to win the pennant. They made a couple of big trades that brought in Joey Jay and Gene Freese. Bob Purkey had come a little earlier. They had some young pitchers in Jim O'Toole and Jay Hook, and the team really took off. They were a lot like [the 2010] Reds, where nothing was really expected of them, and they just kept winning. They never opened much of a lead, but they kept hanging in there. It was one of the most exciting times of my career in baseball.

With my early Reds teams, I was the same age as some of the players and not all that much older than most. I think it was an advantage with some players and probably a disadvantage with others. The veteran players were more used to dealing with older writers and were more comfortable with them. But the young guys on the team— and there were a lot of them—were feeling their way along much as I was. I spent a lot of time with them, and it helped me a lot.

Nineteen sixty-four was a really exciting time because the team was playing well all year, until the very end. It was also a very sad year because Hutch was fighting cancer. He was a strong guy, and people said that if anyone could beat this, Hutch was the guy. He was so tough and so hard.

Early in the season he was doing everything the doctors wanted him to do. He'd been a chain smoker, and then he stopped and seemed to be making some progress physically. But there was a point during the season where he started smoking again, and it was like, "Uh-oh." It was like he had given up, that he knew he wasn't going to beat it. I can't remember, but it might have been Gene Mauch who said, "Hutch showed us how to live, and now he's showing us how to die." That stuck with me for a long time. Hutch just toughed his way through it. He was in such obvious pain every day until he just couldn't do it anymore. Dick Sisler managed the team for the last two months.

The other unforgettable part of that season was the last weekend. We'd gone on a tear and then came home for the final week. The Phillies were in a total collapse, losing ten in a row. We're closing the season against the Phillies, and we have a Friday night game and a Sunday game, but no Saturday game, for whatever reason.

We come into the Friday game a half-game out of first place. The Phillies are the deadest team I've ever seen in my life; they were literally going through the motions. They knew they had blown the pennant, even though they were still alive. We had a lead on 'em, we were up 3–0. Then Chris Short hit Leo Cardenas in the seventh inning, and Cardenas charged the mound. Well, it woke up the Phillies. They came back and beat us, 4–3. After the game, Jim O'Toole and Cardenas got into a big fight in the clubhouse in which O'Toole went after Cardenas shouting "You woke them up!" and Cardenas came back with either a knife or a screwdriver, and they had to be pulled apart.

We're off on Saturday and come back on Sunday. The big thing is whether Jim Maloney, our ace, is going to pitch on three days' rest after throwing eleven shutout innings against Pittsburgh, or John Tsitouris, a middle-of-the-road journeyman pitcher, is going to start. We're going against Jim Bunning. Maloney had started on three days' rest maybe twice all season. I remember Sisler saying, "If Maloney wants to pitch, he's going to be the guy, but he has to want to because he's not used to going on three days' rest."

We had the possibility of finishing in a two-way tie or even a three-way tie. We were all at the ballpark packed and ready to go after the game. And Maloney didn't go to Sisler; he was going to pitch in the tie-breaker on Monday, which never happened. Tsitouris got lit up early and often, Bunning dominated us, and we lost, 10–0. I don't know if this was true, but it was said that Tsitouris came to the ballpark with his car packed with all his belongings and was on his way home before the game was over.

*   *   *

We were a PM paper six days a week and then we were AM for the Sunday paper. Working as a PM guy six days a week, it was almost a nuisance to be an AM guy for Sunday because you're in a routine in the way you cover the team and the stories you're writing. Then all of a sudden you have to shift gears and go the other way for Sunday.

Writing on deadline was something I picked up fairly quickly. One thing that helped a lot was that on my other beats—college football and basketball—the games were played on Saturdays, and I was on tight deadlines.

After a few years, Telecopiers came in, and every writer had to carry around one of these thirty-five- or forty-pound Telecopiers in addition to his typewriter. My paper decided to go to a dictation system, where you'd call into a recorder and dictate your story. That could be done in the press box or late at night at the hotel. That was good in one sense in that you had a lot of time to write. But it also meant that you'd be on the phone forever, spelling out words and giving punctuation.

You knew that the AM guys would have all the basic information in their stories. The thing that Si kept pounding into me was, "If you're not going to get it first, you have to write it better." I took a lot of pride in that. That became kind of a mantra for me. I felt I gave a really informative story. Being splashy was not my way. What I did was solid; that was my key word.

With home games, sometimes I would write in the press box and then drop the story off at the office. We didn't use Western Union at home games, I guess for money reasons. I would drive to the office, drop my story off, and go home. But countless times, I'd be driving home and say, "Why didn't I write *this*? Why didn't I write *that*?" So I'd turn around, go back to the office, and rewrite the lead or the top. That was where I felt my dedication really paid off. If you have time to make it better, sit down and spend another twenty or thirty minutes to make the story the way you really think it ought to be done.

I definitely feel I was a better writer than reporter. You have to be a reporter if you're on a beat, but then you have to know what to do with the information after you get it. I felt my strong point was being able to put out a story that I was happy with and that the readers wanted to read. In the back of my mind, I wanted to please Si Burick. I wanted to make him proud of me.

One story I'm very proud of was about a no-hitter by George Culver, who wasn't one of your more noted no-hit pitchers. It came in the second game of a twi-night doubleheader at Philadelphia in 1968. From a writing standpoint, you'd like to be able to not spend a lot of time on it, because you've had so much to write about already from the first game. I ended up writing my game story primarily about the no-hitter and then a column on George Culver as a person. It got big play, and I got phone calls from both Si and the managing editor.

See, for the last four or five years that I was the Reds beat writer, I also did a column. Si told me to start thinking in terms of being a columnist, because he wasn't going to be there forever. With the Culver thing, I already had a column done, but there was so much good stuff with Culver that I ripped it up and started over. Culver was known as a clotheshorse, and he had all these fancy outfits, a very colorful and flakey guy. It lent itself to a column as well as a game story. I finally wound up dictating that thing at about five in the morning. It was a long but very productive and proud night.

I keep running into people who have never seen a no-hitter. Well, I've seen *eleven* major league no-hitters, and one of them was a perfect game by Tom Browning. I covered seven of them. There was one in particular that stands out, and it has to do with Hal McCoy.

Hal was my backup for the last couple of years I was on the Reds beat. Whenever I needed an off day, I would call Hal and tell him to take the game. So this one week in 1971, I called Hal and told him to take Thursday's game. Well, something came up later where I had to be in Cincinnati anyway, so I called Hal and said, "Never mind. I have to be in Cincinnati anyway. I'll cover the game." And

Ken Holtzman pitched a no-hitter that night for the Cubs against the Reds.

Hal was all over me, saying, "I've never seen a no-hitter. That was my game. . . . How can I forgive you?" and all that. So about three weeks later, I had him pick up another game. Rick Wise pitched a no-hitter against the Reds and hit two home runs. Hal said, "I can forgive you now."

Hal succeeded me on the Reds beat, and I never could have imagined he would stay as long as he did. Absolutely not. I thought he'd maybe move on to a big city paper because he was obviously a very good writer, interesting, entertaining, and ambitious.

By the late '60s, we had Johnny Bench coming on. At one point, we had a battery of Bench and Gary Nolan, and they were both teenagers. Pete Rose was maybe the best hitter in the game. Tony Perez had really established himself as a star. Lee May was emerging as a big hitter. You could see it coming together. Dave Bristol was the manager, and he was a strong developmental guy.

It was really a fun team to cover. Then Sparky Anderson was hired as manager. We had the big breakthrough in 1970 when they won the pennant, then in 1971 they had a total collapse. They lost on Opening Day and never even got to .500 for the rest of the season. Then [general manager] Bob Howsam made the big trade with Houston for Joe Morgan and Jack Billingham, and it was magic from then on.

*   *   *

By 1970 I had never even considered any other job other than newspapers. My life up to that time was geared toward being a sportswriter. I couldn't see myself leaving the newspaper business. Never even gave it a thought. But [the PR job] came up very suddenly. Bob Howsam wanted to talk to me about it, and I said sure. You never want to turn down anything without talking about it; you never know what it might lead to.

I had a meeting with Dick Wagner, who did the interviewing for Howsam. This is a week before Christmas in 1970. At that time our kids were small, eleven and eight. We had recently moved into a new house, and everything was almost perfect in my life. I thought, do I want to move my family, new schools and all that? The PR job sounded really interesting but I wasn't ready to make that kind of decision. I turned them down, and Roger Ruhl was hired.

But the more I thought about it—and I thought about it a *lot* that winter—the one thing about my job was that home games involved a lot of driving. It was always an hour drive into Cincinnati or an hour and a half to Ohio State. Drive, drive, drive, all the time. Because of that, I didn't spend more time with my family when the team was home as opposed to when it was on the road.

The thought of working for a major league team got more and more exciting. I'd always loved the game, the money would have been better, and so on. So by the following year, I said to Howsam, "This was really a tough decision. I hope that if the position ever opens again, you'll consider me again." And he said, "Well, I'll certainly keep that in mind."

Two years later, Howsam called me and said, "Well, are you ready to talk again?" I said yes. I talked to Si about it, and he said, "Well, I really thought you'd do this. I wasn't surprised when you turned it down the first time, but when they came to you again I thought you'd take it. You have a great future here, and you have a great chance to succeed me when I retire, but I realize there's a draw there."

But let me stress this: I was *not* unhappy at the paper, not by any means. The Reds PR job was a fresh challenge, and I was ready for it, when maybe I wasn't ready the first time around. The Reds were the team I'd rooted for all my life. But if that second chance at the job hadn't come around, I'd probably still be at the *Daily News* and be very happy there.

I was *very* comfortable as a beat writer. But the biggest factor [in leaving] was that I thought it was really going to be fun and exciting to work for a major league team, particularly the one I had grown up rooting for. One of the things that helped my success as a PR man was that I knew what the reporters went through. I knew what they were looking for, and it enabled me to help them do their job.

You like to think you could adapt to the changing times. If you'd been a baseball writer for twenty years and the business changed gradually over that time, then yes, I think you could do it. Now, could you have stopped, say, in 1972 and picked it up again in 2002? Then no, I don't think I could have done it. It's a totally different business today.

In those days, pretty much every beat writer traveled on the team charter. You didn't have to make plane reservations or hotel reservations. Today, everything is airline miles and hotel points. Nobody would think of staying in the team hotel if they can get points someplace else. That's changed more than anything, probably. You rode on the team bus to the ballpark, to the airport; you were part of the team on everything.

And yet you still had total freedom. I never felt any pressure, because I traveled with the team, that I had to take it easy on them or overlook things. I never felt that in any way. It was just an accepted thing—you traveled with the team, you stay with the team, and you deal with it.

The reason Hal McCoy retired from the paper was that the *Daily News* made a decision that they were no longer going to cover the Cincinnati Reds. They'd been covered like a home team since 1956 until the end of the 2009 season, and now they don't even cover home games. They don't cover *anything*, not the Reds, not Ohio State, not the Bengals. That's how much the newspaper business has changed. They don't cover things that aren't even a tank of gas away. They've virtually eliminated their sports department. It's sad to think about. Really sad.

16

NICK PETERS

Nick the Greek. Nick from the 'Stick. Nick the Hall of Famer.

The man who covered more San Francisco Giants games than anyone in the team's history—nearly five thousand—handled the Giants beat from 1980 through 2007, but Nick Peters's five-decade sportswriting career began with a two-month stint at the San Francisco Chronicle *back in 1961. Moving quickly to the* Berkeley Gazette, *he served as sports editor there for fifteen years before taking over the Giants beat for the* Oakland Tribune *and its experimental prototype,* East Bay Today, *in 1979. In 1988, Nick joined the* Sacramento Bee *and continued on the Giants beat until 2007, retiring—as he wryly puts it—"on the same day as Barry Bonds."*

Son of a Greek deli owner, Peters earned baseball writing's highest honor in 2009 when he was named winner of the Spink Award. A BBWAA member since 1964 and the author of five books on the Giants, Peters was mentored in his early years by another Spink winner, the Chronicle's *Bob Stevens. During his years on the beat, he was also the Giants correspondent for* The Sporting News *and* Sports Illustrated.

The Bay Area native also covered the Athletics, 49ers, Warriors, the University of California, and three Olympic Games, including an emotional trip to his ancestral home for the 2004 Summer Games in Athens. This jazz lover and world traveler takes pride in maintaining his streak of having attended every Giants home opener since the team moved west in 1958, continuing a baseball love affair that began when he first looked out his bedroom window and saw the lights shining at 16th and Bryant.

My dad's grocery was a few blocks from the San Francisco newspaper offices, so he knew that sportswriters drank, and he was afraid I'd become a drunk. About five years into my job, I drove by his store in my MGB sports car with a blonde. He asked one of my friends, "What kind of a job is that?" My pal replied, "It looks like a pretty good one."

We lived on the top floor of a three-story Victorian home, next to the Bay Bridge. I could see the lights of Seals Stadium, where the minor league San Francisco Seals played, over on 16th and Bryant. We were on 3rd Street, so it was about thirteen blocks away. I could see those lights, and I always wondered what was going on there, as a little kid. I started going to games in 1951 with a buddy from junior high. We bought baseball cards, and I'm still an avid collector. I have millions of cards, and I sort them by stars and teams and years, and it keeps me busy.

My dad took me to my first game, but I didn't start getting interested in baseball until I was about twelve years old in 1951. I worked at my father's store on weekends, and he always had the re-created major league games on the radio . . . the Liberty Network with Gordon McLendon and Al Helfer, where they would do play-by-play, off-the-ticker reports and have canned crowd noise and all that corny stuff. I mention re-created games now to people, and they don't know what I'm talking about. But that's how we got the Yankees and the Red Sox all the time, so I fell in love with Ted Williams and hated the Yankees.

I saw my first televised glimpse of a big league game in 1951 when they put a small black-and-white TV in the auditorium at Aptos Junior High, the playoff game in which Bobby Thomson hit his home run. Seeing the Giants win the pennant on that little screen must have made an impression on me, because ten years later I was covering them.

*   *   *

When I got to City College of San Francisco, I had a teacher named Joan Nourse. Nourse Auditorium is named after her father, who was a city officer. Joan, it seemed, had a pipeline to the *Chronicle*. There were so many people who went from City College, to Cal or Stanford or San Jose State, and then they wound up on the *Chronicle*. She took a liking to me, and I knew my path was being cleared.

At the *Chronicle*, I was the low man on the totem pole. I got to write some headlines, and I wrote one banner, "Spahn Wins 300th Game." That's the only headline that I remember writing at the *Chronicle*.

Bob Stevens was the baseball writer then. The Giants were the only team in town. The A's hadn't come out yet, so with Stevens on the beat, there was no future in baseball writing on the paper. I told Art Rosenbaum, the editor, that I wanted to do some writing. I had been sports editor in junior high, editor of the paper in junior college, and sports editor at San Jose State.

I grew up reading Bob. He had covered the minor league Seals, and he also covered the World Series in those days. The *Chronicle* was the paper of record in San Francisco, and he was the baseball writer of record. I started delivering the *Chronicle* in the early '50s, and I just had an affinity for that paper.

Bob was the ultimate professional in those days. He was a constant. I started reading him in '51, and I read him until he retired in the late '70s. He was my idol. When I decided to become a baseball writer, he was the biggest influence on me.

There was an opening in Berkeley on a four-man staff. The sports editor was a guy named Jim Scott. He'd written a lot of books, and he was prominent in Berkeley, covering Cal sports. When I went over there, I got my feet wet for about two months, then I was drafted into the army for the Cuban Missile Crisis. I hated it because it cut short my career, but while I was in Alaska I went out to dinner and ran into the public information officer. I told him about my background, and he got me into the information office instead of the infantry.

So he saved me. I was also writing for the weekly *Fort Richardson Pioneer* and was twice voted the Alaska Sportswriter of the Year. In my Hall of Fame speech at Cooperstown, I mentioned that the highlight of my career in Alaska was that I was able to see Russia.

While I was in Alaska, I arranged furloughs so I could attend the Giants' Opening Day. I also arranged it so I could go to the World Series in '62, which I covered for the Anchorage paper as well as the

Gazette. Now, I thought that would be an annual occurrence, with all the superstars the Giants had. But if I didn't go to the '62 Series, I would have had to wait until 1989.

*   *   *

When I broke in, the baseball beat was the best job on the paper. They had four or five columnists. Now, the papers have one or two columnists, and that's the prestige spot. The baseball writer doesn't have the prestige that he used to have.

Today, you have to be a columnist to make any money. I never worried about money. I made some money doing freelance work. I worked for the wires; I kept stats. In the NBA, I introduced play-by-play sheets to the Warriors in the early '70s. I had to augment my income because I wasn't being paid much at a small paper in Berkeley. I did the Warriors for UPI, the Giants for the AP, and I was on the Warriors stats crew.

I would have been perfectly happy to have stayed at the *Berkeley Gazette* with a seventy-five-thousand circulation, and it wouldn't have bothered me. I loved the work, and I wasn't driven by ego. I couldn't last today, because you have to be a TV star now. It's a different mentality. I was a quiet kid growing up, and I worried about the work. That's all that mattered to me.

The *Oakland Tribune* made me an offer in 1979. I was the first sports guy they went after, and they told me I could cover the Giants full-time. The lure of being a traveling beat writer made me do it, that's the bottom line. I could cover a baseball team on the road and at home. That was the big appeal. At Berkeley, I didn't travel except to L.A.

When I came on the Giants beat, I was a quiet kid, and I was in awe of those older guys. I didn't make a big splash. The only thing I was known for then was growing a beard around 1966. I was ahead of the curve, but I was in Berkeley, and it was perfectly natural. I remember some of the writers were pretty straitlaced in those days and didn't like it. Bob Stevens never showed me any animosity when I grew the beard.

I was always amazed at Bob's ability to dictate his story after a game. At night games, he would get on the phone with nothing written out and just start dictating. They had early deadlines, so Bob didn't even write. He just dictated over the phone. I never saw anyone else do it like he did.

When I was traveling the beat for twenty-eight years, I was always writing for an AM paper. I had to rewrite for the *Oakland Tribune* when I went to *East Bay Today*, but that was just moving paragraphs around, more or less.

I was always a stickler for making deadline. I think I might have missed three deadlines in forty-seven years of newspaper work. I was thinking of the desk, and I didn't want anybody to worry about it. When I was in Berkeley I was sports editor, so I demanded the same of myself that I did of my writers. I'm always on time, and I get pissed when people aren't, you know?

I think I was a better reporter than a writer. There were a lot of good writers in my day, like Wells Twombly. I knew guys were better writers, but I thought I would have an edge by outworking people. I used to do twelve-hour days in Berkeley. I'd get in early to put out the paper, then I'd go to the Giants game or the Warriors or the 49ers. It didn't seem like a job to me, ever.

I was satisfied with the beat work, because I was able to travel. One of my passions is traveling, so I combined the two. Baseball is the best travel sport because you get into a city for three days; you can hunt around and see things. I did the NBA for one year with the Warriors, in 1979–1980, the year that Larry Bird and Magic Johnson broke in. I hated it. I think I was in Portland on Christmas Day, and that bothered me.

Baseball was the ideal beat job. And it still is, if you're not homesick. I had an understanding wife. My daughter didn't live with me because I got divorced at an early age. But my second wife was very understanding, and she accompanied me on a few trips every year. We made it work.

*   *   *

Competition drove me more than circulation and a quest to be popular. I never shared information with any of my fellow scribes, and I was always looking for a different angle. With competition fading along with newspapers today, it seems that everyone is in bed with each other.

I never wanted to get too close to the players, because I came up in an era where criticism was encouraged and important. I thought that a lot of the old-time writers, as good as they were, were in bed with some of the players, and they protected them. They wouldn't say anything bad about them because their access would be cut off. I never worried about that.

In my early years, the players were pretty good because you had access to them. There were only three or four beat writers, and we all had our moments with the players. You could go up to a Willie Mays and ask him a question, guys like Juan Marichal and Willie McCovey. I had trouble only with Gaylord Perry, because he was from the South, and he didn't like my beard. He always told me that. But now he's more gentle, and he's gotten a lot of anger out of his system. I always knew where he was coming from, and I think he's mellowed. He's very friendly to me now.

I believe the '60s were the best era in baseball because the game was fully integrated by then, and the NL had the edge because of Mays, Clemente, McCovey, Aaron, Orlando Cepeda, Frank Robinson, and Marichal.

Barry Bonds became a sensational story because he became bigger than the team, and I didn't like that. And of course, the clubhouses were always packed when he was chasing records, and that limited your access. And he wasn't a friendly guy, one-on-one, either. At least in his early years with the Giants, you could get a one-on-one with him. But after he became a superstar, every time you went in there, he was surrounded by people, by media, by PR folks telling you, "One more question." I wanted to do my own work; I didn't want to ride on anyone's back to get a story. I just didn't like the commotion.

I know some baseball writers quit because of that. They couldn't take it. They were used to the old days of unlimited access when you could do your own work without much interference. That's not the case anymore, if a player is a big star. I mean, the overkill on the LeBron James thing, his so-called Decision, made me sick.

*   *   *

The beat job wouldn't be as appealing to me today. First of all, only two or three guys travel per team today. The *Sacramento Bee* doesn't cover baseball anymore, so if I were still there I wouldn't be on the beat. The job isn't as much fun. We had six or seven guys traveling with the team, and we did a lot of things together.

I'd like to mention this: baseball fed my love of travel. We would take a train from Montreal to New York. We took trains whenever we could; I wanted to simulate what it was like in the old days. I didn't especially like plane travel, so we drove a lot. I'd take a car, and we'd go from Cincinnati to Pittsburgh, three or four of us.

I also had other interests. In Berkeley, I did jazz interviews and travel articles. I could have been a jazz critic or a travel writer, and that would have satisfied me. Along the way, I interviewed Duke Ellington and Sarah Vaughan and Nat King Cole. I love music, and whenever I got to New York, I'd go to the Blue Note. I wasn't just stuck to the ballpark. I went into cities with a plan to do other things.

I haven't missed a Giants home opener since they moved out in '58. In 2008, after I had retired, I was in Australia. I landed back at the airport at eleven, and the game started at one. That was my closest call.

My biggest story wasn't a baseball story. It was covering the Olympics in Greece in 2004, where I could explore my heritage. I'd been to Greece before; I have relatives there. My dad was the only sibling that came over to America, and the three other siblings stayed in Greece. I have a lot of cousins back there. How do they feel about their famous American cousin? They haven't got a clue. Baseball isn't big in Greece.

My one regret is that I covered the Giants for forty-seven years and I never got a World Series winner. It mystifies me, with all the Hall of Famers they've had, they just ran out of luck when it came to the postseason. I covered Cal for about thirty years, and they never went to a Rose Bowl. I covered a lot of losers, and I didn't have the euphoria of being on the beat with a championship team. I did cover the A's when they won the three straight World Series in the '70s and the Warriors when they won the NBA title in '75, and that's the only taste I've had of success. I don't want to have that reputation!

When I broke in, it was the dawning of the Golden Age of Bay Area sports. The Raiders came in 1960, the A's in 1968, the Giants in 1958, and the Warriors from Philadelphia in 1962. It was a cornucopia of success at the start, so my timing was impeccable.

Winning the Spink Award was a great honor. I was so happy the guys kept putting me on the ballot. I was really flattered and humbled by it. I never aspired to it. It's important to me, but my life wouldn't have changed except from calls from people like you. I got a lot of notoriety, but I didn't need it. I was satisfied with my job, and I didn't have to prove anything.

The day I got the Spink Award, Sandy Koufax, Jim Rice, Eddie Murray, and Steve Carlton all came up to me and congratulated me. I told them, "You guys said more to me today than you did during the fifty years I was a baseball writer."

* * *

In 2010, Nick Peters finally saw the Giants win a world championship, their first in fifty-six years. During the team's emotional October run, their postgame media availability at AT&T Park was held in the newly-renamed Nick Peters Interview Room.

17

GORDON VERRELL

As comfortable at a college baseball field in Long Beach as in the dug-out at Dodger Stadium, Gordon Verrell personified the day-in-day-out baseball beat for two generations of Southern California readers.

The native Californian got his first full-time taste of newspaper work on the Pomona Progress-Bulletin *in 1961. After a two-year army hitch in Virginia, he returned to the* Progress-Bulletin *in 1964.*

Five years later, in 1969, Verrell joined the Long Beach Inde-pendent and Press-Telegram, *his home base for the next thirty-five years. He took over the paper's Dodgers beat in mid-1969 (succeed-ing future Dodgers general manager Fred Claire) and manned it for twenty-seven seasons, from 1969 through 1995. He spanned the ex-ecutive and managerial reigns of Walter and Peter O'Malley, Walter Alston, and Tommy Lasorda. He covered five Dodgers NL pennant winners and the world championship teams of 1981 and 1988.*

When the paper discontinued the daily Dodgers beat in 1995, Verrell covered Long Beach State athletics for nearly a decade before retiring in 2004. A BBWAA member since 1969, national chairman in 1990, and five-time Los Angeles chapter chairman, he served as an official scorer at Dodger Stadium from 2000–2004, using the earn-ings to purchase his beloved John Deere riding mower. A longtime resident of Huntington Beach, he retired in 2004 to Newport News, Virginia, where he dotes on his ten grandchildren.

I considered myself an extension of the fan. That was one way of looking at it. You had that access to the clubhouse that the guy paying for the ticket didn't. I always felt that the guy who went to the game or watched on TV read your story far more closely than the guy who hadn't. He's looking to see if you saw it the way he saw it. That's who you're really writing for.

We missed a road game once, or really played it down or something, and the sports editor told me, "That's only 1/162nd of a season." I came back and said, "Yeah, but 90 percent of the time, that's more important than anything else that's going on today." The way I looked at it, every game, *every* game, was its own drama. Sure, some were duds; a lot of them were. Sometimes you'd write losses that were a lot better than wins.

I think all baseball writers felt that way. You closely guard that beat, and when they want to cut back on stuff, you gotta tell them no, this is baseball. Baseball was it. It's your job. You did it day after day after day, and you acquired a feel for when something was going on, just the way guys were. It's just a feel. So you start poking around.

Like the Steve Garvey–Don Sutton fight in New York. That was really a bizarre day. Milton Richman was in the manager's office talking to Tommy Lasorda, and then all of a sudden there was a scuffle. No other media people were in the clubhouse. Then the press box at Shea Stadium just filled up because Milton put out a bulletin. I remember getting a call in the press box, and, admittedly, none of us knew it. Then you went down and saw Garvey had a black eye. That press box was something, just the New York guys and us on a quiet Sunday afternoon. But by the end of the game, it looked like a World Series.

You kind of evolve into working in the sports department of a newspaper. It started with covering high schools and walking up and down the sidelines in the rain at a football game. I enjoyed that. In fact—and I'm jumping way ahead—I'm covering a high school game in Long Beach years later, and the windows of the press box were so dirty you couldn't see out them. So I said the hell with this and just stood on the sidelines. Somebody who knew me yelled out, "Hey, what are you doing here? You should be with the Dodgers." I was kidding around, and I said, "Hey, this is the most important thing going on because they sent *me* here!" Somebody's gotta cover it, and I'm certainly not above that sort of thing.

*   *   *

My first job out of college in 1960 was in Redlands. The Angels were formed the following year, and I had an Angels press pass. I went to Wrigley Field, and there I am sitting in the back of the press box, watching the guys pounding on the old typewriters. I just sat there looking, and I said to myself, "Man, that would be great." So it just kind of worked its way into my dim head.

I came back to California, to the *Pomona Progress-Bulletin*, after I was in the service in Virginia. Then my life was changed by a game of golf.

One day Fred Claire was playing golf with a bunch of circulation guys. This is in May of 1968, when Ross Newhan left Long Beach to go to the *Times*. Fred left the Pomona paper and got Newhan's old job in Long Beach. The following spring, George Lederer, who had covered the Dodgers since they came to L.A., went to the Angels as their public relations director.

So Claire is playing golf with the sports editor of the Long Beach paper, John Dixon. Dixon mentions to Fred that they had another baseball opening and is there anyone at the Pomona paper who could do it? Fred mentioned Jerry Miles and myself. Jerry said to me, "You're going to get a phone call." I did, and I went down to meet John Dixon and got hired. It was terrific, a great break and all that.

But then we went through about a week and a half of Fred vacillating on whether to stay on the Angels beat or succeed Lederer on the Dodgers beat. Fred finally decided to go with the Dodgers, and I always used to kid him that if he had stayed on the Angels, *I'd* have wound up as the general manager of the Dodgers. So I got the Angels beat.

Then, halfway through the '69 season, Fred gets the job with the Dodgers in the PR department with Red Patterson. So now I've got to make the choice: stay with the Angels or go on the Dodger beat. I figured I'd do the Dodgers because even if something went wrong, if I got sick of it or something, I could say that I'd seen every team and every ballpark in the majors.

Bob Hunter was my mentor. He was a terrific writer back in the old days of the *Los Angeles Examiner*, when the *Herald Express* was a separate, afternoon Hearst paper. He covered the Angels and the Hollywood Stars, and his column at that time was called "Bobbin' Around."

He was really an old-style writer. When Casey Stengel was managing in the Pacific Coast League, he'd come into Wrigley Field, and they had a press room right in that tower behind home plate, and Casey would hold court with the writers all night. Lefty O'Doul with San Francisco, too. Bob was great for telling stories like that. Now I come on the beat and, my gosh, here's this guy who's just about my idol.

Here's really all you need to know about Bob Hunter. My first year on the beat is 1969, and the All-Star Game that year is in Washington. I'm picking up the Dodgers right after the break, in Chicago. I don't know anybody; remember, I was on the Angels beat the first half of that season.

That first day, on the bus in front of the Executive House Hotel in Chicago, we get on, and then Hunter gets on; he'd just flown in from Washington. All he knows is that there's a new guy on the beat. He sat down next to me, and we chatted all the way out to Wrigley Field. That was a real eye-opener for me because, growing up in Los Angeles, I had watched minor league ball at Wrigley Field in L.A. Now I'm going to the real Wrigley Field.

Well, Hunter literally took me by the hand and introduced me to this guy, to that guy, to whoever. Leo Durocher is managing the Cubs, and Hunter said to me, "Do you know Leo Durocher?" I said, well, I'd seen him and stuff, but I didn't know him at all. "Okay," said Hunter. "We're going to meet Leo."

Well, the clubhouse was all the way out in the left field corner, and we go out there. First we saw Yosh Kawano, the clubhouse guy, who's the brother of Nobe Kawano, who worked for the Dodgers. I didn't know that, either. We finally go into Leo's office, and if I remember correctly, the desk was sitting up there, almost like a throne. Leo came out, and there are big hellos and everything. "I want you to meet one of our new writers," Bob said. "Gordie Verrell, one of the good guys." Now, Bob knew me for twenty minutes, and now he's introducing me to Leo Durocher as one of the good guys. That's something I never forgot.

The paper retired Bob. Then the *Daily News* hired him as a columnist, and that may have saved his life, because I don't know what

he'd have done without it. He still made the trips, but he started having medical problems. He went down a few times in spring training,
and they finally gave him a pacemaker. We all went down to see him,
and he's bitching that the warranty for the thing was only fifty years.
He was seventy-eight at the time.

Bob was called Chopper because of the way he chopped his poker
chips in Vero Beach. He'd bail out of the games early and spend the
rest of the night chopping his chips. After he got the pacemaker, he
became RoboChop.

*   *   *

Even after, say, five years, you're still learning what to do, when to
do it, who to talk to. One of the things, early on, was Jerry Holtzman talking to me about the umpires. He said, "On the first game of
a series, knock on the door, say hello, and tell them to have a good
series." I did that nearly every series, and I got to know every umpire
in the National League. I figured, who's closer to the game than the
umpires? I'd get a feeling, a mood, of what was going on. And con-
sequently, where there'd be an incident involving the umpires, I was
the one they'd talk to.

Here's a great umpire story, featuring the late John McSherry.
We're at the Missouri Bar and Grill in St. Louis. We, the newspaper
guys, come in after traveling from wherever we'd been. McSherry
had umpired that afternoon—it was a Sunday—and the next day he
was going to fly on to his next series. The place is packed; it's a
newspaper bar right across from the old *Globe-Democrat*. They had
all the food and drink on one side and a little entertainment on the
other side, and there'd be a girl at the door charging admission, two
dollars or three dollars. Rick Hummel had told the girl that if anyone
came in wearing one of those baseball writers golf shirts—remember
those? We'd charge like five dollars each for them—it was as good as
admission.

Suddenly the gal behind the bar started screaming, and I heard
her say, "That better not be a kangaroo!" Some guy walked into the
bar with a kangaroo! He had it in a gunny sack, and people were petting it and everything. The girl who was at the door came over and
started petting the kangaroo, and then she asked the guy, "Do you
have a koala?"

Well, McSherry went nuts. He said, "If that doesn't tell you all you need to know about a woman! Guy walks into a bar on a Sunday night in St. Louis with a kangaroo, and she wants a koala!" I just fell down when I heard that.

*   *   *

One of the things Bob Hunter always said to me was, "Look, I'm going to get a story. You're going to get a story. We're all going to get our stories." Meaning that, on our own, we'll all get stuff. I remember Mike Marshall, the great relief pitcher. Everybody hated him, but I got along with him great. He was difficult and all that, but I saw him at an old-timers game, and we had a great get-together, and then I saw him in Florida when he was coaching at St. Leo's College.

In 1975, he didn't sign a contract. That was the same year Andy Messersmith didn't sign and wound up turning the whole thing upside down. Now it's sometime in August. Marshall and I got into some sort of discussion about if he ever wanted to manage. I asked him about it, and he gave me an answer, which ended with, "But it'll have to wait because I signed my contract today."

Well, I practically pushed him back into his locker. "You *what*??" I said. So he's telling me how much money he's getting, the whole deal. There was deferred money, which the Dodgers had *never* done before. I thought I had a helluva story, and I know they have to announce it. I get upstairs, read the game notes, and there's nothing. Now, there's no way I can ask the GM, Al Campanis. So I quoted Marshall saying he signed the contract, with "the *Press-Telegram* learned" and all that.

Next day, the club's left for New York. I didn't make that trip. I got a call at about nine in the morning; it's Ross Newhan calling from the airport, "Okay, where'd you get the story?" He'd gotten the paper, and they blew the story up big. Then, after they fly, Ross called me from New York, and he's describing the scene in the lobby of the Waldorf-Astoria. He said the rooms are almost ready, the keys are ready . . . and they have suites ready for Mr. Alston, the manager; Mr. Scott, the traveling secretary; and Mr. Marshall. Ross found out that part of the deal was that Marshall got a suite on the road. This is why you don't miss trips. Yeah, it costs money. But if you're gonna cover the team, you gotta cover the team. And those games on the road count just as much as the games at home.

With Walter Alston, you'd go in and ask him a question, and you got an answer. With Tommy Lasorda, in my mind at least, he felt you were second-guessing him. You had to convince him that, no, this is just what I want to know. Why'd you do this when you had this other guy warming up? Did he have a sore arm? We'd get into more arguments with Tommy, and then the next day, of course, everything was fine. It was just Tommy's nature.

Walter wasn't a colorful guy. One thing Tommy boasted of, and rightfully so, was that he knew the names of every one of his players' kids, including, as he'd say, "Manny Mota's Eight." He knew the names, the kids, and the wives. Walter didn't know anybody's name except for what he *had* to know. He knew my name, but if I was still working in Pomona, he wouldn't have known and wouldn't have cared. That's just the way he was.

Walter would sit in the dugout, night after night, watching batting practice. If you needed to talk to him, there he was. He'd say things like, "That number 27 can really swing the bat." Always the number. We're talking about Willie Mays one time, and Walter said, "God, every time we play those guys, it seems that Willie Mays is always on deck."

Now, how do you say who's better? They both had success, they're both in the Hall of Fame, they both should have won other times when they didn't. In '62 they didn't win with Walter, in '80 they didn't beat out Houston with Tommy, and in '82 they didn't beat out Atlanta. They were both great, in their way. They were totally different, though. You learned a lot of baseball from both of them.

* * *

Vero Beach was my second home. I just loved Vero, loved the town. I was born in Los Angeles, but I was never a big city guy. Vero was a small town where you knew everybody.

There was a guy named Dick Bird, who was a golf pro and the general manager of Dodgertown. He was from Vero Beach, knew everything and everybody, and he put the lid on problems that would arise.

In the early '70s, they still had the old barracks at Dodgertown. They'd just built the new motel-type units. The major leaguers were in the new units, and of course, so were the writers. The minor leaguers were in the old barracks. Now, I'm thrilled that I was in the barracks those first few years. If Sandy Koufax and Jackie Robinson and Duke Snider had stayed in those barracks, it was fine by me.

Tommy Lasorda was managing Albuquerque, the minor league club. Tommy knew I was in one of the new rooms, with a TV, a phone, and all the stuff we didn't have in the old barracks. I'm sure that he went to Dick Bird and told him, "Hey, Gordie Verrell wants me to move in with him. He's got an extra bed in his room." Then Tommy came to me and said, "Dick Bird says I gotta move in with you." I *know* that's how that went down. That's how Tommy got out of the barracks; he was my roommate for one year.

In Vero Beach, you'd get out of bed in the morning, and you were right there. They had the press room, the bar, and all of that. Later it became a conference center, and I guess it still is today, with no team there. I still think that the best thing that could happen to that town would be if the Orioles moved into Dodgertown for spring training. You need an East Coast, cold-weather team in there. People in Baltimore go to Florida. Who in L.A. goes to Florida?

* * *

The day I was elected national chairman of the baseball writers was the day of the earthquake in San Francisco, in 1989. At the Hall of Fame inductions the following year, I'm sitting around the pool at the hotel, writing a column about how "your reporter," meaning me, is going to introduce this guy and that guy. This was when Jim Palmer and Joe Morgan went into the Hall. I was writing that it was a beautiful day in Cooperstown, and, "What can happen now? It couldn't rain, could it?"

Sure enough, it rained. Rained the whole thing out, rained again the next day. They finally held it in the high school gym. I'm sitting in what was considered the green room, looking over my notes and then, about ten minutes before we started, looked around the room. *Everybody* is in there. Ted Williams, Bob Lemon, Koufax and Drysdale, Johnny Bench, Yogi. They're all Hall of Famers . . . and me. Oh, my gosh. What a moment.

I would get a kick out of when Dick Young and Jerome Holtzman would go at it in the writers' meetings. They were so dedicated to their cause, it was inspirational to watch them battle. And they were all battling for the same thing. . . . It was all about access. They did it like they were in a courtroom: "Would the chairman please . . ." and all that. There would be a rant, and then the other one would say, "If it may please the membership . . ." It was passionate and wonderful to see. Those two guys championed our cause beautifully, about clubhouse access and our importance within the game. They'd argue with each other a lot but ultimately about the same things.

There were guys on the beat when I was covering who didn't particularly like the game. I'm not going to mention any names. It was a job, but it was an honor to take this great game and write about it. You can oversimplify it by thinking that all you did was write about a bunch of guys playing ball. But that's what you did because people paid money to watch those guys play. But it was never about the money. A guy making an error still had to 'fess up to it whether he was making $5,000 a year or $500,000 a year. You're asking him the same questions that the guy in the fifth row wants to know.

It takes a toll, and it's a twelve-month-a-year job now. My competition came from other papers, for the most part. Now you're competing against television, the Internet, whatever. You can get a call at four in the morning, and there's an outlet where you can put your stuff out there, unlike having to wait for the next day's paper.

What I had a hard time with was days off. They play baseball every day, and you're out there every day. When I was told I'd get a day off, well, how can you take a day off? And it started in spring training. Well, I wasn't going to Key West or Disney World on my day off. I was going to the ballpark. I might not have to write, but something's liable to happen where I'll have to call the desk. There's stuff that's happening every day that's important to the baseball writer . . . but maybe not to the guy on the desk. I had a hard time with that; I still would.

You are the guy from the *Long Beach Press-Telegram*, and you report what's going on, just like the guys on the Lakers beat or the Rams beat or the Kings beat. Baseball's every day, and you cover it every day. You have to be in that locker room every day.

That's one of the things that bothered me about writers being official scorers, where you're paid by the league. My thought was that you're on deadline, then you go downstairs, and you have only fifteen minutes. If you spend ten minutes of it arguing—or even discussing—a call, you're not doing your job for the paper. So it didn't bother me at all when they said no more scoring for the writers. The way they have it now, where the only thing you're doing is scoring, that's the way it ought to be.

I loved the game, truly loved the game. I watch my grandkids playing in the youth leagues, and I get a kick out of that. I also watch the local team here in Newport News. It's baseball, and it's also the people.

The paper pulled the plug on the baseball beat after the '95 season. The next year, I go out to cover a Long Beach State game instead of going to Vero Beach. I'm out there on the campus field, and I'll tell you, it was the same deal. Watching them hit ground balls, the sounds, the smells, the grass, the whole deal. Baseball's baseball. The only thing wrong with it was those damned metal bats. I hated those things then, and I still do.

18

BILL MADDEN

Every year, for decades, Bill Madden attended the annual induction ceremonies at the Baseball Hall of Fame. In 2010 he went to Coopers-town once again, this time as the Spink Award winner.

It was the climax of a forty-year career in baseball writing, which started for the New Jersey native in 1970 at UPI in New York. A protégé of Milton Richman, Madden moved to the Daily News *in 1978, taking over the Yankees beat for nine years starting in 1980. In 1988, he became the paper's national baseball columnist, a position he maintains today. He has covered a total of thirty-five World Series and has also specialized in long-form pieces such as his 1997 feature on Tony Horton, the ill-fated Cleveland first baseman who abruptly left baseball after suffering a nervous breakdown in 1970.*

A BBWAA member since 1972, Madden was the New York chapter chairman in 1980–1981, and made the then-controversial deci-sion to end the legendary baseball writers show. Early in his career, he established himself as one of the early authorities on the baseball collecting business, with a column in The Sporting News. *Madden is the author of five books, including a best-selling 2010 biography of Yankees owner George Steinbrenner.*

I guess I came up with the name Foofs, probably when I was at UPI. Remove the Foofs! It's a combination of a fool and a goof. It was a word I created for the people who didn't belong in the press box, pseudo–radio guys from pseudo–radio stations that no one really knew or knew whom they worked for.

I've always said I've been probably the luckiest guy in the history of New York baseball writing because I had the two best mentors you could possibly have . . . Milton Richman at UPI and Dick Young at the *Daily News*. If you asked, people would probably say I was more of a reporter than a writer. This all goes back to Young. Young always told me that the most important thing is to talk to your readers and give them something they don't know, something they can't get off television and can't get in the other papers. In other words, be a reporter. That's my first instinct.

I was weaned to be a sportswriter by my father. He owned a plumbing supply company, and he would always talk to me about Dick Young. The problem was, my father wouldn't allow the *Daily News* in our house. He considered it a scandal rag. But he had it on the counter down at the County Plumbing Supply in Hackensack. The plumbers would come in, and they'd all bring the *Daily News*, and that's where my father got access to it. He'd never bring the paper home; he'd just tell me how great Dick Young was.

We had the *Herald Tribune* delivered, and my father would make me read it, especially Red Smith, Tommy Holmes, and Harold Rosenthal. My father knew the history of the New York papers, and he knew all about Stanley Woodward, the legendary sports editor of the *Herald Tribune*.

The great story about Woodward was in 1948 when Leo Durocher switched from the Dodgers to the Giants in what still may be the biggest in-season baseball story ever in New York. The editor of the paper told Woodward, "We're taking the Durocher story up front," meaning that they were going to put it on the front page of the paper. To which Stanley Woodward looked at him and said, "Why would you take a great story like that and bury it on Page One?"

I'd use that story whenever they wanted to take one of my stories and put it up front. There's a lot of pride within the sports section. We always believed we carried the paper, not the other way around, and that people buy the newspaper to read the sports first and then get to the rest of it.

*   *   *

How I got to UPI is a classic example of, "It's not what you know, but who you know."

I was at the University of South Carolina on a track scholarship, but after one year, I decided to just be a student. I really wanted to write and went to work for the school paper. I covered the basketball team because they were all New Yorkers, and I knew all those guys. The coach, Frank McGuire, was famous for what was called the underground railway, bringing in recruits from the New York area.

My senior year, I was going to summer school, finishing up my credits, and working part-time for *The State* paper in Columbia. One day the sports editor, a guy named Herman Helms, said, "Billy, Coach McGuire's on the phone. He wants to talk to you."

I get on the phone. How you doing, Coach? He said, "Look, Billy, I don't have a lot of time here. I just got off the phone with Jack Griffin in New York, and you've got the job." Jack Griffin was the sports editor at UPI.

Now, the previous winter, I had been in New York at a hockey game, and at a bar I ran into Dana Mozley, the hockey writer for the *Daily News*. I introduced myself and asked, "How does a guy like me, working in South Carolina, get a job in the newspaper business in New York?" He laughed and said, "Don't even waste your time writing to the *News* or the *Times*. They're not going to hire anybody out of college. What you should do is write to the wire services. They hire people from all over the country. You grew up in New York and went to school in the South. You'd be perfect."

He gave me the name of Jack Griffin at UPI. I wrote to him then totally forgot about it because I never heard back. Now it's the following summer, and Frank McGuire is telling me that I got the job. I said, "Coach, I don't understand. I didn't use you for a reference." He said, "Well, you should have, you stupid bastard. Don't you know that when I was the coach at St. John's, Jack Griffin was my ballboy? Now, you better call Jack Griffin before he changes his mind."

I call Griffin immediately. He laughed and said, "I came across your letter, and as soon as I saw 'University of South Carolina,' I made up my mind that there was only one person on earth that was going to decide whether you got this job or not, and that person was Frank McGuire."

*   *   *

Baseball was my first love, but I would have done anything at UPI. I got my BBWAA card in 1972 and covered a lot of home games. I didn't do any traveling until 1975, when I went to my first spring training with Milton Richman.

Milton was very strict. You never wanted to do anything that would embarrass yourself or UPI or, by connection, Milton. You were always fearful of him because he lived such an exemplary life.

Milton had a lot of different sayings that I'll always remember. The first one was, "Billy, always have your dime," which in those days was what it cost to make a phone call. You'd be somewhere, and if something happened, you'd run to a phone booth and phone it in to the office in New York. That was his first credo: always have your dime.

He taught me how to approach players. He was always very polite and introduced himself even though the players all knew who he was. He was almost fatherly in the way he conducted his interviews.

When I was at UPI, I read *The Sporting News* religiously like everyone did. I got to know a lot of their people through Milton, one of whom was Lowell Reidenbaugh, who was the managing editor and one of the greatest newspaperman I ever knew.

Back in the '50s and into the '60s, *The Sporting News* had these little, tiny ads for baseball card dealers. There were two or three of them; one was named Gordon B. Taylor and another was named Marshall Oreck. They had little ads saying, "Write in for what you want." This was before card stores or anything else. It was a very loose-knit hobby, nothing like the sophisticated thing it is today.

I was one of the few people whose mother didn't throw my baseball cards away. So I called up Lowell Reidenbaugh and said, "I've noticed these little ads for baseball card dealers. Did you ever think of maybe having a column dedicated to baseball cards?" He called me a few weeks later and said, "Send me a sample column." I did, and the next thing you know, he said, "I want you to do this once a month, a column on baseball cards or collecting."

Then Lowell made the column twice a month. About four or five years into it, all of a sudden, the same kinds of columns were popping up in papers across the country. You had card stores going up everywhere. By the mid-eighties, Jim Beckett came out with his card catalog, and this thing just went crazy. I don't want to sound egotistical, but the fact of the matter is that it all started with my column in *The Sporting News*. It was the first mainstream column dealing with sports collecting, mainly baseball.

I wrote about all sorts of memorabilia. In fact, just last year [2009], I wrote a piece assailing the Phillies for putting out the two worst World Series press pins ever, in 2008 and 2009. The next time I see Dave Montgomery, their president, I'm gonna ask him, "What's wrong with you guys? You've been in the World Series two years in a row and did the two worst World Series press pins ever."

It's another reason why baseball isn't what it once was. It's become so corporate. You've got these marketing people, young kids put in these positions who don't know the history of anything like World Series press pins. They don't have a clue that one of the central displays in the Hall of Fame is the World Series pins and the championship rings. If they only knew, if Dave Montgomery only knew, that his cheap, Cracker Jack–box press pins are on display up there next to the Yankees pins, which are beautiful because they know the tradition, they would be appalled.

*   *   *

I was around the *Daily News* people all the time because we were in the same building with them, on 42nd Street. UPI was on the twelfth floor, and the *News* was on the seventh floor. I was pretty well known then because I was UPI's principal baseball writer; I was at the World Series and the winter meetings every year. Dick Young and Phil Pepe and other guys at the *News* would love my stories about Milton.

In 1978, the *News* was looking to hire a baseball writer to back up Pepe on the Yankees beat and Jack Lang on the Mets beat. It just kind of evolved. Young wanted me over there, and to have Young as a mentor after working for Milton, well, you just couldn't have asked for anything better than that.

One of Young's favorite credos was, "Always take care of your beat man." I never forgot that, especially after I became a columnist at the *News* and I would make sure that whatever I got, I gave to the beat guy. In 1984, the Yankees signed Ed Whitson as a free agent. Young called me at home and said, "Aahhh, look, aahhh. They just signed this Whitson guy, three-year contract. Just write it." I said great, is there anything else? "Nahhh, nahhh," he said. "Just write it."

"Well," I said. "I just have one question. What's our source on this?" "Source?" he said. "*I'm* your fucking source!" He had gotten it from Steinbrenner, but he gave it to me because I was the beat guy. Always take care of your beat guy. That's what I was taught to do.

Another thing Young would say was, "Don't be a fucking Hemingway. We don't need any essayists here. Talk to your readers." My style has always been to be as much like Young as possible, in that I try to talk to my readers and get to the point.

I knew I was ready to be a beat guy. It was something I had aspired to my entire life. When the *Daily News* hired me, I was the one guy who was never gonna miss a deadline. At UPI, my deadline was every minute. Most of the stories I did for UPI I dictated over the phone. There's no better training ground than the wire services. I tell that to people today, and they don't even know what the wire services are.

The only thing was, I didn't quite realize what the competition was going to be like. There wasn't anybody more formidable on the Yankees beat than Murray Chass at the *Times*. Then you had Henry Hecht at the *Post* and Moss Klein at the *Star-Ledger*. Moss didn't miss a thing. The best thing I had going for me was that Pepe, who had been moved up to columnist, had also been in that competition. Pepe was a great mentor. He taught me the ropes of the beat, and I always had him to lean on.

I also had no idea what the Steinbrenner factor was going to be. Every time George brought Billy Martin back, it was a new nightmare for all of us. You never knew when something was going to happen.

You couldn't leave the hotel bar until Billy left, and even in that case it didn't always hold up, like in the famous fight in 1985 with Ed Whitson, which continued upstairs in the hotel. I'm dictating my story to the paper, and I hear this commotion outside. There's Billy pounding on Whitson's door down the hall from me; he's in his underwear with his arm in a sling. I feel like I'm back at UPI, dictating a play-by-play of the fight.

The problem with George was that he was an equal-opportunity leaker, with whomever he felt like leaking stuff to on any given day. Then you'd have to clean up the mess. You'd get a call from your editor—"How come this is in the *Post*? How come they have Steinbrenner quotes and we don't?"—and it would be George leaking stuff.

Even if the Yankees were going great, George would be up to something. It was like being a doctor on call.

In 1982, George fires Bob Lemon after fourteen games, after he'd promised him he'd be the manager the whole year. They went through forty-seven players, three managers, five pitching coaches, and three hitting instructors. They wound up in fifth place with seventy-nine wins. Without question, the craziest Yankees year ever.

*　*　*

I would say there were two stories I'm most proud of. One was at UPI, at the 1975 winter meetings at the Diplomat Hotel in Hollywood, Florida. This was when Bill Veeck was trying to repurchase the White Sox. The team was bankrupt; John Allyn was trying to sell them. It was one of those meetings were nothing was happening and we were all bored stiff.

The third day into the meetings, I was sitting on the floor at the end of a hallway with Dave Nightingale of *The Sporting News*. We realize in this hallway that what we thought was a wall was actually only a partition. We heard these voices behind the partition, and it turned out to be the American League meeting. The person speaking was John Fetzer, the owner of the Tigers. I'm listening to this whole thing through the partition.

Fetzer was saying, "I don't like the son of a bitch any more than you guys do, but dammit, we told the guy to go out and get his financing in order. He came back to us and got it in order like we told him to, now we've got to take another vote!" It turned out that the American League had voted Veeck down, and now here's Fetzer, the most respected of all the owners and the polar opposite of Veeck, telling them that they have to vote again.

I'm writing everything down as Fetzer is speaking. I ran over to Milton. Milton's by a phone booth—he had his dime, remember—and I said, "Milton, I've got this unbelievable story. I was sitting by this partition and I overheard the entire American League meeting. They voted Veeck down and then took another vote and voted him in." I give Milton all my notes, and he started dictating the story back to New York. Before the owners got out of the meeting, it was on the wire, Fetzer's exact words! They went crazy. Bob Fishel, the PR man, threatened to have me sanctioned by the baseball writers. Veeck even mentioned it in one of his books, calling me "a young cub reporter from UPI."

The other one, ironically, again involving the White Sox, came in early 1984. They had something called the free agent compensation draft. Basically, it was ultimately what resolved the 1981 strike in that teams that lost free agents could get some kind of compensation. It was a draft in which all the teams could protect around twenty-five players or so in their entire organization.

The White Sox had lost a free agent, and they were the first team to pick in this compensation draft. I had a source, and he called me the day before the draft and said, "I know who the White Sox are taking, and you're not going to believe it." I said, "Who?" And he said, "Tom Seaver." I couldn't believe the Mets would leave him unprotected. "Well," my source said, "I've talked to the White Sox people, and tomorrow they're going to take him."

So I called up Roland Hemond at the White Sox, who has been a dear friend, and Roland would never confirm anything like this. Then I called the Mets, and I asked Jay Horwitz, "Look, I've got a tip on something that is very big, and I've got to get a confirmation on this thing, but you've got to promise me you won't tell any of the other writers. If you do, I'll have you assassinated." So Jay tracked down Frank Cashen, the general manager, who was at a cocktail luncheon.

I said to Frank, "Look, I have this on very good information that you've left Seaver unprotected." Frank said, "I don't know how you would have known that." I said, "I can't tell you how I know it, but I need a confirmation." Frank confirmed that he did, indeed, leave him unprotected.

I said, "I have more bad news for you, Frank. You're going to lose him. The White Sox are taking him." There was silence on the other end of the phone, and finally Frank said, "Well, I don't know what to say. I can't confirm any of that," and he hung up. Sure enough, that's what happened.

Nobody in Chicago had a whiff of it; nobody in New York had a whiff of it. At the time, it was a huge story . . . the Mets leaving Tom Seaver unprotected and losing him, again, for the second time in six years! Later on, Frank explained that the reason they left Seaver unprotected was that he was thirty-nine years old, he was a Mets icon, and the Mets figured they were safe because no one would do that to them. But Hemond's philosophy was that any time you could add another front-line pitcher, you do it. When he saw Seaver's name on the list, his eyes bulged.

* * *

In 1997, I did the piece on Tony Horton, the Indians first baseman who completely dropped out of sight after his nervous breakdown. I was probably more proud of that story than anything I've ever written at the *News*. When I was putting that story together, I almost felt like a detective. One clue after another, connecting all the dots.

In the mid-'70s, when I'm still at UPI, there was a guy named Shelby Whitfield, who was a broadcaster for the Washington Senators. He wrote a book called *Kiss It Goodbye*, which was all about how Bob Short kidnapped the Senators and moved them to Texas. Shelby was on a book tour, and he stopped in New York. Milton told me to go out and meet with Shelby and his publicist.

During the course of our interview, Shelby said, "I couldn't get this in the book because it really didn't have anything to do with the Senators, but during the course of my writing, I had a lot of dealings with Alvin Dark, Ken Harrelson, and Gabe Paul of the Indians. This is maybe something for you because no one has touched this story. If I were you, I'd look into Tony Horton. Do you remember him?" Sure, I said. "Well," he said, "you notice how he's no longer in baseball? That's what you've got to look into."

I went to Milton and said, "Shelby Whitfield told me there's a great story that no one has written, about what happened to Tony Horton." Milton said, "Billy, don't go near that story. Leave it alone." I'm saying to myself, "Wow. If there's anyone with a nose for news, it's Milton. And he's telling me to leave the story alone?" So I did.

Now almost twenty years go by. I'm at the *Daily News*, and this Tony Horton thing is still in the back of my mind. When I was on the Yankees beat, I didn't have time to do a long, enterprising story like this. When I got off the beat, I did occasional long pieces, and it came back to me. I said to myself that I gotta find out what the hell this Tony Horton story is all about.

So I started making phone calls. I knew Ken Harrelson very well because he'd been a Yankees broadcaster. He told me part of it. I called Alvin Dark, the Indians manager at the time, and he told me his part. Gabe Paul was in failing health. Russ Schneider, who was the Indians beat writer back then, gave me a lot of background. I got all these people and found out that Horton had a mental breakdown, but I still didn't have the one final touch as to why he never came back, and why the Indians kept putting out these cryptic press releases about him still recovering.

Schneider told me that some of the Indians players back then stayed at this place called the Blue Grass Motel, outside of Cleveland. I asked Russ if the place was still there. "Nah," he said. "They tore it down years ago. But the guy who owned the place is still in Cleveland." And he gave me his name: Larry Mako.

I looked the guy up, called him, and said, "I'm doing a story on Tony Horton and I'm trying to find out what happened to this guy." "Oh," he said, "I'll never forget that night as long as I live."

Then he told me the whole story. Horton held out that spring because he felt he deserved a raise. He was insanely jealous of Ken Harrelson. Harrelson was a popular guy whom everybody loved; Horton was more of an introvert. He went in for his raise, and Gabe and Alvin tell him there's no money for him. Finally they said that if you don't come to spring training, we're just going to give your job to Harrelson and do without you. He signed the contract, and a few days later, Harrelson slid into third and broke his ankle. That's what set him off.

Now it's late August 1970. Mako told me that one night he came out of the hotel to a car parked outside, and there's Tony Horton with his wrists slit. Mako told me he called the police and the hospital, and the next day Horton's father and the Indians officials came in, cleaned out his room, and, he said, "That was the last we ever saw of him."

Sam McDowell, the great pitcher who later became a counselor for Major League players, told me that part of Horton's treatment afterward was that he could never have anything to do with baseball. I guess that's why Milton didn't want me to pursue the story. In those days, baseball didn't like to have stories like that uncovered, and Milton may have been concerned about lawsuits. I checked with Gene Orza at the Players Association and found out that Horton had never collected anything off his pension. That's how thoroughly he cut his ties with baseball.

Finally, we sent a stringer to Los Angeles, where Horton lived. He knocked on the door, and his father answered. The stringer said, "I'm looking for Tony Horton." The father said, "I don't know if he's here," and just as he said that, here came Tony Horton out of the garage. His father told him, "There's a reporter here to talk to you." Tony said, "Not interested." His father said, "He wants to talk to you about baseball," and Tony said, "Definitely not interested." That was the end of it.

Finding the motel owner was the key to the story, since the suicide attempt was never revealed. I guess why I'm so proud of that story is that it probably never would have come out if Milton hadn't told me, "Billy, stay away from that story." I never had anyone tell me that before. That's why I never forgot about Tony Horton.

*   *   *

I had a very tumultuous two years as New York chapter chairman in 1980–1981, which included being in charge of the show at the writers dinner. The problem was that the show was losing its appeal for a lot of reasons. In the old days, the baseball writers didn't have anything to do in the wintertime. They had plenty of time to put these shows together. They were very good, very clever, and people loved them.

But by the time I took over as chairman, it was like pulling teeth to get anyone to come to the rehearsals. Young would walk in and say, "Ahhhh, I'm doing this song," hand you the music, and you had to fit it into the show somehow. A couple of the previous chairmen had arranged it so that they would sing the signature song at the end of the show, and it was awful. It just wasn't working. I made up my mind that we weren't going to have a show anymore.

Once I made that decision, I said, "Well, what *are* we gonna do?" We had to come up with something that was both entertaining and baseball driven. Someone tipped me off to a comedian named Dennis Blair, who was playing at Dangerfield's. He was very clever and funny; he did a lot of baseball stuff. I went to Dangerfield's with Moss Klein, talked to Dennis, and said, "Look, this is what I need you to do. I need you to save my ass, that's what I need you to do."

Blair was delighted to do it because it was an opportunity to get his name out there. I told him I needed four or five baseball songs with funny lyrics. We went back to Dangerfield's, and he auditioned for us, and I said, "This is perfect, exactly what we need." He was great, but the only problem was, he wasn't the old writers' show.

At the end of my two-year reign of error as New York chairman, we have this roast for the outgoing chairman at the Diamond Club at Shea Stadium. And here comes Young; he's the last of the speakers. He had had a few red wines that night and said, "Well, I know at these roasts it's always traditional to say a lot of funny things about the guy and rip him, and then at the end we say we don't mean any of it and that he's really a good guy. Well, I can't do that tonight. Billy, all I can tell you is . . . you coulda done better."

There was a silence in the room. People were aghast; they couldn't believe it. Here's my mentor up there, putting me down in front of the entire chapter. I was crushed, all because I had gotten rid of the show.

For a good year, I was devastated. I never got over it. I talked to Young's friends and said, "How could he do this to me? I was his guy." They all said, hey, that's just Dick. I said, "Yeah. I know, but geez. Getting rid of the show was no big deal. It was lousy, people were walking out. It had become a joke."

The following year, when we had the next roast, Young got up and said, "Last year, I said a lot of bad things about Billy Madden. I just want to say in front of everyone that I apologize to you." I said to myself, wow. This had to be the first time Dick Young has ever apologized to *anybody* in public.

*   *   *

Obviously, the Spink Award is the culmination of my career. I've covered every Hall of Fame induction ceremony since 1979, and it's going to be very strange being on the other side.

About fifteen years ago, when Bud Selig was the acting commissioner but not the official commissioner, he didn't go to the inductions. I think it might have been a jealousy thing, or something where they didn't want him giving out the plaques because he wasn't officially the commissioner. I told him, "Bud, it doesn't matter. You should be there. The Baseball Hall of Fame induction day is baseball's High Holy Day of obligation. Everybody should be there."

It's the most important day in baseball. When I got off the beat at the *Daily News* and created the national baseball columnist job, they wanted to bring in Michael Kay to be the Yankees beat writer. I said I'd be interested in this national columnist job because it'll give me a chance to do all of baseball, not just buttonhole myself into the Yankees. But I did ask that a few things be written into the deal: number one, that I have exclusive coverage of the Hall of Fame ceremony. As a baseball writer, that's something I need to be at every year.

I could be a beat writer today, but I'll say this. You gotta be young, and I don't mean Dick. You gotta be young. What beat writers have to do today . . . there's no comparison. When I was the beat writer, I was responsible for writing, basically, the game story and a short notebook. I mean a *short* notebook; at times it was, like, five lines. We called them Yankee Doodles, remember? Four or five little lines, and that was it.

Not only that, but we traveled with the team. We flew on the team charters, didn't have to worry about airport security or making your own plane or hotel reservations. Everything was done for you. The writers today, they have to handle all the logistics of getting to all these places, plane reservations, hotel reservations. Then they have to write a long game story, a long notebook, blogging, Tweeting, it's endless. It's back to the wire services where you're on the job twenty-four hours a day. I know I could never do it now, but I guess if you're twenty-one and just starting out, you do it.

Another thing is that the relationship between the writers and the players today is so different. I'd hang out with the players in the hotel bar, and you'd pick up all kinds of stuff. The players today, first of all, it's hard to find them even in the clubhouse, not to mention outside the clubhouse. And there are so many added people around. In the old days, it was just the five or six beat writers, and that was about it. There's no interaction, no relationship whatsoever, between the players and the writers anymore. That makes it even harder for these beat writers today, because they don't have the same access to the players that we had.

It extends to off the field, too. All the baseball people went to events like the All-Star Game and the World Series. Now, none of them go. They'd have parties and brunches, and it was a baseball writer's smorgasbord. It'll never be like that again. It's become a marketing event.

The one thing that we writers still have that's enabled us to maintain a sense of the power we had in the old days is that we still have the awards. TV has been trying, year after year, to get our awards away from us, or to have us sell them. We've kept them our domain. That still separates the baseball writers association from any other association or guild of journalists. But there's no question that, with the demise of newspapers and the rise of the Internet, we've had to change our constitution to bring website writers into the association.

The Hall of Fame is still the number one thing, no question. I've always said to people that I don't see how any right-minded person could say that the baseball writers haven't done an exemplary job for the Hall of Fame. It's because of us, because it's so hard to get in, that people care about the Baseball Hall of Fame like no other. A lot of these other Halls of Fame, nobody even knows who's in them or who does the electing.

But with the Baseball Hall of Fame, there will be arguments until the end of time about who should be in and who shouldn't be. I think Lang said this first: we should be proud of the fact that people complain about who we *don't* put in, rather than who we *do* put in. Because it's so hard to get in, that's why it's so meaningful.

19

WAYNE MINSHEW

Donald Davidson, who spent a lifetime in baseball as the legendary traveling secretary of the Braves, once wrote, "Wayne Minshew enjoys baseball as much as any reporter I've known."

Born in Alabama and raised in Georgia, Minshew's career path in baseball followed in the best traditions of Southern storytelling. A former pitcher at the University of Georgia and a pro briefly, Minshew's sportswriting career began with one year at the Americus (Georgia) Times-Recorder *and five years (1961–1965) in Florida at the* Jacksonville Journal.

In September 1965, Minshew arrived in Atlanta, hired by fabled sports editor Jesse Outlar at the Atlanta Constitution. *The following year, he became the* Constitution's *first beat writer for the newly arrived Atlanta Braves.*

For the next two decades, Minshew would become a major symbol of Braves baseball. In thirteen years on the Braves beat (1966–1978), Minshew covered the club from its arrival in the South to its 1969 NL West title to Hank Aaron's unforgettable quest for home run number 715 through the early, tumultuous days of Ted Turner's ownership. He also served as the longtime Atlanta correspondent for The Sporting News.

In mid-1978, "Shew" left the Constitution *and embarked on an eleven-year career with the Braves (1978–1988) as their director of public relations and promotions. Today, he lives in semi-retirement in Calhoun, Georgia, and serves as the executive director of the Calhoun-Gordon Council for a Literate Community. But he'll still reach back into his past and recall a remarkable man known to a se-lect few as Mr. A. Diefendorfer, or how an eccentric comedian named Professor Backwards gave him the biggest scoop of his career.*

I go back and read some of my old stuff with Google searches once in a while. Some of it I cringe at, and some of it I'm very proud of. I would not classify myself as a great writer but as an interesting writer who played up good angles and had good insight. To me, the great-est pleasure came from popping something that nobody expected, causing conversation, and setting people on their ears. That was the biggest kick I got.

I always had an angle in mind and knew which way I was going, usually. Except the night Hank Aaron hit his 715th home run. I just stared at my typewriter and that blank piece of paper for what seemed like hours. Now, it was probably only maybe three or four minutes, but it seemed like forever.

I grew up in a mill town in Georgia, about seventy miles from At-lanta. The mill team played in the Northwest Georgia Textile League, and that was the weekend entertainment in those days, preceding television. There wasn't any Little League or uniformed kids leagues in those days. Our early idols as kids were those mill town players. As I got older, I'd go to the ballpark and shag flies for them.

I learned my first swear words at the ballpark. The big one, you know? I brought it home, and my mom barred me from the ballpark after that. I often wondered which direction my life would have taken had I not disobeyed my mom, because I kept going to the ballpark.

Those guys knew how to play; a lot of them were ex-professionals. They got jobs in the mill. Usually they wound up as painters, but their primary job was playing baseball. They probably made more money playing for the mill team than they did in the lower profes-sional leagues of those days.

I read the *Times-Recorder* about the Textile League and about the Atlanta Crackers minor league team, when Jesse Outlar, F. M. Wil-liams, and Furman Bisher covered them. Bisher was a great writer. And Jesse Outlar was one of the best game reporters, for both base-ball and football, that I ever read. He was probably a role model, al-though I wasn't aware of it at the time.

My brother and I would put our bats across the handlebars of our bicycles and go looking for a game. If we only had two or three guys, say, we'd play a game called "Catch 'em in a Pickle." We'd put one fielder at third base, one at home, and the runner would put himself in a pickle and try to get out of it. If we had four or five guys, we'd hit on a certain side of the field, to keep it in play. We'd choose up sides and play all day long, and that's something you don't see anymore.

I was a junior at the University of Georgia, without a major. I went to my high school baseball coach, Ralph Toggle, and I said, 'Coach, I'm a junior in college, and I don't have a major. What the hell am I gonna do?" He said, "Well, why don't you major in journalism and be a sportswriter?" It was as simple as that. In the back of my mind, I knew that I wrote well in high school and college, with English papers and things like that.

I signed with the Cardinals and played a year of pro ball in Hobbs, New Mexico, in 1958. I played one year and didn't do real well. I had a good strikeout-to-innings record, but that was about my only positive mark. But I played against Tony Cloninger and Denis Menke, who were both on the Braves when I started to cover them. I once got a bunt hit off Tony, and one night I struck out Menke with the bases loaded. Later on, they both refused to remember that moment. But they did spread the word that I played pro ball.

As a former player, I believe you can get away with writing things that other writers can't. Ballplayers respect people who have been there, so that really helped my career. At least it gives you a head start.

*   *   *

I started my writing career in Americus, and the fun part was I would pitch batting practice to the high school team. Then I would umpire the games, and then I would write it. One thing was sure: the umps never got ripped in my game stories. One of the players in Americus was Dan Reeves, who later, of course, was a great NFL player and coach. We became great friends.

I covered Triple-A ball in Jacksonville for four years. The first year I was there, they were the first Houston Colts farm club, and they were awful. As a gimmick, the last week of the year, I signed a contract and pitched a game with them. I pitched five scoreless innings against the Dodgers' Greenville team. Of course, that made the rounds.

It was the best training ground I could have asked for. I used to pitch batting practice on the road, and that stood me in good stead. In fact, this may make me sound like a house man, but when they won the International League in '62, they threw me in the shower.

We had good ball clubs in those days. The first year we were a Cleveland farm team, it won the International League pennant. We had Vic Davalillo as the star of the team, and Ben Geraghty was the manager. Then, later, it was a Cardinals farm team, and Harry Walker was the manager, and he really became a great friend later. In fact, Harry allowed me to hang around in the clubhouse while he held team meetings. The equipment guy tried to throw me out once, and Harry said, "No, he's all right."

I helped Harry negotiate a trade once. My first year in the majors, Harry was managing Pittsburgh, and he asked me if I thought that Bobby Bragan, who was the Braves' manager in their first year in Atlanta, would be interested in a Don Schwall-for-Billy O'Dell trade. I said I'd ask him about it, and Bobby said he was interested. So I wrote a story saying that the trade was going to be made, using the usual "reliable sources" line.

I had been working in Jacksonville when Jesse Outlar called me and asked if I wanted to be a general assignment guy with an emphasis on college sports. That's when I was hired at the *Constitution*. To cover the Braves, they had hired a guy named Jack Williams, who was at the University of North Carolina in their public relations department. He had worked at the *Constitution* before, and he came back to the paper with the intention of covering the Braves. But he missed North Carolina so much—it was his home state—he went back and didn't stay in Atlanta.

Meanwhile, the trial of Milwaukee County against the Braves, in which they tried to prevent the team from moving, came down to Atlanta for some hearings in 1965. I covered those, and ultimately that's how I won the job of covering the Braves. I'll admit I knew much more about balls and strikes at the time than I knew about law. I felt lost. The Milwaukee paper sent a legal guy down to handle their coverage, and this guy kind of guided us through it. He was a big help. I didn't really look upon it as an audition to get the Braves job. I looked upon it as being out of my element, in a room hearing testimony. I can barely remember what I wrote.

When I got the Braves beat in '66, I looked upon it with some trepidation, but my years covering Triple-A ball really helped.

Wilt Browning of the *Journal* and I at the *Constitution* were the original Braves beat writers in Atlanta, and we got along great, although we competed hard. In those days, the most dreaded words that a reporter could hear were, "Where were you on this?" That's when you knew you got beaten on a story. You'd get a phone call at home or a memo saying, "Where were you on this?"

Jesse Outlar was a great guy to work for, as long as you did your job. He was sort of a Bobby Cox of sports editors. If you did your job, you never heard from him, except to say, "Good job" and things like that. He let me know when he liked my stuff, which was great praise because he was a great writer himself. I still think he's the greatest football game writer I've ever read. Furman Bisher, I'm told, was a little tougher over at the *Journal*. He stayed on you a little harder.

In those days, I didn't feel I had to teach the readers baseball as much as I had to remind them that this was the major leagues and there were superstars in both clubhouses. After games, if the star was on the opposing team, then I'd go and talk to him. I'd always try to cultivate the opposing managers, be friends with them, and use them as sources. That was the approach I took . . . not necessarily to teach them anything, because Atlanta had a great baseball history. The two sports editors—Jesse and Furman—always went to spring training and the World Series.

I still have dreams about deadlines. Most days, you'd write for at least three editions. You'd do a plug for the first edition, which hit the streets about six or seven. Then you wrote a running and a top for the state edition, and then you'd write a sub for the final edition. Besides all this, you wrote notes and little sidebars, so we must have written two thousand words a day, on a typical game day.

There was a lag of about forty-five minutes between the time you filed your story to the time that you got it in the paper. First you had to hand your copy over to the Western Union operator. Then he'd send it; then it had to go through a line operator back at the office. The best operators would correct your mistakes and save you without your even knowing it. Then it had to be set in type and finally printed. Again, it took about forty-five minutes. Now it takes about two seconds.

Leads were important in those days. I remember writing one in the first year [1966] where I copied the old "Spahn and Sain and pray for rain" line. Ken Johnson and Denny Lemaster were the only two pitchers who could win that year, so I wrote something about, "Johnson and Lemaster and three days of disaster." Spahn and Sain are still remembered more than a half-century later. My line lasted about twenty-four hours.

* * *

The early Atlanta Braves were good copy. Eddie Mathews was the ultimate professional team guy, very old school. Hank Aaron, while he was quiet, was always cooperative. Gene Oliver was the resident wit. Joe Torre was, too. He'll admit today that he was a fat catcher. A scout told me once that the Braves would never win as long as Torre was the catcher because he couldn't get down and block low pitches. Joe was great copy.

So it was a fun club to cover, but it was a plodding, slow kind of team that waited on the long ball. They didn't have much pitching. One of the best quotes I got in that first year was in Billy Hitchcock's first game as manager, when he replaced Bobby Bragan. It was in August, and Denny Lemaster pitched against Sandy Koufax, who was in his last year. Lemaster finishes his warm-ups, and Oliver is catching him. Oliver walked up to Lemaster and said, "Hold 'em to a run, and we'll play for a tie." That was the best quote I had all season.

There were more than fifty thousand there. Then we had this long rain delay. Felipe Alou hit a home run, and then Jim Lefebvre hit one in the eighth inning to tie the game, if I remember right. And then Mathews hit one in the bottom of the ninth to win it, and Mathews had just been put back into the lineup by Hitchcock. Bragan had benched him, and Hitchcock had reinstated him. Mathews and Bragan did not get along at all. In fact, a lot of people didn't get along with Bragan, and parties broke out all over the clubhouse when he was fired. It was a big day all around.

Hank Aaron was such a class act. He did get some hate mail during the home run chase, the few fanatics and bigots and people like that. He came into Atlanta and got wild cheers from the beginning. He was just a class act from Day One.

I remember the first time he held out; it was for $25,000. Can you imagine that? That would be tip money today.

Aaron won me over early. You know, the writers were the official scorers in those days. I was in the clubhouse one day, and Gene Oliver was fussing over a hit that I didn't give him. Hank came by, laughed, and said, "Well, tell me, Gene. If he'd have given you that hit, that would get you to what, about .240?" Gene just got up and left.

The 1973 season ended with Hank having 713 home runs, one away from tying Babe Ruth's record. Donald Davidson and the people who ran spring training knew it was going to be a zoo the following year. So they put Hank in a condominium away from the team hotel, and they registered him as "A. Diefendorfer." Donald told me, and I was the only newspaperman who knew. That lasted all that season; he was registered in each road hotel as A. Diefendorfer. It was the only way he could get any privacy.

Number 715 was such a great moment that I thought it was important to background it. So I sent early copy about how Hank spent his day. He watched soap operas, and this and that. I felt what was important was what was going through his mind during that day, what he did to make the day go by. I sent in my copy early and then wrote the game story on top of that.

The feeling was that everybody just *knew* that Hank was going to hit the homer that night. There was no question in anyone's mind that you talked to, except maybe Hank's. I don't know if he knew it. But everybody just knew he was going to hit the homer that night. That's how people made their plans. I mean, Stan Hochman knew he was going home to Philadelphia after that night; he always said that.

When Hank hit it, I had a blank sheet of paper in the typewriter, and the words wouldn't come. I went down to the press conference. Some small-town guy asked Hank what he thought he had done for baseball. That got some giggles, but I thought it was a great question. Hank answered by saying that he hoped it brought positive attention to the game and helped all the way around. He talked about how happy he was that it was over and now he and his teammates could go back to playing ball.

When I got back to the press box, I wanted it to be classic. Finally I just settled on whatever came, that Hank Aaron cut off a slice of baseball history or something like that. It'd never win an award, but I got it in. I was there until about 3 a.m. that night; I was filing stuff for *The Sporting News* and a couple of other people. It was a long night. It got Hank the Magnavox endorsement and got me about $3,000 extra.

It didn't win any awards or anything like that, but my paper liked it. They played it out on the front page. For a long time—and I don't know if this is still the case—the paper displayed the ten most important front pages in its history and hung them in the office lobby. That was one of them. Of course, it was more the moment than the writing, but at least I wrote it. I was very proud of that.

* * *

In those days, breaking stories was a big deal, more so than today. I don't think they care about it today. ESPN scoops the *Journal-Constitution* all the time now. But in those days, breaking a story was the biggest kick you could get.

The biggest story I broke, as far as the Braves were concerned, was Ted Turner buying the team in late '75. I got tipped at the winter meetings, and I wrote the first story about Ted buying the Braves.

What happened was that most of the Chicago syndicate that owned the team—the Bill Bartholomays and Potter Palmers and those guys—wanted to get out from under. Bill worked out a deal where he remained as chairman of the board, and today he's still listed as chairman emeritus. Ted liked to say he bought the team for a thousand dollars down and a thousand a month.

It showed what a visionary Ted was, because he could already see that satellite in the air televising games all over the country. He knew the team had to get better sooner or later, and when it did, he knew he was going to have some very popular programming.

When Ted first bought the club, he'd call me twice a week at home. Just informational stuff, you know? I remember one night he called and said, "Hey, what are you doing?" I said, "Well, I was about to watch a movie on TV." He said, "What are to going to watch?" and I said, "*The Longest Yard.*" He said, "Oh, I've always wanted to see that. What channel is it on?" And I said, "Yours."

Ted gave me a story early on where he wanted to rename the team the Eagles. That played out for a week or two. He'd give me stuff in exchange for information, he was that savvy. When I was on the paper, he'd introduce me as his best friend. Then when I worked for him, it was "Hey, you." He was a great PR guy, and he knew how to play you.

By 1978, we had gotten a new managing editor, a young boy wonder type who didn't believe in long beats. He switched everybody around. But this was what I wanted to do; I wanted to be a baseball writer and not a general sportswriter. He promised me that whatever major event happened, whether it was in New York or wherever, I'd go and cover it. I didn't know if I should believe him.

In the meantime, the Braves' PR man, Bob Hope, with Ted's blessing, offered me the job as his assistant. That sounded really good to me. I wanted to stay in baseball and try that end of the game, so I took the job. The managing editor had said, "Now, I don't want you to go off half-cocked and take another job." Two days later, I went off half-cocked and took the job with the Braves. It was a great experience. I wouldn't trade my days in either job.

With the Braves, we were also the promotions department. That was different from most teams. We'd put together the promotional and giveaway schedule. Then Bob Hope left to go to Coca-Cola less than six months after I got there, so my title became director of public relations and promotions, both major jobs.

*   *   *

You know what was great? There were the fraternities in each profession, especially the baseball writers. They share information, network and things like that. I remember getting sick in New Orleans once, and Joe Durso wrote my story for me.

The BBWAA, to me, is the best writers organization that exists. They pick the major awards that mean as much as any in sports, because I think they're the most valid. You actually see the players play; you discuss their credentials around the batting cage and in dugouts. You can feel their value because you're out there watching them. One year I got a ballot for the Heisman Trophy and returned it because I hadn't seen the players play, and I didn't feel qualified to vote.

The coverage today I find very, very provincial. I don't think the Atlanta guys have stepped into the opposing clubhouse in the last three or four years. I don't know if it's because they have to produce so much copy or what, but you're not even sure if they know the guys on the other team.

But you *have* to know the other guys. It's good stuff and adds to what makes the game popular. I did the town with Ernie Banks one night in Chicago, and man, you talk about doors opening! Then I ran into Pete Rose one day in Cincinnati when Hank was sitting on 2,999 hits, and Pete said, "Tell Hank that if I catch his 3,000th hit, I'm throwing it out of the ballpark."

*   *   *

I felt like I was in a dream in a lot of ways, although a lot of people would be too cynical to admit that. But from childhood, this was my dream. First I wanted to make it as a player, obviously, but that fell through when I wasn't good enough. But to make it at all made me kind of a big man in my old mill village hometown. I felt successful, and my old town was proud of me.

My strangest scoop was a football story, oddly enough. I got tipped that Ray Graves was going to be fired as coach at the University of Florida in 1970. The thing that makes this unusual was that I had a friend named Jimmy Edmondson, who was Professor Backwards. Now, you're probably too young to remember this, but he was on *The Ed Sullivan Show* all the time. He wore a cap and gown in his act and all that.

I knew Jimmy and the president of the university were close, and I called him and asked if he would call the president to verify it. He did, and sure enough it was true, and I went with it. Then it occurred to me that the source of this great story was a guy named Backwards.

I just thought of another great line. One year we went to spring training with three or four knuckleball pitchers . . . Phil Niekro and Hoyt Wilhelm and a few others. Back then, there was a controversy over whether you should start a knuckleballer or pitch him in relief. That was a big thing. We're playing the Expos, so I went over to Gene Mauch in the other dugout and asked him, "Gene, if you had a knuckleballer, what would you do? Start him or relieve him?"

And Mauch said, "Neither. I'd trade the son of a bitch to Atlanta." That was the best quote I got in my whole career.

20

STAN HOCHMAN

Stan Hochman joined the sports staff of the Philadelphia Daily News *on June 9, 1959. More than half a century later, he is every bit a Philadelphia icon as cheesesteaks and the Mummers Parade.*

After working on papers in Texas and San Bernardino, the Brooklyn native was hired by legendary Daily News *sports editor Larry Merchant. Hochman was on the Phillies beat from 1959 through 1966, working alongside two Spink winners, the* Inquirer's *Allen Lewis and the* Bulletin's *Ray Kelly. He covered the Phillies' record twenty-three-game losing streak in 1961 and the infamous September collapse that cost them the 1964 NL pennant. On the beat, he chronicled the stormy tenures of two lightning rods of Phillies history, Gene Mauch and Richie Allen.*

Hochman was promoted to general sports columnist in 1966 (succeeded on the Phillies beat by future Spink winner Bill Conlin), and remains today a daily habit in Philadelphia with a regular column in the Daily News *and numerous TV and radio appearances. A BBWAA member since 1959, Hochman is a three-time winner of the Pennsylvania Sportswriter of the Year award as well as a member of the Philadelphia Jewish Hall of Fame (2002) and Philadelphia Sports Hall of Fame (2008). The man who portrayed himself in* Rocky V *can also tell you a little something about teaching Richard Burton how to play pool.*

Larry Merchant gave me only two pieces of advice when I showed up in Philadelphia. First, he told me how to get to the ballpark and where to park. Of course, that was an adventure at Connie Mack

Stadium. They had a cop assigned to the street a block away, where the writers parked, and he'd watch the cars.

The second piece of advice was that his philosophy was to inform the readers, entertain them, and every so often, surprise them. That's what I've followed for the last fifty years. That's what I think about when I sit down to write.

I'm a Brooklyn guy. Born in Brooklyn, grew up in Brooklyn, went to New York University, was a Mel Ott fan before the other kids in the neighborhood pummeled me and told me I had to root for the home team. I was a Giants fan, but when the Dodgers signed Jackie Robinson, I became a Dodgers fan.

I became a sportswriter because I couldn't dance. I'm at NYU and it's an all-male campus. On Fridays they would bring the young women from Vassar or Barnard or Columbia to the student union building for a dance. I was very much ill at ease, so I wandered up to the second floor and walked into the newspaper office, where a guy looked up from his desk and said, "You here to work?" I said, "What have you got in mind?" He said, "We need writers and reporters. We need someone to cover the student council meeting tomorrow night." I said, sure, I'll try it.

I served most of my two years in the army at Camp Gordon, Georgia. I read the two Augusta papers and felt, like any New Yorker would, that I could do a better job. I wrote the sports editor a letter saying that I could cover events for him, even though I was in the army. Friday nights I covered high school football, and Saturdays I covered the University of Georgia games at Athens. I also soon heard that there'd be an opening for sports editor at the afternoon paper when I got out of the army.

The South Atlantic League baseball season began, and here came Jacksonville with Henry Aaron playing second base and a fellow named Horace Garner in right field, to play the first integrated baseball game in the state of Georgia.

Aaron hit a home run his first time up, and then the game was halted because the fans in right field were throwing rocks at Horace Garner. The two managers met at home plate and decided that the only way the game would continue would be if they put Garner in *left* field, where he'd be standing in front of the segregated, black bleachers. They played the game to a conclusion, and my story didn't go over too well, I think. I called the rock-throwing fans "yahoos."

Shortly thereafter I was called in and they said, "Hopkins . . ." I knew I was in trouble because I had been there three weeks and the editor didn't know my name. He said, "We're not going to promote the sports editor." So I left.

I had a license to teach in New York City, but I didn't want to teach. So I checked in *Editor & Publisher* and answered a blind ad for Region Two, and it turned out to be Brownsville, Texas. That began my Texas odyssey: almost five years in Brownsville, Corpus Christi, and Waco.

A sportswriter on the Waco staff was applying for a job in San Bernardino because he was a movie buff, and he wanted to get close to Hollywood. I asked him if it would be all right if I applied, too, and he said yeah. I got the job. The Dodgers had just moved to Los Angeles, and possibly I could dazzle them in San Bernardino and then get a job in L.A. Two weeks after I got there, two of the four Los Angeles papers folded, and a lot of good people were out of work.

I stayed in San Bernardino for about a year and a half. We covered the big races at Santa Anita and Hollywood Park, the Rams, and the Dodgers. I was a big fish in a little pond out there, but it wasn't satisfying enough. I wanted to get to a big city. Then I got lucky. A college classmate of Larry Merchant's sent my stuff to Larry in Philadelphia. Larry was looking for a baseball writer because his guy had missed too many deadlines, and he hired me.

*   *   *

My introduction to Philadelphia was that I got three overtime parking tickets in my first week then went on a twelve-day road trip. I put my car in a garage across the street from my apartment, and they disconnected the odometer and drove it around the whole time I was gone, stole my golf clubs and binoculars out of the trunk. I was going to call back to San Bernardino to see if my old job was still there. But my brother, who has since passed away, said I hadn't given Philadelphia a fair chance and that I shouldn't be so hasty.

I didn't feel I was ready for something as big as the Phillies beat. I had covered a few Dodgers games at the Coliseum, but no, I didn't have any experience as a beat writer on a major league team, as awful as that team was. Keep in mind that this wasn't a contender that I inherited. The very first game I covered in 1959, they lost and fell into last place and never got out the rest of the season. I thought it was my fault, then I realized they were in last place on merit.

I felt a little overmatched in the beginning. But I was very lucky that Ray Kelly was the kind of guy he was. Ray took me under his wing, showed me the ropes, and looked after me. We both loved horse racing. Ray went out of his way to make me feel comfortable. It was just the three of us—Kelly of the *Bulletin*, Allen Lewis of the *Inquirer*, and myself—that traveled with the team.

The Phillies had brought back Eddie Sawyer to manage. He's pretty aloof and distant. Robin Roberts looked at me early on and said, "I'm used to baseball writers being older." Little did I know I would age quickly. There weren't high expectations, and people knew it was a bad team.

The crossroads came the very next spring, in 1960, my first spring training in Clearwater. Sawyer describes Ted Lepcio as the worst-looking major leaguer he'd ever seen. Then he takes Wally Post and Harry Anderson out of the starting lineup, based on the way they looked in batting practice.

In those days, Cincinnati had the honor of playing the first game of the season. The Phillies open in Cincinnati. Roberts gives up five runs in the second inning, but Sawyer lets him bat for himself in the third, and he winds up striking out with two out and two men on base. They lose 9–4, and the three of us approach Sawyer and asked him why he let Roberts hit for himself. Why didn't he use a pinch-hitter? Sawyer dismissed us and said Roberts had a history of coming back in the late innings, that kind of thing.

The next day is a day off, then they're going to open at home. Sawyer tells us he's quit. We asked him why. "Because," he said, "I'm forty-nine and I want to live to be fifty." That summed up how awful that team was. Andy Cohen, one of the coaches, managed one game and then they brought in Gene Mauch. Mauch looked around at all these solemn faces and said, "Why is everyone so sad?" We said, "You'll find out." And he did.

Working the Phillies beat with Lewis and Kelly, I soon discovered a routine that worked for me. Most days we rode the team bus to the ballpark. It would leave the hotel two-and-a-half hours prior to game time. I found I could talk to players while they dressed and during batting practice. I would spend time in the home team clubhouse looking for column ideas, establishing relationships.

We'd get nasty mail, mostly postcards, written in crayon by a crank who disliked the Phillies ownership and felt that we were in their pocket. So he'd address the cards to "The Three Stooges—Lewis, Kelly, and Hochman," at whatever hotel we were at. We're in St. Louis at the Chase Park Plaza. One day an embarrassed front desk man hands us this postcard and says, "I'm sorry. This has been here a couple of days. We sent it to the wrong room." It turns out that the Three Stooges—the *real* Three Stooges—were appearing in St. Louis, and they had sent the postcard to them. They said, "This can't be for us." So we were getting mail that had been sidetracked to the Three Stooges.

When the Phillies played in San Francisco, Candlestick Park hadn't been built yet. They played at Seals Stadium, and at night, when the wind was blowing in the right direction, you could smell the brewery behind it. When we were downwind from the brewery; it made for an interesting night.

In the second row of the press box, there was a handsome guy who looked like Jeff Chandler, the actor. His name was Rod Ryan. I was using a blue Olivetti portable, and I would come back up from the clubhouse and start typing. When I finished a page, I'd hand it off to Rod. He had this wooden box and a telegraph key, and he'd send it in dots and dashes to the Western Union office on Locust Street in Philadelphia.

Back there was a little guy (let's say he was vertically challenged) who, of course, was named Shorty. He'd sit there with earphones on and translate the dots and dashes into words. Then, when the story was finished, Shorty would get on his bicycle and go over to 23rd and Arch, which was where the *Daily News* offices were, and deliver my copy.

That was just in San Francisco. In the other cities, we had the Western Union operators with the big Teletype machines. You'd hand the operators your story, and it would come out in strips, like ticker tape. Back in Philadelphia on Locust Street, it would come out in one strip after another, and you'd paste it up until you had a page of copy, and Shorty would ride it to the *Daily News*.

In Los Angeles, the Dodgers played at the Coliseum. We didn't always write there; we wanted to get back to the Ambassador Hotel, where the Phillies stayed. We'd go to our rooms and write and then go to the front desk and call Western Union to come and pick up our copy.

One day Ray Kelly took his story to the front desk at the Ambassador. There was a new guy at the desk who didn't know much about newspapering or baseball. Ray said to the guy, "Guard this with your life." Well, at four in the morning he got a call from his office wondering where his story was. Ray said, "I took it to the front desk for Western Union hours ago!" They said, "You better check." He went back and, indeed, the guy was guarding it with his life. He didn't let it out of his sight, didn't give it to Western Union. So Ray had to dictate to his office, and he made deadline!

*   *   *

Connie Mack Stadium. It was musty and old, and it was in a tough neighborhood. If a fan parked two blocks away, some kid would be standing there and he'd say, "Watch your car for a quarter, mister?" And you better give him that quarter, otherwise you'd come back and find your tires punctured. For the media, they had one small lot where a cop watched over your car.

There was an elevator to the press box, and I think the capacity was about four people. It was just like a closet on pulleys. That's how you went down to the clubhouse. The press box had the best milkshakes and Tastykakes in the League. A man named Mike would make milkshakes to order for the writers. He had a little cubicle in the back of the press box and they always had all the Tastykakes you could eat.

At the end of the 1959 season, Merchant declared that the Phillies would no longer pay our airfare and hotel rooms. When I started on the beat, the Phillies picked up the tab and distributed meal money. Larry put an end to that. He got management to give us our independence.

Being married was an adjustment, as far as the beat was concerned. We'd go to spring training together, but after that, I was on the road for at least eighty-one days. The good news was that I was going to some cities I'd never been to. The bad news was that I was by myself and away from my family. I missed my daughter's first steps, and I felt badly about it.

That all began in the off-season after my first year of covering, in 1959. I got an invitation to attend a Public Relations Association luncheon at the Bellevue-Stratford Hotel. The principal speaker was

Bill Shea, a New York attorney who was threatening to form a third major league, the Continental League. The Dodgers and Giants have left. Shea and his friends applied for a new franchise in New York and were turned down. So Shea said okay, we'll show you, we'll form our own league and steal your players.

That made a good off-season story, so I go to the luncheon. A young woman doing public relations for the hotel delays the luncheon so I can interview Shea. I go back and write a column in which I *don't* mention the name of the hotel, nor do I mention the name of the group Shea was talking to. I just mention the newsworthy aspects of the Continental League.

Of course she's furious. Three weeks later, I see her at the Army-Navy Game press party, at one of the other hotels she worked for. I tap her on the hip and say, "Do you remember me?" I get a twenty-seven-minute lecture on the ethics of journalism. I'm so impressed I asked her out. She was busy that week, but I asked her out again the next week. A year later, we were married at the Bellevue-Stratford.

*   *   *

The Phillies had that historic twenty-three-game losing streak in 1961, historic to the point where I'm running out of ways to describe what's happening. So I decide I'll change my point of view.

I go out to 20th Street, where the kids used to wait for home runs over the right field wall, and I spend the game out there. That day, I write about the kids listening on their transistor radios. Then I go up into the scoreboard; a fireman and a schoolteacher are in there looking through a little window and listening to Byrum Saam broadcast the game. Then I did the first aid room. Who's getting hurt or sick watching this dreadful team play? I think I covered five of the twenty-three losses from places other than the press box.

Gene Mauch was the most eloquent baseball guy I've been around. He really studied the game, knew it, knew how to turn a phrase, like, "Extraordinary people do extraordinary things." Or, say, if Johnny Callison was in a slump, he'd say, "He's going to hit .300. Look at the back of his baseball card." He was so inventive.

One of the first things he did was switch the bullpens. When he took over, the Phillies used the left field bullpen at Connie Mack but were in the third base dugout. So he switched them to the right field bullpen so he could see it from the dugout. Then he had his bullpen catcher, Bob Oldis, take a towel out there. If there was a runner on first and the guy hit the ball toward the right field wall, Oldis would wave the towel so the runner would go from first to third. Little things like that.

At the same time, he was so devious. When the visiting team took batting practice, he would stand behind the batting cage to see if the batter was standing close to the plate or far away, checking out his stance, anything to give his pitcher an edge. Well, Leo Durocher came in once with the Cubs and saw Mauch standing there while the Cubs were hitting. Leo took a fungo bat and started firing balls off the back of Mauch's legs. Mauch absorbed about three or four shots and then realized he'd better get his ass back to the dugout.

Mauch studied the rule book more than anybody I'd ever met. He once karate-chopped Jerry Grote of the Mets across the wrists when Grote dared to pursue a foul ball into the Phillies dugout. He was right; the rules said you go into the opposing dugout at your own risk. They changed the rule after that.

The nightmare of 1964. Johnny Callison first pointed it out. On the last long road trip, in mid-September, guys showed up with these rifles and shotguns that they had bought in a gun shop in Houston. They had them in L.A., which was the next stop on the trip before they came home. Callison shrugged and said later, "They were spending the money before we got it." And he was right.

Callison got sick, and Mauch put him in once as a pinch hitter during the losing streak, and he got a hit, and he was so weak he couldn't even zip up his warm-up jacket. Bill White, the Cardinals first baseman, zipped it up for him, in one of the great displays of sportsmanship. That tells you what kind of a guy Bill White was.

The position players basically stayed the same during the slide. Callison stayed the same, Tony Taylor, Ruben Amaro. It was the pitchers who were being quizzed all the time—Bunning and Short and hold the fort—about what Mauch did to the rotation. Depending on whether the guys liked Mauch or didn't like him, that's the kind of answers you got. In my view, he did screw up the pitching rotation. There's no doubt in my mind. Pitching was their downfall.

I kept a diary of that season. I was going to write a book, a diary of the '64 season. The *Daily News* had agreed to print some excerpts with the publisher. The paper would have first shot at it, and then the book would come out. Well, as they began to lose, Ray Hunt, the managing editor, came over to me, dusted the ashes off his cigar, and said, "If they blow it, we ain't interested."

I said, "Wait a minute! What about the nightmare finish?" He repeated, "If they blow it, we ain't interested." There went the book. For me, personally, it was a kick in the teeth.

Plans had been made, tickets had been printed, we were going to do special editions. Larry Shenk, the Phillies PR man, bless his heart, had made the seating arrangements. Then they lost ten in a row.

I'll never forget. We finish the season in Cincinnati while the Mets are playing the Cardinals. I'm sitting next to Jimmy Cannon. At that point, he wasn't well. He had turned really grumpy, and no one wanted to sit next to him. I said I would. I mean, this is my boyhood hero, the guy I grew up reading in Brooklyn. It was Cannon, of course, who uttered the famous line, "Baseball, gentlemen! Baseball!" when the Chipmunks were chattering a little too much for him.

Mauch had avoided Cannon in spring training either that year or the year before, so Jimmy Cannon had no use for Gene Mauch. I think, secretly, he enjoyed watching Mauch suffer. That's what I remember about the final days of '64. People wanted to know how Mauch took it. Mauch was tranquil, truly calm, to the point that it puzzled me. How could he be so calm when this dream is collapsing all around him? That's how he was.

With Richie Allen, you've got to go back to 1963, when he's called up at the end of the season. He's wearing a tweed jacket with leather patches on the elbows, and wing-tipped shoes that were kind of orange. I described the way he's dressed, writing, "Dressed like that, he better be able to hit. And this guy can hit."

Now, fifteen years later, Dick and I are talking in spring training. He says to me, "When I first came up, you made fun of my clothes." I said, "Dick! Did you not read the last line? I said you could hit." He said, "That's not what hurt. Making fun of my clothes hurt." So there's a guy that kept that in his mind for fifteen years!

Richie was an independent guy, totally independent. His father vanished early on; he wasn't real good with authority figures. He felt the Phillies had screwed him over, putting him in Little Rock at a time when integration was a hot topic. All these slights and insults, he just harbored and kept them inside. He had a great year in '64 playing a tough position, third base. And that tremendous power! He had the look of a Hall of Fame player.

Both of his brothers played in the majors, Hank and Ron. I once went up to Hank when Dick was hitting something like .311. I said, "Gee, Hank. If he just followed the rules and conformed a little bit, maybe he'd be hitting .340." Hank looked at me and said, "If you made him follow the rules, he might be hitting .211." That stayed with me. After that, I didn't hammer away at Richie. I just let him do his thing.

*   *   *

It's late 1963, I've just come back to Philadelphia after covering the Yankees-Dodgers World Series. Ray Hunt, the managing editor, approaches me and says, "We're going to send you to Mexico." I said, "Really?" He said, "Yeah. They're making a movie in Puerto Vallarta called *The Night of the Iguana*. It's going to be a carnival because John Huston is the director. Richard Burton's in it, and he's shacked up with Elizabeth Taylor. Ava Gardner is in it, and she once had a fling with the husband of Deborah Kerr, who's also in it. Sue Lyon, who was in *Lolita*, is there with her boyfriend. We're going from a nickel to a dime in price, and we need a circulation booster. You're it. Don't tell the movie company you're coming, just show up."

I show up, and they're a little surprised to see me, but they're thrilled to get some publicity. They'll help me line up interviews, with the exception of Ava Gardner, who has it in her contract that she doesn't do interviews. I taught Richard Burton how to play nine-ball pool, in the only pool room in town at the time.

Did I mention there were no telephones there? The movie company had a ship-to-shore phone that you would crank up. That was their communication with the United States. But the hotel had no phones, so I couldn't talk to my wife or anyone.

I stayed there ten days, interviewed everybody except Ava Gardner. A woman named Grayson Hall was nominated for Best Supporting Actress in that movie. Well, her real name was Shirley Grossman and her mother lived around the corner from me in Philadelphia! So she became my pipeline and told me what was going on behind the scenes.

The crew loved me because, since there were no newspapers or TV, they wanted all the details about how the World Series turned out. As it turned out, Burton had a fascination with baseball. Honestly. He had appeared in *Camelot* on Broadway and had played on their softball team in the Broadway Show League. First time up, he hits a home run. He wanted to retire on the spot.

Burton had all these questions. Why was the mound sixty feet, six inches away? Why were the bases ninety feet apart? He and I got along great. He was a man's man and a great storyteller. Liz looked at me kind of suspiciously. She had had enough of Philadelphians, what with Eddie Fisher. She didn't have much use for me. I gathered enough material and then I got homesick. I decided I would sneak home, because the office figures I'm going to be there two weeks.

I went home early but didn't dare go out because the *Daily News* delivery trucks had my picture on the side: "Our Man in Puerto Vallarta." At that time, we lived on the second floor of a duplex behind the Art Museum. Years later, we were with the woman who lived downstairs from us, and somehow the subject turned to my covering *The Night of the Iguana.* I mentioned that I came home early and never went out, and this woman was so relieved! She sighed, wiped imaginary sweat off her forehead, and said, "I have to tell you. I heard a man upstairs all that time and I thought it was none of my business. I know Stan's in Mexico." She had kept that secret all those years, then she finally realized it was me!

*   *   *

Even though the *Daily News* was strictly an afternoon paper, I was the fastest gun in the East, and I say that without bragging. I could go to a clubhouse after a game, interview whom I needed to, come back up, and finish before the morning paper guy was finished with his story. I didn't linger, even though I had plenty of time before deadline.

The only time I ever got writer's block was after Jim Bunning's perfect game at Shea Stadium in 1964. I had to climb out of Shea; they had locked the gates. I just choked. It was the first game of a doubleheader, and I hadn't even put a dent in it by the time Rick Wise won the second game. I read that story now, and I'm embarrassed.

Somehow I got the story sent, but when I packed up and got ready to leave, the gates were all shut. Bad day. A perfect game! I guess I wanted to write a perfect story, and I didn't even come close.

I couldn't have done the beat my way anymore. Just the logistics of it have changed so dramatically. There were times, especially on the road, where I had a player one-on-one for as long as I needed him. It could be thirty minutes, forty minutes. We'd both get there early, and I'd pull up a chair, and we'd talk. The chances of that today are slim to none. My approach to baseball writing would be logistically improbable, if not impossible, today. I came along at the right time.

I became friendly with some of the opposing players and had a terrific relationship with Willie Stargell, Joe Morgan, Frank Robinson, Vada Pinson, Willie McCovey.

On the other side of the coin, I had problems with Bob Gibson. His wife wrote a book about baseball, and I was critical of it in a two-sentence item in a notes column. Bill White made sure that Gibson saw it, and the next time I walked into the Cardinals clubhouse, Gibson screamed at me, implying the criticism was racist. He yelped, "If Nancy Seaver had written that book you wouldn't have ripped it." I told him gently he was wrong.

He didn't talk to me for about fifteen years. The one-sided feud ended when Joe Torre suggested a truce about the time Gibson became eligible for the Hall of Fame. "You probably won't vote for me anyway," Gibson sneered. "You'd be surprised," I told him.

21

JOE GIULIOTTI

Joe Giuliotti, a friend once said, was so wired into Boston that "he could pick up the phone at one in the morning and get anybody, from the mayor to the police chief to Carl Yastrzemski."

"Joe Gil" became woven into a city's fabric through more than a decade as a cityside reporter. Starting as a teenager with the now-defunct Daily Record *in 1951, he was a full-time reporter by the end of the decade. Through a series of mergers, Joe worked for the* Record American, *the* Herald American *(in the early '70s), and, finally, for the reborn, post-Murdoch* Boston Herald *starting in late 1982.*

In 1972, the tough, no-nonsense Giuliotti found a new home in sports and put the reportorial instincts honed on the street to use on the most prestigious beat in New England. He covered the Red Sox for nearly three decades, first as beat writer (1973–1995) and then as the Herald's *first national baseball columnist (1995–2000).*

A two-time Spink Award finalist and a BBWAA member since 1973, Giuliotti and his straightforward style chronicled the Red Sox's rise from a quaint New England tradition to a worldwide phenomenon, usually in direct competition with the Globe's *Peter Gammons. While covering the Sox, he was also (amazingly) the beat writer for the hockey Bruins during the mid- and late 1970s.*

Joe Gil's half-century in journalism ended with his retirement from the Herald *in 2000, but his involvement in sports remains as strong as ever. He was an official scorer at Fenway Park through 2008, and for the last decade has served as assistant men's hockey coach at Shawsheen Valley Tech High School in suburban Billerica.*

was a much better reporter than writer. *Much* better. I learned from some of the best on the news side: How to ask questions, how to dig facts out, how to separate bullshit from the truth, how to not be conned by people.

You know, the *flowery* writer, well, he never existed. You didn't have time to sit down with your thesaurus and lay out your paragraphs. You had to get it into the paper. That's what I learned in news: you had to get the damn thing in. Otherwise you'd miss an edition, which I never did in my life, thank God. So I probably could have been a better writer if I could have missed an edition or two by taking my time. But you didn't have that luxury.

I don't care how good you are. If you don't have contacts, you're just an ordinary person. I made contacts and realized that was the way to go. I just made contacts and kept up with 'em.

I loved being a news reporter. In those days—and I hate to use that term—we had rewrite men because the editions came so quick, one right on top of the other. We were a morning paper, and the reporter didn't have time to go out, cover a story, come back in, and write it. There just wasn't time. So you called in to the rewrite man, gave him the facts, and he wrote the story.

I started at the *Daily Record*, which became the *Record American*. Then in 1971, when the *Herald Traveler*, which was one of our competitors, went out of business, we bought their building and moved into it. Then we wound up as the *Herald American*. Now it's just the *Herald*, since Rupert Murdoch bought it in 1982.

I was a senior in high school looking for a job. We had a Catholic newspaper in our town called the *Pilot*. One of my best friend's parents worked for the *Pilot*, and so did he. On Thursday, when the paper came out, he'd take copies of the *Pilot* around to the other Boston papers: the *Globe*, the *Herald*, the *Record*, and so on. When he came into the *Record*, the guy in charge of the office boys asked him if he had any classmates who needed a part-time job. So my friend asked me, I said yes, and the rest, as they say, is history. This is in 1951.

In those days, you had to serve your time. I put in six years as an office boy, and then I became a reporter in 1957. I was a general assignment reporter, and I did everything. We didn't have many specialists at our paper. It was a Hearst paper, and we had tight budgets. You name it, I covered it . . . the statehouse, City Hall, everything. But most of my work was in crime.

Now, you never turn down a promotion. I was offered a job as a rewrite man. I really didn't want it, because it meant going from nights to days. But I took it, and then I missed being out on the street. Something would happen, and you'd be helping out on the phone inside, but I really want to be out there on the street.

Then around 1972, a job opened up in sports, where you did all your own writing. Here was a chance to be on the street and also be able to write. That's why I went into sports. You had the time to go to an event, cover it, give it to Western Union, and have them send it into the paper. On cityside, you didn't have that luxury. You'd be knocking on peoples' doors asking if you could use their phone. I missed being on the street, and I wanted to write, and here was the opportunity to do both.

I always said that if I were ever a sports editor, I would want a guy with at least five years' experience in news before he came to work in sports. Back then, a team would give you a press release, and a lot of times you'd take it as gospel. No, you had to check it out, and a lot of times you'd find out that it wasn't accurate. So my training in news was invaluable. I had some great editors, too. That was a big, big plus.

By 1973, I was the third man on the Red Sox beat at the *Herald American*. We had Bill Liston and Fred Ciampa, both of whom have passed away. They sort of split the beat, and I was the sidebar guy, doing the jockstrap stuff, that sort of thing. I took it over full-time in '75.

I was more than qualified. I mean, the beat is easy. After dealing with tough cops and prisoners and stuff, the baseball beat was really a piece of cake. But you still wanted to learn, get yourself established, and then drive it home if you had to.

I just hung back and learned from a lot of the older guys. I just listened to them. I didn't come in as a big mouth, saying that I was going to own the world one of these days. I just sat back, lay in the weeds as they say, observed, and watched. I did that most of my first two years, probably. That's how I eased myself in.

We had a great guy named Larry Claflin, who had been a beat writer at the old *American*, before all the mergers. He was a monster help to me. I'll never forget, Larry said to me when I was first starting, "There are two things that people here are interested in: home runs and Carl Yastrzemski." And he was absolutely right. That's all the Red Sox did, hit home runs.

The road was an adjustment. On cityside, you'd drive to wherever in New England then drive home at night. The road was interesting and different. I always said that the perfect job would have been covering baseball without having to travel. I hated traveling. I didn't mind flying, but I just hated the rush. In the end, that's what got me to say enough's enough. Plus, everything was changing at the time, with the evolution of the business in the '90s.

I always had a good rapport with players. Don't ask me why, maybe it's because I didn't bow down to anyone or kiss anyone's tail. You got a job to do, I got a job to do. If you don't like my job, my complaint department will be open once a day, because I was always in the clubhouse three hours before a game. If I was there any later than three hours before, I'd consider myself late for work.

I told it like it was and didn't sugarcoat anything. Now, I had my arguments and disagreements, sure. But I had a good rapport with players and managers, even some of the old-time managers. Gene Mauch was supposed to be a hard-ass. Well, Gene Mauch was a pussycat if you stood up to him.

Too many baseball writers were afraid to stand up to these people, because they looked at them like gods or something. I never did. Maybe that's why I got along, I don't know. On cityside, you dealt with cops, prisoners, convicts, thieves, and everything. Now I come into sports, and I'm supposed to be impressed because you can hit a baseball? Doesn't impress me at all. You do your job, and I'll report the facts of what you do, good or bad.

I always wrote for an AM paper. The PM people had plenty of time. I was at my *best* on deadline. I was one of the fastest writers on the paper. That goes back to my training in news.

Say we go to the West Coast. You'd write a pregame story, you'd write running, you'd write an early notebook, then a sub-notebook. Then at midnight another sub-notebook, then sub the story at 1 a.m. You had to keep all this stuff down, and it was all rush, rush, rush. If you asked me what I put down on paper sometimes, I wouldn't know. As they said one time when I was in news, "The story's no good in your typewriter."

When we moved into the old *Herald* building, we had the biggest circulation in New England, about 450,000 papers a day. The higher-ups then changed their thinking, and we went after the Republican

Herald readers, of which there were only about 140,000. In going after them, we ignored the base we had, and that's when we started losing circulation. We were basically called the "race track paper": we'd have the race results and whatnot.

The guy in the street bought the *Herald.* Before the lottery, they'd have the daily number, and people would be lined up at street corners at eight o'clock at night waiting for the early edition so they could see what the number was. We were the blue-collar paper, and the *Globe* was always for . . . well, as Howie Carr, one of our columnists, called them, "the bow-tie bumkissers."

*   *   *

As far as me and Peter Gammons, I think Red Sox fans should be so thankful that they had two people like us. When I worked, I never put myself out there, which was probably my mistake. I let Peter do the politicking and going on all the TV shows. I just stayed in the background. But neither one of us ever slipped up. We wouldn't dare slack off. Peter worked twenty-five hours a day and I worked twenty-four and a half. I think the readers of both papers benefitted from it.

Of course, we always had small staffs. We worked for Hearst, and they operated on a shoestring budget all the time. You'd go to a game, and there'd be one guy from our paper, and I'd be up against three or sometimes four or five from the *Globe.*

Peter had a ton more space than I did. Peter would have, let's say, a hundred lines to fill, and I'd have forty. Or Peter would have a hundred lines for the lead and fifty for the notebook, where I'd have forty and twenty. It was hard, but you had to get the same stuff in. That's where writing for a tabloid always helped me. It's hard to go from a standard writer to a tabloid writer, because you'd develop diarrhea of the mouth at a standard paper. At a tabloid, you had to say the same thing in as few words as possible.

I enjoyed traveling with Peter, I enjoyed covering with Peter, I enjoyed beating Peter, and I'm sure he enjoyed beating me. But that didn't happen too often. My pride wouldn't allow me to get beat.

I figure that you work hard, you pay attention to what you're doing. You may miss minor things, but you'd never miss anything major. I didn't, and Peter didn't. That's why we got along. We'd never argue with each other; we'd travel together. We didn't socialize much on the road because we were two different people, as far as going out after dark. Peter would go back to the room and start making calls. I'd want to go out and have a few scotches. But when crunch time came, we were both there. I enjoyed Peter. Peter made me better, and I'd like to think I made him better.

Not to sound conceited or anything like that, but there were so many stories and things I broke. I had a former night sports editor who would call me at home during the off-season and say, "Joe, I need a Red Sox story, but I need one that'll lead the paper." And I'd say eight or nine times out of ten, I'd deliver it. There was a time where there wasn't a major story in New England that I didn't break, when I was at my best, even when Peter was around. I had contacts, I broke stories. There weren't many stories I broke that didn't . . . well, maybe one.

The only story I broke that didn't pan out was one that my sports editor sort of pushed me into. It was around '76, when Fred Lynn and Rick Burleson and Carlton Fisk and those guys had their contracts run out. My sports editor said, "I want you to write a story that Fred Lynn is gone." I said, "I don't have anything to support that." But, he said, look at all these offers he's getting, look at this other stuff, and so on. So I wrote the story to the effect that Fred Lynn was probably gone, and the next day he re-signed with the Red Sox.

I actually had a conversation about it with Lynn; he sort of misled me, which he later apologized for. That was maybe the one black mark on my career. Now, if you look at a thing like that today, Chrissake, you'd be a hero if you wrote that. Today they write that this guy's going here and that guy's going there, and they never go.

*   *   *

I don't think there's enough digging today by the beat writers. It's almost like they accept what's presented to them. I'll give you an example. The Red Sox just signed Bobby Jenks as a free agent [in late 2010]. That came out of the blue. Carl Crawford's signing also came out of the blue. That never happened before. Gammons and I would always have broken a story before it was announced by the Red Sox. That doesn't happen anymore, and I don't know why.

You can't say, "They're putting a big lid on it." That goes back to my old premise about making contacts. I don't think these guys today have any contacts, I really don't. They may have them, but they're the wrong kind because they can't tell them anything. That's why I say it's a little provincial. There's nothing that comes out that you don't already know about.

Right now, over the course of the off-season, every player in the league gets traded five times. Every paper has everybody traded or "sources said" or that stuff. It's kind of ridiculous in a way because if you kept track of every deal that's in the paper, maybe 2 percent of them work out.

Writers today have to do their TV and radio shows before they write their own stories. Now, I worked for the Red Sox flagship radio station, and my job was a fifteen-minute pregame show, basically to talk about the pitching matchups and what happened the day before.

The agreement I made before I accepted the job was, "Look, they could be shooting each other in the locker room before the game. Don't even ask me about it. That's for my paper, that's not for the radio, so don't even ask me." I wouldn't do it, and I'd get ticked off at people who did because you'd have a good story, and why put it on the radio? Radio's only giving you pocket money; your main job is the paper you work for. If you didn't work for that paper, you think the radio station's going to hire you? Absolutely not.

You ask me about 1986 and the Dave Henderson game and Game Six against the Mets. There were so many twists and turns. You know, when you're *there*, you're writing, and you're doing your running, you really don't know what's happened. You're just *reacting* to what's happened.

Both Game Six against the Mets and the Carlton Fisk game in '75 ended way after midnight, so you couldn't write more than running. You're so into it, and you have to do so much. I probably took it upon myself to do more than I had to do. I wanted to fix up my notebook, for instance. I see notebooks today, and it's all pregame stuff. I hated that. Pregame stuff was for the first edition, but once the game starts, you should have some live stuff in your notebook.

As I said, it's no good in your typewriter. You gotta get it on paper and get it in. Then after the game you go out and have a beer and start thinking about it, or you're up in a plane at two in the morning and you say, "Oh, my God. Did I have the right score of that game?" Everything is a blur.

I was on the Bruins for five or six years. Back then there was an off-season in baseball. Outside of your Sunday notebook, you didn't write many baseball stories. At our paper, that probably changed in the '80s. The sports editor, Bob Sales, wanted a baseball story every day during the off-season, and that was unheard of. Before that, that's how you could cover two beats.

In 1974, I covered the Stanley Cup Finals where the Bruins lost in six games to the Flyers. Game Six was in Philadelphia. It was a Sunday afternoon, and they lost 1–0 to end the series. I came home Sunday night, went into the office, looked at the schedule, and started the next day on an eleven-game homestand with the Red Sox. That doesn't happen today.

Back when I did it, the hockey players were so much better to deal with. There weren't many millionaires. I think Bobby Orr had just broken the $100,000 mark. He was one of the first, before the WHA started and stole all the players. Hockey players never made much money. Their background was basically as Canadian farm boys, and they appreciated everything they had. Baseball players thought that they were owed what they were getting, the money and the adulation. Hockey players weren't like that. Even today, you can see the difference.

We never had a baseball columnist at the *Herald*. The *Globe* did, with Peter. I told my boss that we should have a baseball columnist, but he didn't want anything to do with it. Then we had a change in sports editors, and the first thing the new guy—Mark Torpey—did was ask me, "Do you still want to be a columnist?" And I said absolutely.

He also said, "There won't be much travel," because I had made it known that I had wanted to cut back on travel. Well, it was as much travel as I had on the beat, but I didn't mind it because I was doing something creative, something I wanted to do.

I used to read columns that had a lot of quotes in them. The whole column would be quotes from some athlete. I always believed that the column should be an opinion or an analysis, and if a quote helps it out, then yeah. I'd write ten columns in a row without one quote in them. That's what I thought a column should be: analysis and opinion.

They talk about blogging and Tweeting. Basically, we did that anyway, especially when we were on the road and perhaps an hour or two before. You had to constantly be feeding the paper stuff, constantly updating. I don't think it would be that much different. No, not at all. A little more work, maybe, but work never hurt anybody.

I think I could do it today. I don't know if I could step right into it, but once you get into the swing of things and figure out how to do it, how to cut a corner, maybe to get this or that done, then, yeah, I think I could. What is it? It's gathering facts, putting them together in story form. Now it's easy to send. I remember on the West Coast it would take you three to six minutes to send one page on a Telecopier. Now, two seconds and you get ten takes in. So I think I could do it; I think I'd even enjoy it. If they fire me from my hockey job, I may consider trying to get back.

People always ask me what's my biggest thrill in sports, and I can't separate them. It's all a blur. But in March 2008, in the Eastern Massachusetts Hockey Championship, my team was playing the top team from the southern region of the state. All of a sudden I see a scramble around the other team's net, and the red light goes on, and I said, "Holy Moses!" That's the biggest thrill I've ever had in sports: we won in overtime and went on to play in the state finals in Boston.

22

BOB HERTZEL

If there's an unofficial BBWAA record for membership in the most chapters, Bob Hertzel may very well hold it. His forty-plus-year career has included stops (and memberships) in Atlanta, Cincinnati, Cleveland, Washington/Baltimore, Pittsburgh, St. Louis, and New York. And, as he kiddingly points out, he's outlasted three of his employers—the since-departed Cleveland Press, St. Louis Sun, *and* Pittsburgh Press.

The bouncy, energetic Hertzel was the chief chronicler of Cincinnati's fabled Big Red Machine for a decade (1969–1978) with the Cincinnati Enquirer, *a period over which the Reds won four National League pennants and two World Championships. Following his Cincinnati stint, he covered the Indians for the* Cleveland Press, *the Orioles for the* Washington Times, *the Pirates for the* Pittsburgh Press, *the Cardinals for the* St. Louis Sun, *and the Yankees for the* Bergen Record. *A BBWAA member since 1966 (when he covered the newly transplanted Braves for the* Atlanta Journal*), he has covered six no-hitters and every World Series from 1969 to 1978 and again from 1982 to 1995. He's the author of four books, including two collaborations with Pete Rose.*

New York–born and New Jersey–bred, Hertz is still on the job today, covering the Pirates for the Fairmont Times West Virginian *and contributing to the Baseball Prospectus website. He serves as an official scorer at Pittsburgh's PNC Park, where the working conditions are usually much more comfortable than on a rainy, cold night in Boston in 1975, when he was the scorer for one of the game's most famous home runs amid a near-empty press box.*

The first year I was in Cincinnati, Pat Corrales, the Reds' backup catcher, was my next-door neighbor. Every morning I'd get a knock on the door about ten o'clock, and Pat Corrales would be standing there. He'd have the newspaper under his arm, a cup of coffee in his hand, and he'd say, "Let's talk." We'd sit, and he'd say, "Now, what did you write this for?" He'd be upset about a few things, but that's tough, you know? But there would be other things in there that I'd overlooked, and he'd go through that. You learned not to take everything at face value. So we'd sit there for a half hour. That would *never* happen today.

I definitely think I was born to write. I can't tell you why. It's just always come ridiculously easy for me. It's been one of the great pleasures of my life. I won a fifty-dollar award in a junior high school essay contest that the *New York Daily News* ran. Unfortunately, I don't recall what deep subject I attacked, but I'm sure it changed the world. All the writing awards I've won since—and I've won a few—never included money.

When I was ten years old, I joined the Little League team in Englewood, New Jersey. Richie Scheinblum, who would have a pretty good major league career, was on the same team, and we became best friends. I learned really quickly about the power of the press. I was a catcher, and I wasn't very good. Lo and behold, I wake up one morning and find out that both I and Richie Scheinblum had been traded. Not only that, but I read in the *Bergen Record* that this ten-player trade in the Little League was done because the team that traded me was unhappy with their catcher, which happened to be me. I spent three days crying.

On that Little League team, our coach was a woman, Janet Murk, and to this day I maintain she was the best hitter I've ever seen. She played in the women's league during the war; she was the real deal. She was the one who suggested to Richie that he become a switchhitter. And Richie became a wonderful hitter, hit .300 a few times and made the All-Star team in '72. He wound up being traded to Cincinnati when I was covering the Reds, and the first thing he said to me was, "Remember, I'm a year younger than I really am," because I think he had lied about his age when he signed.

When I was in high school, I had a teacher named Sarah Winfrey. She recognized that I had a talent, made me sports editor of the paper, and eventually steered me to the University of Missouri. So I was not only playing but also writing about myself. Talk about controlling the message! One time I was phoning in a story to the *Hudson Dispatch* about a game I had caught. I went 0-for-3 as usual, but our pitcher, Bruce Hulin, threw a three-hit shutout. The lead was, "With Bob Hertzel calling a wonderful game, Bruce Hulin threw a three-hit shutout . . ."

There was another fellow in New Jersey, Dick Stahlberger, who was the public relations man at Fairleigh Dickinson University. He allowed me to go with him to games, file stories, and keep stats. I was sort of his right-hand man while I was still in high school.

I was a pretty good high school ballplayer, but when they threw me that first curve ball, I realized that writing was a lot easier than playing baseball. I played through my freshman year at the University of Missouri and then gave it up.

*   *   *

I read the newspapers religiously. I knew every baseball statistic there was, which is funny because now I don't know any. I was so fortunate to be able to read Jimmy Breslin, Jimmy Cannon, Dick Young. Breslin was wonderful in the way he wrote about people. Young was great as a reporter, pulling no punches. I fell in love with that. Then when I read Jim Murray, that gave me a whole new love, trying to do interesting things with words.

I left the University of Missouri and went to Wilmington, Delaware, to work for the *News Journal*, writing high schools and golf from '64 through '66. I went from there to the *Atlanta Journal*. The Braves were moving there, and I wanted to write baseball. Furman Bisher, the editor and great columnist, hired me as a golf writer. I was going to be only the third golf writer in the paper's history. The first was O. B. Keeler, who was Bobby Jones's biographer. Then Ed Miles covered for thirty years, and now here I come. But I wangled my way into covering baseball.

Now, you think that you know everything there is to know about writing baseball. Well, let me tell you. . . . When you're a rookie, you're a rookie, and it doesn't matter. I had more lessons down there . . . I don't even know where to begin.

Bob Gibson pitched a great game in Atlanta, a three-hitter, but gets beat on a home run by Felipe Alou. Denny Lemaster pitches a one-hitter and wins the game. My assignment is to interview Bob Gibson. Now, the guys that took Pork Chop Hill during the Korean War had an easier job than interviewing Bob Gibson after he got beat in a game like this. I go over and, of course, ask him the ultimate question you shouldn't ask: "Bob, what was the pitch Alou hit?" Well, let's just say I never asked that question again. Bob Gibson taught me that in no uncertain terms.

That was one lesson. Here's another. The Giants come to Atlanta for one of their first times ever. This is 1966, at the height of all the civil rights stuff. There had been a story in the paper earlier that they felt was somewhat racially hot. To be honest with you, I don't recall exactly what it was about. My job is to do a Giants sidebar, but the only one who's talking to the media is Tito Fuentes. I got what I thought was a nice little story, but of course, the paper didn't want a story on Tito Fuentes. I had gone to Willie Mays, and he was on the training table. We chatted a little, and I tried to interview him, but he just said to go talk to the manager, Herman Franks. So I didn't get anything out of Willie.

Now I go back to the paper, and they tell me not to write Tito Fuentes but about how the Giants wouldn't talk. So the next day I get to the paper at 5 a.m. because it's an afternoon paper. I also laid out the paper, and I came up with what I thought was the greatest headline ever written: "Say Hey Says Nay All The Way." That led the sports section.

The next night, Mays comes up, and they're booing him. Willie hits a ball so far you couldn't have gotten to it with a five-dollar long-distance call. Next time up, there's a lot less boos. The time after that, the fans are cheering him, and I'm certain that they're all looking up at the press box and booing me like I'm a jerk. I learned you don't pick on the great stars too often and get away with it.

Another time I went to the hotel to interview Sandy Koufax. This is also in '66, Sandy's last year with the Dodgers. They had gotten in really late the night before, and now here's young Mr. Robert Hertzel in the lobby of the hotel, dialing Sandy Koufax's room at 8:30 in the morning. Let's just say that interview lasted about a minute and a half, and I didn't do much of the talking. It was Sandy Koufax teaching me about major league travel and how players aren't very friendly at 8:30 in the morning.

* * *

I was in Atlanta until '68. The Cincinnati Bengals started in the AFL, and I went to the *Dayton Daily News* to cover them. I did some Reds stuff as well.

Lou Smith was the legendary Reds reporter at the *Cincinnati Enquirer*. He had worked there for thirty-five years and was one of the real characters of the business. Bill Ford was the backup writer. He wanted the top job and was thrilled the day Lou Smith retired in 1968.

Now, the legend is that Bill Ford got off the airplane for spring training in March '68, looked around and said, "Will this damned season ever end?" Bill had an awful time. He had married late in life, had a family, and the travel got to him because he didn't do all that much traveling as the backup guy. He did one year and wanted to quit. They went looking for a baseball writer, and here I was, fifty miles away in Dayton. I got the job and joined the *Enquirer* in '69.

When I came on the beat, there were four traveling papers: the *Enquirer*, the *Post*, the *Dayton Daily News*, and the *Dayton Journal-Herald*. Bucky Albers was the beat writer for the *Journal-Herald*, and we used to call him Three-Fingered Albers because he had lost two fingers in a farm accident when he was a kid.

The veteran on the beat was Earl Lawson of the *Post*. Jim Ferguson was the beat man for the *Dayton Daily News*, Si Burick was the sports editor there, and Ritter Collett was sports editor at the *Journal Herald*. Both Burick and Collett wound up in Cooperstown as winners of the Spink Award, as did Earl Lawson. Hal McCoy also won it, but he came along a little later in Dayton. The Dayton papers were very good, and of course the Cincinnati papers put everything they had into the Reds beat. It was the plum, it was what people talked about in the city, and of course the Big Red Machine was just starting to be born at that point.

Crosley Field was one of the great old ballparks. The clubhouse was actually a little building under the stands, inside an outer fencing. One day, Dave Bristol, the manager, got so mad at Chico Ruiz that he yanked the pay phone off the clubhouse wall and threw it out the window. To get to the field from the clubhouse, you had to walk through the stands. The press box was up on the roof. One year we had a fierce tornado that tore across I-75, and here we were up on the roof in this cardboard press box, thinking we were all going to be done in.

That first year with the Reds was kind of amazing. We had back-to-back no-hitters with Jim Maloney and Don Wilson of Houston. There are guys who cover baseball their whole life and never see a no-hitter, and I got two in two days. That was when Wilson charged the Reds dugout, screaming after the no-hitter. Earlier in the season, the Reds beat Wilson 14–0, and the Reds were taunting him and making fun of him all during that game.

It was a great team to cover. They stayed in the pennant race the entire season until a guy named Keith Lampard hit a home run off Wayne Granger to beat them in the Astrodome right at the end. It was a team that was just starting to find itself.

It was interesting dealing with Sparky Anderson. His first year, 1970, the Reds won seventy of their first hundred games. They had a wonderful team, and he was along for the ride at that point. Pete Rose, Johnny Bench, Lee May, Tony Perez, Bobby Tolan . . . you didn't have to do a lot of managing with those guys, and he knew it.

One night in San Francisco, I'm out with Dave Burgin, who was a columnist with the *San Francisco Examiner*. It was a very drunken night, as will happen in downtown San Francisco. In the course of our evening, I told him that I didn't think Sparky should be Manager of the Year. I said that he really didn't do anything. All he did was platoon Bernie Carbo and Hal McRae. The rest of it was pretty much a team that was really ready to win.

I get up the next morning, and Dave Burgin is quoting *me* in his column, saying that Bob Hertzel thinks that Sparky Anderson, who I have to deal with every day, shouldn't be Manager of the Year! I don't know why he did this, but I go right to Sparky, before he's even seen this in the paper. I'm starting to explain, but as only Sparky can, he says, "Bobby, you're right. I haven't done a damn thing." I mean, he could have been pissed, *really* pissed.

In '70, all of the pitchers got hurt late in the season. When they played Baltimore in the World Series, the whole staff was a mess, and they couldn't compete. Now it's Christmastime, and we're sitting around the office at the *Enquirer*. A Christmas card arrives, and we open it. . . . Who the hell is this? It was signed "George Anderson." We have no freaking idea who George Anderson is for two days. Then I figure it out. . . . It's Sparky! Sure as hell, Sparky had signed his cards "George Anderson," and nobody knew who he was.

After the Reds made the trade with Houston—the trade that truly made them the Big Red Machine—there was one writer who was sure that this was the worst trade in the history of the Cincinnati Reds. And that was me. Lee May? Tommy Helms? How could they trade Jimmy Stewart? I mean, Joe Morgan was a .260 hitter. He had trouble with his manager, Harry Walker. They gave up May, a great guy who hit thirty-nine home runs the year before, for a guy many perceived as having a questionable attitude.

But who knew? Who knew that Morgan was going to become a Hall of Famer? Who knew that Jack Billingham was going to be a big winner? Who knew that Denis Menke would be able to play third base? Who knew Ed Armbrister would lay down the bunt that led to one of the most famous plays ever? Who knew that Cesar Geronimo would be a terrific outfielder?

Bob Howsam, the general manager, was so freaking mad at me! But I absolutely lambasted that trade. I thought it was just awful. I wish I had some of those clippings now, because I would laugh my ass off.

*   *   *

I was never intimidated on the beat. Maybe it's the New Yorker in me, but the fact that I had a sound background made me feel that I belonged. I felt secure in my baseball knowledge and my ability to deal with people.

I never had a problem with deadline writing. That was always my strength. I could bang out a story in twenty minutes, tops. It would be eight hundred words and at least decent. You could read it, laugh at it, learn something, and you wouldn't criticize the English in it. I was very prolific; I would write a lot of words, a lot of stories. I worked ten years in Cincinnati and missed two games.

There's a secret to writing on deadline, and it wasn't anything that anyone told me or that I learned. You have to be able to recognize and organize what's important and put it in order, even before you go down to the clubhouse. Often, what you learn in the clubhouse will change what you're planning to write.

One of the things I always felt I had a knack for was pregame. Nowadays, they don't let you in the damn clubhouse until 3:30 for a 7:00 p.m. game. In those days, you could get in there much earlier. I remember when I was in St. Louis, I'd sit there with Whitey Herzog, and he'd be in his underwear drawing lines on a piece of paper . . . different colored lines of where guys would hit the ball. Now, you do that all with computers, but he was way ahead of that. He had it all done on a sheet of paper.

If you were smart, you didn't do much talking, and you'd do a whole lot of listening. That's the whole idea. You listen to these guys. *They* have the knowledge. You'd come across guys like Joe Torre who were absolutely wonderful to deal with. If you went out early enough, you'd sit around with them, and you'd be amazed at how much you'd use in that night's game story. More often than not, what you got before the game was better than what you got after the game.

Baseball is different from every other sport because of the relationships you have with the players. There's so much time spent with them. In those days you traveled on the team plane. There were relationships built that today's journalists wouldn't understand. You had to learn how to deal with people who were not only your friends but who were also professionals, and maybe you weren't always going to write nice things about them.

Dave Concepcion messed a game up one night. I'm on deadline, and I don't have time to soothe Davey's feelings. I have just enough time to get a quote or two. I went up to Davey and asked him what the hell happened. He started off with, "Oh, you never talk to me when I do good . . ." and in a way, he was right. In a locker room with Bench, Perez, Morgan, Rose, and Foster, you didn't go to Dave Concepcion a whole lot. But two minutes later, he told me exactly what I wanted, and I went upstairs and did my story. It was because of the relationship we had, rather than having a nasty, knee-jerk reaction toward someone he didn't know and trust.

The writers don't make the kind of money to live in the same neighborhoods as the players anymore. But in the apartment complex I lived in, Ray Washburn, Bobby Tolan, Pat Corrales, Woody Woodward, they all lived there. I drove to spring training one year with Jim

McGlothlin—he lived across the street. It was just different; there was a community. Now, when I go into the Pirates locker room, there might be three people in there because there are so many rooms to hide in. You went into the locker room with the Reds, and everyone would be there. You'd get stories about their past, not even stories that you'd write. Just two guys talking. It made the life great.

*   *   *

I am a much better writer than a reporter. I say that with a lot of regret, because Dick Young was one of my idols. For whatever reason, I was never one of those people. If I got a story first, that was fine. But I always felt I'd rather have a story ten minutes after deadline than ten minutes before. If someone else got it, I can't do anything about that. I could at least write it well. Today, with the Internet, it's very hard to be first with anything. It's more important to be accurate and right than just getting the scoop.

There are a lot of people who disagree with me, I know. I was always more interested in people, in people's reaction to the game, than with who was signing what contract and what trades were being made. I didn't much care that Joe Blow hit a game-winning home run. What I cared about was how he reacted to hitting the home run. I always felt that the losing locker room was a better room than the winning locker room. There was nothing better, no more emotion, than to go into a losing room. I'm sure talking to Bob Gibson that day, if I had handled it right, would have been a better story than that of the winning pitcher.

I liked good lines. The Reds once traded Angel Bravo for Al Ferrara. Ferrara was a funny guy, a racetrack guy. He had played with the Dodgers, and Buzzie Bavasi would hold back his salary or else he'd blow it all at the racetrack. We're in San Diego, and there's an ordinary pop fly to the outfield. Ferrara circled under it like he was dizzy then made a diving catch. Afterward I went into the clubhouse and said, "Al, what was that?" He looked at me and said, "What did you expect for Angel Bravo?" That was such a good line that I didn't care what else happened in the game.

When Carlton Fisk hit his home run in Game Six of the 1975 World Series, there may have been three people in the press box at

Fenway Park, the three official scorers: Charley Feeney, Clif Keane, and me. It's after midnight, it's cold, it's wet. It was just a miserable night.

Back then every ballpark had a press room where they served alcohol—great places to sit and talk after games. During the World Series, everybody had gotten out of the cold and went back into the press room, where a wonderful guy named Tommy McCarthy took care of us. A lot of writers will tell you that they saw Fisk's home run live, but let me tell you, I *had* to see it live because I was the official scorer. I looked around at that moment, and there were only a few stragglers in the press box.

It's 1978, the off-season. I'm doing a story on the baseball writers awards, and I need to talk to Sparky. I call him, and we talk for about a half hour. But all the time, I sense there's something wrong. Because all the time he's talking, he's referring to the Reds as "they," not "we." I hang up the phone, turn to the guys in the office, and say, "You know what? Sparky's just been fired." And they said that's impossible. I said, "Nope, I'm telling you. He's been fired."

Now, I couldn't write anything. I couldn't bang it down, but it came out later that day. Dick Wagner, the general manager, met with him at the hotel at the Los Angeles airport and fired him. He'd won ninety-two games that year. I don't know if it was my writer's intuition or whatever. It was just so weird, and it came from just knowing somebody really well. That just wasn't Sparky on the phone that I had talked to.

*   *   *

Baseball is baseball. Given my background and my love of the game, I could do the beat today. I did it up until '95, and it was my decision, basically, because I didn't like New York.

But they ask an awful lot of these guys. They're pretty much on call twenty-four hours, with the Internet. What I don't like now is that these guys miss a lot of games. I really felt like I had to be at the game every day because baseball is a game that goes from day to day. What happened yesterday doesn't end yesterday; it carries over into the next day. If you're not there every day, you may not know it. Whether it be a fight in the clubhouse, or something said between two managers, or something like that. The more you're there, the more you're part of it, the better off you are.

Look, I never lived a normal life. But I lived the life I wanted to live. I lived a life that I enjoyed. I was doing what I wanted to do. I felt I was informing and entertaining a lot of people who were interested in the same things I was. It was a pretty good life, a life I wouldn't trade.

I really enjoyed the people, from the Sparky Andersons to the Chuck Tanners to the Jim Leylands. Even Alex Johnson, who was impossible to deal with when he played for the Reds. Alex had this thing against all writers, and in particular Earl Lawson. Lawson would walk into the clubhouse wearing one of those Reds floppy hats, and Alex would say, "Who shit and put a hat on top of it?" Even as hard as he was, there were still redeeming features about a guy like that. When Earl had his heart attack, the first person to ask about him was Alex Johnson.

23

RICK HUMMEL

It was a hot summer night in Milwaukee, and two guys were talking baseball in the press box at old County Stadium. Suddenly, from the other end of the box, a voice cried out, "Hey, Commish!"

Both Bud Selig and Rick Hummel turned around.

Such is the respect, admiration, and affection held throughout the game for Hummel, the 2006 Spink Award winner and a pillar in the unmatched legacy of St. Louis baseball.

For decades the leading baseball writer in what is arguably America's best baseball city, Hummel commandeered the Cardinals beat for the St. Louis Post-Dispatch *for twenty-four years, from 1978 through 2001. He's been the paper's national baseball columnist for the past decade, still a must-read for the red-clad residents of Cardinal Nation.*

A four-time winner of the Missouri Sportswriter of the Year Award, Hummel has covered each of the last thirty-five World Series as well as the last thirty-two All-Star Games. He served as the BBWAA's national president in 1994, is a member of the Hall of Fame's Historical Overview and Screening Committee, and, for good measure, was nominated for a Pulitzer Prize in 1980.

Groomed for success in his early years by another Spink winner, the fabled Bob Broeg, "the Commish" has presided over baseball venues ranging from two Busch Stadiums to the writers' wing at Cooperstown to a marvelous, legendary hangout called the Missouri Bar and Grill.

don't think people in Boston or New York would wear the team colors every night and feel as if they were expected to do so. They wear them because they want to. If you don't wear red here, people are looking at you cross-eyed like, "What's wrong with you? Where's your stuff?"

You're an out-of-towner if you come to a game here and you're not wearing red. That either means you're rooting for the other team or you don't care, and not caring is worse.

I don't think St. Louis was necessarily a better baseball town than anyplace else until the '80s. I mean, they had good teams, but they weren't selling the place out. Then the Cardinals of the '80s played a game that was unlike any game played anywhere in a long time.

First, they had the artificial turf. Second, they had guys who could run. They distracted pitchers, made plays in the field, and pitched well. They hit a home run once in a while—a couple of home runs a week, maybe. It was a totally different game. The Cardinals hadn't won for, like, fifteen years, since the great teams of the '60s. It was almost chilling to watch them play; nobody else had teams like that. With the turf, the game was totally different.

That's when St. Louis took off as a baseball town. That separated St. Louis, back then. They were drawing crowds of three million when it was a true turnstile count. The American League was using tickets sold, the National League was using the actual people in the seats, and St. Louis was way ahead of any market their size, and most other markets, too.

People here appreciate hustle and ingenuity. If it looked like you were trying, they were for you. If you weren't, you'd get booed. I've had guys who played for the Cardinals tell me that if they had taken a half-step or showed a little less than 100 percent effort, they'd get booed, and they knew why.

* * *

When I was in high school in Quincy, Illinois, my driver's training instructor was named Melvin Tappe. He was a big star in Quincy, played minor league ball, and then became a broadcaster of the high school games. His twin brother was Elvin Tappe, who was one of the rotating College of Coaches the Chicago Cubs had.

During one of our driver's training sessions, I mentioned to Melvin that I might like to become a broadcaster someday. He said, "You know what? I think most of these broadcasting jobs are going to go to former athletes. What you really ought to do is become a sportswriter." I figured that was kind of interesting.

I didn't do much with it until I went to Quincy College, three blocks from where I lived. I decided I'd work for the school paper. It worked out fine for the first year, although there was one problem: I didn't know how to type. So my mother, who was a professional typist, would type all my articles for me, and I'd take them over to the school paper.

That wasn't fair to her, so I took a typing course my second year. Then I applied for the journalism school at the University of Missouri and went there for my junior year. I had worked a couple of summers at the *Quincy Herald* as a general assignment reporter, which helped me a lot. It gave me a good perspective of what journalism is all about. I did everything there, a lot of grunt work, answering the phones and writing obits.

I did sportswriting at Missouri, went into the army, and came to the *Post-Dispatch* in 1971. But no, I didn't always want to be a sportswriter. I did want to be a sports broadcaster. But now I think I wouldn't have been a good sportscaster because maybe I wouldn't have had the ability to fill time like you have to.

My draft number was a hundred-thirty-something, so I was probably going to get drafted. I enlisted in the army as an information specialist. While I was at Missouri, I got to know a few of the people at the *Post-Dispatch*, like Bob Broeg and Dave Dorr. I went into information training at Fort Benjamin Harrison, Indiana, and learned to write the army way, which isn't necessarily how to write the newspaper way. Then I was stationed in Germany and did a lot of writing and broadcasting for the Armed Forces Network.

Later I wound up at Fort Carson, Colorado, and worked at the division newspaper. The lady who ran the operation was a real high-powered woman who had all the generals in the palm of her hand. Her name was Irene Posner. I'd been there about a year, and the army realized that I hadn't been formally assigned anywhere, so they called one day inquiring about me. I said, "Irene, I think this is for you."

She got on and she said, "Uh huh . . . uh huh . . . uh, huh. . . . Well, he's not going." And that was the end of that. I stayed there for two years and then got out of the army.

*　*　*

I started applying to papers. I had chances to go to Dayton, Memphis, and here in St. Louis. I thought maybe I should start out at a small town and work my way up. I didn't know if I was ready for St. Louis. The *Post-Dispatch* called me in for a tryout, which was mostly desk work, and offered me a job after just two days. I took it, not really knowing what I was getting into.

I started off writing high school sports, like you should do on any newspaper. I started doing some baseball in '73, moved up to the number two job, and then got the Cardinal beat in '78 when Dick Kaegel became the sports editor and went to *The Sporting News* after that.

I did some games in '73 when Neal Russo had some issues. Then I backed up Kaegel and Ed Wilks for a few years. Dick asked me in '78 if I wanted to do it full-time, and I didn't know. He said, "Why don't you try it for the rest of the year?" I did it and got through it okay.

I don't think I was ready for it at all. You just learn by the seat of your pants. Guys like Russo helped me and told me things about how to deal with people. Broeg and Kaegel did too; they said you can't let these people intimidate you. You have to stand your ground, and if you're right, you're right. I haven't had too many brushes with confrontation, but I wasn't ready for it. I'm not sure I'm ready for it now!

When the *Globe-Democrat* folded and St. Louis became a one-newspaper town, I think it made it easier for me on a daily basis as far as interacting with the manager and the players. You didn't have to joust with anybody for time.

I made myself, and rightfully so, compete with KMOX Radio, which was an incredibly powerful operation for baseball. At one time you could shake a stick at a bunch of great sportscasters, and anyone worth his salt had worked there. Those were the people I was competing against: Jack Buck and Mike Shannon and Bob Costas later on, all those guys. They were dialed into stuff that I wasn't dialed into, so I tried to raise my game to their level, to get the same network of contacts they had. You weren't competing with just newspaper people anymore. I can't think of any station that was more powerful or had the breadth of knowledge of the people who worked there.

There's not really been any other sport here in St. Louis that's captured peoples' interests on a consistent basis for any longer than eight or ten years. The football Cardinals were big for a while. The Rams were big for a while, and now they're not as big. The Blues were big, and then they weren't, and now they're getting better.

But the Cardinals, every year, have had a consistent following. That was due in large part to their location; for almost fifty years they were in the westernmost and southernmost city in the major leagues, before expansion and teams moving to the West Coast. So their crowds were based largely on people from out of town, and still are. People from all over plan weekend vacations here to watch baseball.

Also, the success of the teams of the '40s, both before and after the war, with Stan Musial and Red Schoendienst and those guys, even though they didn't draw really well. They didn't really start drawing until Whitey Herzog took over in the '80s. That was the difference.

*   *   *

I didn't work on a heavy deadline when I started because we were a PM paper back then. Then we made the switch to AM in 1984 when the *Globe-Democrat* was still going, and then it became a race to the finish; one of us wasn't going to make it. We just made it by a nose; we could have folded just as easily as them. We used the same building and the same presses. I'm not sure what the determination was, but we survived and they didn't.

Was I a deadline guy? No, but it didn't take long for me to learn how to be one. Now I love it. I'd rather have an hour to write a game than four hours anytime. You can organize your thoughts faster, be done quicker. You tell yourself that you try to make every story the best you can, although the Pulitzer committee probably won't be meeting in any special sessions to determine your eligibility. You just get it in, and you make a lot of people happy. . . . You make the desk happy, you make the truck drivers happy. Everybody's happier that you didn't take an extra fifteen minutes to make a prize winner out of it. I like deadlines a lot. I'm sure I missed a lot whole potload of them, too.

I think I'm a lot better reporter than a writer. I don't think I was ever a real good writer. I think I was good, but I think I was a better reporter. It's because I've always tried to tell the readers something that they didn't already know. That's been the one thing that maybe . . . I don't know if that sets me apart, but that's my goal every day. I've read hundreds of better writers than I. I don't think there are hundreds of better *reporters* than I.

What Bob Broeg did most for me was pat me on the head and tell me I was doing a good job, when I really needed to hear that from somebody. He didn't tell me how to do it. He might tell me who to talk to for a story, but he never told me how to do it. He just said, "This is good," or, sometimes, when he didn't say anything, you knew it *wasn't* good. He wasn't really hands-on, but he was real supportive. He'd go behind the scenes for me a little, too. He'd talk to somebody and say, "Hey, we have this young reporter here doing a story on so-and-so. Can you help him out?" It was a big deal without it being a big deal.

Bob wanted me to become sports editor when he retired. He thought he was grooming me for that all along, not necessarily the baseball beat. When Bob retired, I kind of had a choice to make. I was never really offered the sports editor's job, but if I wanted it, I could have had it, I think. I didn't want it; I was happy doing what I was doing.

When Bob was the sports editor, he'd write his columns, but he didn't make up the schedules or things like that. He had assistant editors doing that for him; Bob wouldn't have been a good schedule maker anyway. At the time he retired, it looked to me that the sports editor didn't do a heck of a lot of writing, which was what I wanted to do. When I was growing up, the sports editors did everything; they wrote, they organized, they did whatever else it took. That's not the case anymore.

One thing Bob told me off the bat was to get to know the manager. I've basically had only four managers to deal with in St. Louis: Red Schoendienst, Joe Torre, Whitey Herzog, and Tony La Russa. I can't think of any situation like that, other than maybe the people who covered the Dodgers when they had Walter Alston and Tommy

Lasorda for something like fifty years in a row. I can't think of another situation with that kind of continuity. I'm not sure I could have covered a team that had fourteen managers instead of four, over the forty years. Heck, some teams have had *twenty-four* managers over forty years!

Every ten years, it seemed, Red would manage for a little while. It was like an old family friend had returned; hey, Red's here, we're gonna be okay! Red would answer all your questions, but when you checked your notebook, you didn't have all that much. He was cooperative enough, and every now and again there'd be a good nugget in there.

Whitey Herzog used to carry newspapers as a kid and knew about the newspaper business. He read them avidly and did not care for talk radio, TV talk, or that stuff. We got along famously in that regard. Whitey was very media savvy, as was Joe Torre, having been a broadcaster between managing jobs.

Torre knew what people wanted, what they were looking for. You'd say, "I'm looking for an off-day story," and he'd tell you, or he'd just volunteer it. Most guys, when they know they have an off-day coming up, are thinking about spending time with their family or playing golf. Not Joe.

The home run chase with Mark McGwire in 1998 was hard on both of us. There was a media frenzy with him the previous year when he hit fifty-eight homers for two teams, coming over from Oakland. He came up to me one day and said, "When they told me I was coming over here, the guys out there said that the only guy I had to talk to was you. What's the deal with all these people asking me stuff every day?" I said, "Don't hit so many home runs. We're not used to seeing that stuff."

The next year, the out-of-town guys were coming in, and they had to write something every night whether he hit a home run or not. McGwire didn't feel compelled to talk to them when he didn't do anything; he didn't much enjoy it when he did. We established sort of a pool reporting system where I would go interview him after the game and report back with whatever he had to say. I was embarrassed to bring some of that stuff back to these guys, but at least they had something to tell their editors—they had a quote or two. I didn't sign up to be the pool reporter; I have enough trouble keeping up with myself. So that part was hard.

The Pulitzer nomination came in 1980 when I had done some stories on Garry Templeton. This was when the Cardinals had hired Dal Maxvill to be an infield instructor, and Tempy, for whatever reason, thought he didn't need that kind of instruction. He was unhappy with his contract; it was a bunch of other stuff. I wrote three or four stories in spring training about it.

I think Ed Wilks just put it up there because he thought I had done some good work. I never thought it was Pulitzer-worthy or anything like that. I was merely nominated; I didn't win. It was a nice thing, but I didn't know much about it or why Ed did it.

*   *   *

You look at that list of Spink winners . . . Damon Runyon and Grantland Rice. Come on! I mean, you put my name in a sentence with those guys, and it doesn't take too long to figure out which one doesn't belong. That was the most impressive part about it. Then there were the guys I knew, like Jim Murray, who was always real nice to me.

I'll never forget the esteem Red Smith was held in. In the 1981 Montreal–Los Angeles playoff series, Jerry Reuss was going to pitch against Steve Rogers in Game Three. They were both St. Louis guys; they had pitched against each other in high school, and that was the thrust of my story.

Before the game, Joe Durso escorts Red Smith up to meet Steve Rogers. Red says, "My pleasure to meet you." And Steve says, "No, no, no. *My* pleasure to meet *you*." I'll never forget that. I'd never seen that with a sportswriter before or since.

So to be on that list with those guys. . . . I go up there now and look at those pictures of all the winners, and I still don't believe it. I'm not saying I never thought I had a chance to win, because guys I had worked with were going in. I figured maybe someday it would happen to me, so it didn't come out of the blue. I was hoping to be considered, at least.

It changes your life. In a small big city like this, I go to the ballpark, and not more than three or four days go by where somebody doesn't ask me for my autograph. That's very flattering. I would never think of not doing it. I know ballplayers get besieged all the time, but it's new territory for me.

Two longtime guys on our staff, Bob McCoy and Gary Mueller, were responsible for calling me the Commissioner. Part of it stems from the office pools, the football pools. I'd run those. But more significantly, we used to have this APBA football board game we'd play. The boards were very complicated, and I ended up running it because I was the only one who could read the game boards.

We had a league of nine teams, then went to twelve, and then sixteen before we disbanded after three or four years. I would have to go to all the games because I knew how to read the boards, whether my team was playing or not. I was sometimes traveling thirty or forty miles to guys' houses. It would be a big deal; we'd have lunch and everything. That's how I became the Commissioner. We also had a bowling league and a softball league, but it really started with the table football in the office.

The amazing thing is that it's been passed along from player to player, from generation to generation. Players on this year's team call me Commish. They've just heard it. Matt Holliday, who barely knows me, calls me Commish.

Boy, there are some famous stories about the Missouri Bar and Grill. Places like that don't exist anymore. The only thing close might have been the Short Stop Bar on Sunset Boulevard in Los Angeles, at the bottom of the hill when you come out of Dodger Stadium.

The Grill used to be a *Globe-Democrat* bar. We used to have a bar called the Press Box right across from us. The Press Box folded, and we started going to the Grill; then the *Globe* folded, and it became our bar. The umpires used to go in there a lot. Then I brought the sportswriters in. They had a neon message board, and they'd put the writers' names on it; that was a big deal.

In the 1985 playoff series with the Dodgers, the lady who still works there, Tina Miller, got caught in the postgame crush when Ozzie Smith hit his famous walkoff home run. In all the excitement she got pushed down and broke her ankle.

She hobbled into work that night because she knew all her friends would be there—the L.A. guys like Verrell and Terry Johnson and Steve Dilbeck and that whole crew, and all the national guys. The place was packed, and Tina was hobbling around, working on a broken ankle! Then we decided we'd all take over behind the bar and give her the night off. We lost a bunch of money; people would order three shots, and we'd pour five.

After a while the owners made up hats and shirts that said, "Missouri Bar and Grill, BBWAA headquarters." It was just that for a really, really long time. I don't go there very much anymore. I don't drink anymore, but if I did, I'd be there every night. I'd put three hundred dollars on the bar and tell the bartender to just tell me when it ran out. That's how we started parties.

I don't know of any other place like that. It wasn't exactly Toots Shor's, but you could get a sandwich or a steak at 2:30 in the morning, which was unprecedented anywhere except maybe in New York. The Grill was probably one of the reasons I won the Spink Award— all those beers I bought for all those guys over the years.

*   *   *

I don't think I could be a beat writer now, as far as the travel is concerned, especially with St. Louis not being a hub for a lot of airlines like it used to be. To be responsible for blogging and everything else that goes into covering a team now, I think it would be too draining.

Now I work all the home games and about twenty road games. On the road you're responsible for everything: gamer, sidebar, blogging. That part of it. . . . Writing constantly from three hours before the first pitch to a couple of hours afterward is very draining. No, I couldn't do it on an everyday basis. I could do it on a one-third basis.

I don't see a lot of young guys lasting in this. If they do, it's more because they enjoy the blogging and Tweeting aspect. I think they feel more empowered to put themselves out there rather than what they're covering. That's what those things are, I guess. I don't want people to know what I'm doing twenty-four hours a day, nor do I think they would even care. The whole process has changed, and it changed because of ESPN, the Internet, and talk radio.

Everything has combined to make the players more suspicious of people in our business, and I don't blame them, because there's a lot of people they don't know or don't have any contact with. So it isn't nearly as much fun as it used to be. That's life in general, I guess. You can't fight it; you just have to try to do the best you can.

*   *   *

Every time I see an old movie depicting a sportswriter, where they're typing away and yelling "Copy!" I think about how easy it must have been back then. Well, maybe it wasn't easy, but you didn't have to worry about the phone lines working or your laptop working or the Internet connection. All you needed to do was change a ribbon. Do that, and you were golden.

APPENDIX:
THE J. G. TAYLOR
SPINK AWARD

B aseball writing's highest honor is the J. G. Taylor Spink Award, given annually by the Baseball Writers' Association of America for "meritorious contributions to baseball writing." The award is named in memory of the legendary publisher of *The Sporting News*, who was the first recipient in 1962.

The annual winner (selected among three finalists) is voted upon by the BBWAA membership via mail ballot. Several years in the award's early history featured multiple winners. While not considered "enshrined" members of the Baseball Hall of Fame, the Spink winners are permanently honored in the Hall's "Scribes and Mikemen" display at Cooperstown. A similar award, the Ford C. Frick Award, honors the game's greatest broadcasters and was inaugurated in 1978.

Finalists for the Spink Award are announced at the All-Star break in midseason, with the winner announced at the winter meetings and formally honored at the following summer's Hall of Fame inductions. In 2007, the designated award year was changed to coincide with the annual Hall of Fame induction ceremony; hence, there is no winner listed for 2007.

The list of Spink Award winners:

YEAR	WINNER(S)	PRIMARY HOME CITY
1962	J. G. Taylor Spink	St. Louis (*The Sporting News*)
1963	Ring Lardner	Chicago, New York
1964	Hugh Fullerton	Chicago, New York

YEAR	WINNER(S)	PRIMARY HOME CITY
1965	Charles Dryden	Chicago
1966	Grantland Rice	New York (syndicated)
1967	Damon Runyon	New York (syndicated)
1968	H. G. Salsinger	Detroit
1969	Sid Mercer	New York
1970	Heywood Broun	New York
1971	Frank Graham	New York
1972	Dan Daniel	New York
	Fred Lieb	New York
	J. Roy Stockton	St. Louis
1973	Warren Brown	Chicago
	John Drebinger	New York
	John Kieran	New York
1974	John Carmichael	Chicago
	James Isaminger	Philadelphia
1975	Tom Meany	New York
	Shirley Povich	Washington
1976	Harold Kaese	Boston
	Red Smith	Philadelphia, New York
1977	Gordon Cobbledick	Cleveland
	Edgar Munzel	Chicago
1978	Tim Murnane	Boston
	Dick Young	New York
1979	Bob Broeg	St. Louis
	Tommy Holmes	New York
1980	Joe Reichler	New York (national AP)
	Milton Richman	New York (national UPI)
1981	Bob Addie	Washington
	Allen Lewis	Philadelphia
1982	Si Burick	Dayton (Cincinnati)
1983	Ken Smith	New York
1984	Joe McGuff	Kansas City
1985	Earl Lawson	Cincinnati
1986	Jack Lang	New York
1987	Jim Murray	Los Angeles
1988	Bob Hunter	Los Angeles
	Ray Kelly	Philadelphia

YEAR	WINNER(S)	PRIMARY HOME CITY
1989	Jerome Holtzman	Chicago
1990	Phil Collier	San Diego
1991	Ritter Collett	Dayton (Cincinnati)
1992	Leonard Koppett	New York, San Francisco, Oakland
	Bus Saidt	Trenton (New York-Philadelphia)
1993	Wendell Smith	Pittsburgh, Chicago
1994	(no award presented)	
1995	Joe Durso	New York
1996	Charley Feeney*	New York, Pittsburgh
1997	Sam Lacy	Washington, Baltimore
1998	Bob Stevens	San Francisco
1999	Hal Lebovitz	Cleveland
2000	Ross Newhan*	Los Angeles
2001	Joe Falls	Detroit
2002	Hal McCoy*	Dayton (Cincinnati)
2003	Murray Chass*	New York
2004	Peter Gammons*	Boston
2005	Tracy Ringolsby*	Kansas City, Seattle, Dallas, Denver
2006	Rick Hummel*	St. Louis
2008	Larry Whiteside	Milwaukee, Boston
2009	Nick Peters*	San Francisco, Oakland
2010	Bill Madden*	New York
2011	Bill Conlin*	Philadelphia
2012	Bob Elliott*	Toronto

*Living winners as of June 1, 2012

ABOUT THE AUTHOR

Dennis D'Agostino has been one of the sports world's most respected public relations executives and historians for more than two decades. His most recent prior work, *Through a Blue Lens: The Brooklyn Dodger Photographs of Barney Stein* (Triumph Books, 2007) followed his highly acclaimed *Garden Glory: An Oral History of the New York Knicks* (Triumph Books, 2003). His first book, *This Date in New York Mets History* (Stein and Day, 1982), is still considered one of the definitive works on the club's history three decades after its publication.

D'Agostino worked on the New York sports desk of The Associated Press from 1978 to 1983 and then served as assistant public relations director of the New York Mets from 1983 to 1987, earning a World Championship ring in 1986. His twelve-year tenure with the Knicks (1987–1999) earned him the 2000 Marc Splaver/Howie McHugh Tribute to Excellence Award from his peers in the NBA PR Directors Association for long and distinguished service to the league and media. He is currently the team's official historian. A member of the Society for American Baseball Research, he also serves as a statistician/historian on ESPN's, Fox's, and Turner's coverage of Major League Baseball and the NBA.

A native of Brooklyn and a 1978 graduate of Fordham University, D'Agostino now lives in Huntington Beach, California, with his wife, *Los Angeles Times* sports columnist Helene Elliott, the 2005 winner of the Hockey Hall of Fame's Elmer Ferguson Award for distinguished hockey journalism.